THE BAR/BAT MITZVAH PLANBOOK

Also by Ellen Robinson Epstein

Record and Remember: Tracing Your Roots Through Oral History

THE BAR/BAT MITZVAH PLANBOOK

Foreword by Rabbi Richard M. Yellin

JANE LEWIT AND ELLEN ROBINSON EPSTEIN

STEIN AND DAY / *Publishers* / New York

Tikkun page reprinted with the permission of Ktav Publishing House, Inc., from *Tikkun Lahkori'im* (Revised Edition), copyright © 1946 by Fannie Scharfstein, copyright © 1969 by Ktav Publishing House, Inc.

First published in 1982

Designed by Yowa Graphics
Printed in the United States of America
Stein and Day/*Publishers*
Scarborough House
Briarcliff Manor, N.Y. 10510

Library of Congress Cataloging in Publication Data

Lewit, Jane.
The Bar/Bat Mitzvah planbook.

Bibliography: p.
Includes index.
1. Bar mitzvah. 2. Bat mitzvah. I. Epstein, Ellen Robinson.
II. Title.
BM707.L48 296.4'424 81-48459
ISBN 0-8128-2861-5 AACR2

Contents

Acknowledgments

בֶּן זוֹמָא אוֹמֵר אֵיזֶהוּ חָכָם הַלּוֹמֵד מִכָּל־אָדָם

"Who is wise? He who learns from every man . . ."
—Pirke Avot IV: 1

A book such as this only could be written with the assistance of many people with Jewish interests at heart. Friends, Jewish professionals, and parents from around the country helped us with their ideas, personal concerns, and original suggestions. We wish to express our gratitude to each of them, above all, Anne Reich and Joshua Youlus. We especially appreciate the efforts of several rabbis who reviewed the manuscript to assure that information is accurate and useful for today's Bar/Bat Mitzvah parents.

We certainly want to thank all our children, Abigail, Benjamin, and Phoebe Lewit along with Jeremy, Asher, Barak, Dina, and Kira Epstein, whose cooperation enabled us to complete this undertaking. While Abigail's Bat Mitzvah in 1978 helped prompt the writing of this book, we hope and expect that this planbook will still be helpful in 1994 when Kira becomes a Bat Mitzvah! A special word of thanks to our husbands, Robert Lewit and David Epstein, who gave us continual support and encouragement in this project and in everything we do.

Foreword

by Rabbi Richard M. Yellin

Every rabbi, in his duties as a spiritual adviser in a congregation, is called upon at one time or another to help plan a family's celebration of a Bar or Bat Mitzvah. Jane Lewit and Ellen Robinson Epstein have written the perfect guide to assist the rabbi and his congregation in counseling families as they prepare for the unique ceremony of celebrating religious maturity.

The book focuses on the Bar or Bat Mitzvah as a Jewish religious occasion. For parents planning the ceremony, this guide is meant to be used in conjunction with your synagogue and spiritual leader. The authors are very sensitive to the individual customs of the synagogue that, in the final analysis, must be respected by those who are sharing this mitzvah with the synagogue community.

Any family using this guidebook and implementing its suggestions will be able to wed the ethical insights of religion to a meaningful and tasteful event. *The Bar/Bat Mitzvah Planbook* ensures that a moment in time, filled with emotion and commitment, will be linked to tradition and cherished forever.

Preface

Help! Help! My Child is Having a Bar Mitzvah.

Recently, a friend called, full of questions and seeking advice, bewildered about how to plan for her eldest child's Bar Mitzvah. She was in a thirteen-month countdown and overwhelmed by the prospect of organizing this special occasion. The only aspect of the occasion that was firm in her mind was the date. How could she, who is tense when serving dinner for eight, plan a Bar Mitzvah celebration that might involve ten times that number? Her phone call gave us the incentive to write *The Bar/Bat Mitzvah Planbook.* We were tempted to subtitle this book *A Guide for the Perplexed,* but that would have been taking too great a liberty with Moses Maimonides. Clearly, many families can benefit from a simple, creative guide to the Bar/Bat Mitzvah ceremony and celebration.

Across the country, there are children preparing for this ceremony from many different backgrounds, reflecting the breadth of the American Jewish community today. Wherever your family finds itself along this spectrum, you can be comfortable knowing that there are many others like you, who are offering this special opportunity to their children. The rich heritage of Judaism encompasses a variety of religious beliefs and traditions. While some customs are commonly followed, there is a great diversity in practice. This planbook should serve as a helpful guide in organizing your Bar/Bat Mitzvah. It is not intended to give a single answer but, rather, to suggest what can be done. You have the opportunity to choose what is relevant, meaningful, and in keeping with your synagogue's practices. We suggest that you consult your rabbi, religious school director, or other leaders in your congregation as the appropriate authority to guide your decisions.

This guidebook will enable you to follow a timetable, ask the right questions, plan with confidence, and even anticipate the unexpected. We have specific practical suggestions for preparing your child, choosing a date, selecting the invitations, acquiring the traditional ritual items, organizing your guest list (with charts and timetables), providing hospitality for your out-of-towners, extending the festivities with a party, and arranging for the Bar/Bat Mitzvah to be held somewhere other than your synagogue. We realize that some readers will know a little more, and some a little less, about the Bar/Bat Mitzvah. Some of you will find it useful to read every page of this book; others may dip into it here and there to help resolve one point or another. It is with the latter possibility in mind that we have occasionally repeated small bits of information at appropriate points. With this planbook in hand, you can now anticipate your child's Bar/Bat Mitzvah with joy. Here's how to do it.

Bar/Bat Mitzvah Background

Bar/Bat Mitzvah Background

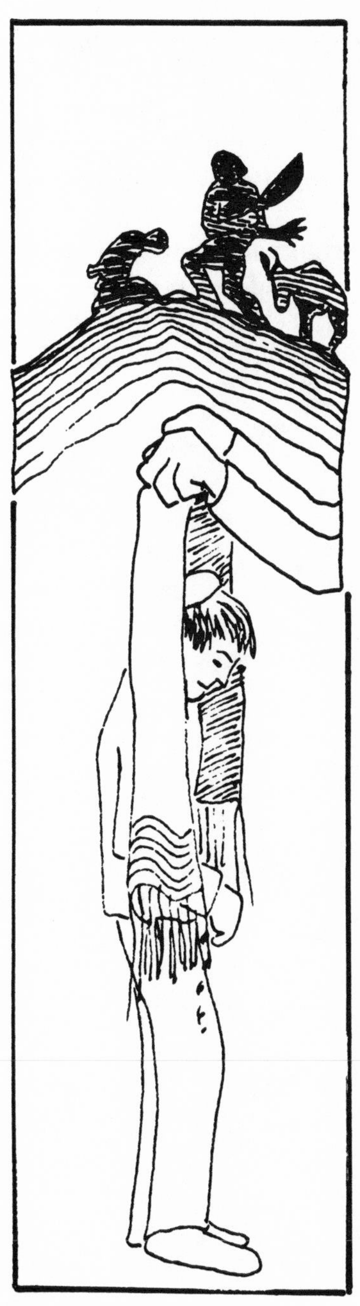

Why Hold the Ceremony at All?

Why should your child have a Bar or Bat Mitzvah? Through this ceremony your child gains an identity with his heritage and community, recognition of personal achievement through study, and a sense of self-confidence. Judaism is not only a religion but a way of living which enhances our lives. By learning its literature, language, prayers, and customs, a youngster can share more fully in this tradition. Equally important is the use of ritual to mark and celebrate the transition from one stage of life to another. We recognize, as did our ancestors, the importance of punctuating our life cycle with ceremony. A contemporary Bar/Bat Mitzvah ceremony is a link in an unbroken chain of thousands of years of Jewish tradition. Every Bar/Bat Mitzvah can be understood as a symbolic renewal of Abraham's covenant with God.

The Bar/Bat Mitzvah ceremony is a very personal experience, often having a profound effect on the young person involved. However, it is not a private event. The Bar/Bat Mitzvah ceremony gives your child an opportunity to acknowledge publicly the significance of this occasion for himself and for his role in the Jewish community.

As the youngster affirms a commitment to lead a responsible Jewish life, the Jewish people are renewed and strengthened. The celebration takes place because the Jewish community rejoices as another young person chooses to identify with it. This is the fundamental reason for the ceremony and celebration at the time of the Bar/Bat Mitzvah.

Educating one's children and passing on Jewish tradition is essential if our rich heritage is to be perpetuated. A *midrash* (folk story) tells of a despot who asked, "How can we overcome the Jewish people?" The perceptive reply of his councilor was, "Go up and down before their houses of study and houses of worship. If you do not hear the voices of children chanting, you can overcome them. But, if you hear the chant of children, you will never subdue them."[1] It is said that the pillars on which the world stands are its schoolchildren. All this reflects how the hopes of the parents and the expectations of the community rest on the promise of the next generation.

All groups within the American Jewish community, Orthodox, Conservative, Reform, and Reconstructionist, view the Bar Mitzvah as an important step in the life of the younger generation. In today's world, parents from varied backgrounds, with different levels of Jewish experience and identification, are preparing their children for the Bar/Bat Mitzvah ceremony. To understand the significance of a Bar/Bat Mitzvah, one must explore the history and meaning of this rite.

The term *bar mitzvah* literally means "son, or subject, of the commandments." The child is entering a new stage in life, one marked with new obligations and new privileges. The child assumes responsibility for observing the teachings of the Torah and gains the right and obligation of taking a full role in the Jewish rituals in the home and synagogue.

1. Azriel Eisenberg, ed., *Bar Mitzvah Treasury* (New York: Behrman House, 1969), p. 301.

The Tradition of the Bar Mitzvah at Age Thirteen

Why does a child become a Bar Mitzvah at age thirteen? The origins of this ceremony are obscure and are not mentioned specifically in the Torah. The Talmud records that at the time of the Second Temple (520 B.C.E.–70 C.E.), it was traditional for the sages to bless a child who had reached the age of thirteen and who had fasted on Yom Kippur. A midrash tells us that Abraham was thirteen when he heeded God's call to leave his father's home, turn from idol worship, and enter into a personal covenant with God. Similarly, the twins, Jacob and Esau, reached the critical turning point in their lives at age thirteen. It was then that they separated—Jacob to study the Torah and become known as Israel, and Esau to follow the ways of idolatry. In Genesis 34:25 "Simeon and Levi . . . took each *man* his sword . . ." According to Rabbinic tradition, Levi was thirteen when he was referred to as a man, thus marking the transition between boyhood and adulthood.

In the *Pirke Avot* (Ethics of the Fathers), which describes fundamental Jewish teachings in epigrammatic form, it says:

> At five years, the age is reached for the study of Scripture; at ten, for the study of Mishnah; at thirteen, for the fulfillment of the commandments . . . [5:24]

By the time the Talmud was compiled (sixth century of the Common Era), rabbis universally recognized that the thirteen-year-old was obligated to follow all the commandments and be responsible for his actions. At that time, a thirteen-year-old male was also viewed as an adult, in terms of legal matters. His vow was valid and he could participate in a *Bet Din* (religious court). Giving further authority to this ceremony, the sage Rashi stated that Bar Mitzvah should be considered as obligatory as the biblical laws given Moses at Sinai.

Perhaps the significance of age thirteen was influenced by earlier puberty rites. By the second century Eleazar ben Simon noted that a father was responsible for his son only up to age thirteen. Thirteen typically marked the onset of sexual maturity, a time when childhood was left behind. The sages of the *Mishnah* (Code of Jewish Law) added a spiritual dimension to this purely physical change. They noted that the threshold of thirteen for a boy, and twelve for a girl, brought with it not only puberty but also the *yetzer hatov,* or good inclination. No longer would a child's behavior solely be dominated by instinct and inclination for evil, *yetzer hara.* He is now guided by his own spiritual strength and therefore responsible for his behavior and the consequences of his actions. Therefore, a father can recite a benediction at his son's Bar Mitzvah, *Baruch shepetarani me'onsho shel zeh,* or Blessed is He who has freed me from responsibility for this child's conduct. Now the child's moral sense is deemed to be sufficiently developed for him to know right from wrong.

In the late Middle Ages, the Bar Mitzvah evolved into a form which closely resembles the ceremony of today. It developed within the context of Judaism as a community-based religion. The Bar Mitzvah was a public demonstration of a youngster's new role as a member of the adult Jewish community with the obligations and privileges that this entailed. The celebration was marked when the Torah was read the first time after the child's thirteenth birthday. Thus, the tradition of Bar Mitzvah at thirteen was firmly rooted.

In Eastern Europe, the ceremony usually took place as the boy was called up to the Torah on a Monday or Thursday. A significant part of the ritual was the boy now putting on *tefillin* (phylacteries) for prayer. In Western Europe, the Bar Mitzvah was usually on Shabbat, with the boy being called up to the Torah to read the *Maftir,* the final portion, and the accompanying *Haftarah* from the Prophets. In Germany, customs developed further, with boys conducting part or all of the synagogue service and possibly reading the full Torah portion of the week. Interestingly, for the Marranos of Spain and Portugal, who had to live as secret Jews, Judaism was first introduced to the next generation at Bar Mitzvah age, since it was felt that a boy of thirteen could be trusted to be discreet. In this way, with only secret observance, a Jewish heritage was preserved for over 300 years.

The Bat Mitzvah

The ceremony of Bat Mitzvah is a relatively recent addition to Jewish practices. (The word is pronounced "baht" in Sephardic Hebrew and "bahs" in Ashkenazic Hebrew.) Antecedents existed in Jewish tradition which for centuries had acknowledged that girls reached religious maturity at age twelve, although there was no specific ritual to mark this coming of age. However, in New York City on Saturday morning, May 6, 1922, a historic event took place at the Society for the Advancement of Judaism. Here at the center for the Reconstructionist movement, then a branch of Conservative Judaism, the eldest daughter of Rabbi Mordecai Kaplan became the first American girl to experience a Bat Mitzvah ceremony. Previously, under Rabbi Kaplan's leadership, the Reconstructionists had begun to recognize women as part of the minyan of ten needed for a prayer service. The growth of women's rights in this period had led to the passage of the Nineteenth Amendment to the United States Constitution in 1920 which granted women the right to vote. In America, the time was ripe for the Bat Mitzvah to take its place alongside the longer established Bar Mitzvah. Offering the Bat Mitzvah ceremony was an effort to give a Jewish girl an opportunity comparable to that of a Jewish boy. Over the years, the Bat Mitzvah has become an accepted part of the tradition of many synagogues. Today many congregations offer one course of instruction for all children, culminating in either a Bar or a Bat Mitzvah ceremony. The service is the same, with the young person called to chant from the Torah and Haftarah.

However, other congregations feel that different rules should apply for girls and boys. Egalitarianism does not necessarily mean that Jewish women and men have identical religious roles. Distinctions are meant to be understood in a positive way for they reflect the congregation's interpretation of the separate functions for women and men within the Jewish community. Following this belief, some synagogues hold the Bat Mitzvah ceremony only on Friday night. Sometimes girls are allowed more latitude to develop a creative, personalized Bat Mitzvah observance, perhaps not possible in the straightforward, prescribed nature of the usual Bar Mitzvah ceremony. Chanting the Book of Esther on Purim or leading a Tu b'Shevat service with its special prayers and songs are two innovative alternatives. Others encourage young women to demonstrate their achievement and commitment by delivering a learned speech or Torah discussion, known as a d'rash or d'var Torah. These celebrations often do not take place in the synagogue. Occasionally, such a ceremony is known as a "Bat Torah," marking a girl's coming of age though not identifying the rite of passage with the Bar Mitzvah.

Clearly, Judaism has changed in many different ways to accommodate the concept of Bat Mitzvah. Many older Jewish women are seeking to experience the Bat Mitzvah ceremony, which was not available to them in their youth. Hence, there is a growing movement for adult Bat Mitzvah classes throughout American Judaism today. Much has happened since the early 1920's when Rabbi Mordecai Kaplan referred to his four daughters as "four good reasons" to institute the Bat Mitzvah as part of Jewish ritual.

Choosing the Date

Choosing the Date

Many congregations give parents the opportunity to request a Bar/Bat Mitzvah date or to list several possible choices. Some congregations have so many children reaching the age of Bar/Bat Mitzvah at the same time that they cannot schedule the ceremony on the Shabbat following each child's birthday. While a Friday night or Saturday morning Bar/Bat Mitzvah is most common, it is also possible to hold this ceremony at a different service. Your synagogue leaders may be willing to consider options for a Bar/Bat Mitzvah to be held on Shabbat afternoon, a festival morning, or other times that services are customarily held in your synagogue. It typically is the role of congregational leaders or someone designated for that job to decide when each Bar/Bat Mitzvah is to be scheduled. A friend of ours who sets the Bar/Bat Mitzvah schedule for his synagogue acknowledges that coordinating the various requests requires the patience of Job and the wisdom of Solomon. If you are able to request a Bar/Bat Mitzvah date rather than having one assigned, here are some factors to consider.

At What Age Does a Child Become Bar/Bat Mitzvah?

It is customary for a boy to celebrate his Bar Mitzvah at age thirteen. In Jewish tradition, this age was viewed as the beginning of religious responsibility. Girls, who usually mature earlier, were considered to reach this point at age twelve. Some congregations today insist that all children experience this ceremony at the same age—thirteen. This also serves to keep a balanced religious school program with all students moving to the level of Bar/Bat Mitzvah when they are in the same school grade. You should check with your own synagogue leaders to find out how they view the Bat Mitzvah date. Do they schedule the ceremony as early as the twelfth birthday, the thirteenth birthday, or some date in between? If you have some flexibility here, consider the maturity of your own daughter and her readiness for the Bat Mitzvah experience, which marks her coming of age.

Whether for a daughter or a son, many parents have independently noted that significant growth takes place after a child has experienced the Bar/Bat Mitzvah process: the study, the preparation, and the synagogue ceremony. In addition to the physical changes which may be taking place at this time, the religious passage is accompanied by an emotional and psychological maturation on the part of the young teenager. This confirms the great wisdom and insight in Jewish tradition which marks this age for a public religious ceremony. The timing acknowledges the many changes which occur in this transitional period. The experience thus has a profound impact on the Bar/Bat Mitzvah as he or she enters adolescence.

Your Child's Hebrew Birthdate

It is traditional to hold the Bar Mitzvah right after your child's thirteenth birthday on the Jewish calendar. This calendar reckons the months according to the moon and differs significantly from the Gregorian calendar in use in the United States. To follow Jewish tradition, consult the Hebrew-English calendar in the Charts and Timetables section at the end of this book. First, check the year of his birth. Then find his exact civil birthdate. The chart will render the Hebrew equivalent. Working with the Hebrew date, now ascertain its thirteenth anniversary on the Hebrew calendar and its corresponding secular date.

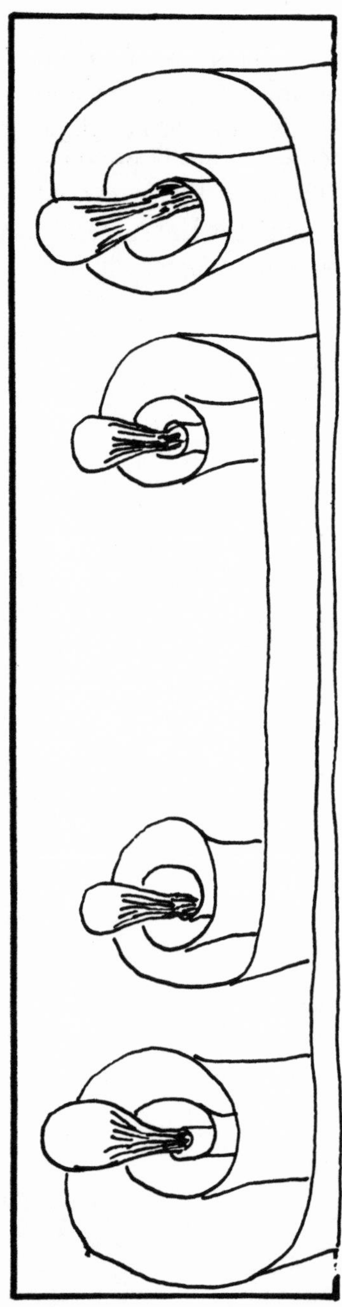

The Yearly Cycle of Readings: The Torah and Haftarah Portions

The Torah is divided into portions so that a different section is read each week; the entire cycle of readings fills a calendar year. At the holiday Simchat Torah, on the 23rd of Tishri (usually in September or October), Jews celebrate completing the reading of the Torah scroll while beginning the next cycle without interruption. Each week, along with the specified Torah portion, there is a selection known as the Haftarah, from the Prophets, or *Nevi'im.*

In many congregations, the Bar/Bat Mitzvah child chants the Maftir, the final section from the week's Torah portion, and the accompanying Haftarah. This pattern of participation is traditional, having evolved in this form approximately 500 years ago. Publicly reading from the Torah and Haftarah is a demonstration of preparation and commitment to the Jewish community.

The Hebrew-Civil calendar in the Charts and Timetables section of this book can tell you which Torah portion is scheduled for each week of the year. A *Chumash* typically will have an index listing the names of all the Torah portions in order.

In looking for a Chumash, it may be helpful to know the variety of words used to refer to this book. Chumash is a Hebrew word and comes from the same root as the Hebrew word for "five," *chamesh,* referring to the five Books of Moses—(the Torah). This is how the Torah also became known as the Pentateuch, from the Greek root for five. Below is a list of Torah portions in the annual cycle, starting from the beginning, Genesis. After the name of each portion is a brief description of its contents.[1]

1. The descriptions were compiled from the following sources: "Adas Israel Chronicle," Adas Israel Congregation (Washington, D.C., 1979–1981). Arthur Chiel, *Guide to Sidrot and Haftarot,* Ktav (New York, 1971).

Description of Torah Portions

BOOK OF GENESIS/*BERESHIT*

1. BERESHIT Gen. 1-6:8
This sidra begins with three simple but very important Hebrew words, "*Bereshit barah Elohim* . . ." "In the beginning God created . . ." Here is the most important teaching of Judaism: that there is a God and that He is the Creator of all life.
2. NOACH Gen. 6:9–11:32
Unlike other accounts of massive floods in primeval times, the biblical account alone underscores the ethical foundations of civilization. The world was destroyed because of selfishness.
3. LECH LECHA Gen. 12–17:27
Abraham hears the call to leave his father's house, to search for a new way of life.
4. VAYYERA Gen. 18–22
Abraham's love of God is tested. He is impelled to offer his son as a sacrifice, which God rejects. The rejection of human sacrifice is a milestone in the growth of civilization.
5. CHAYYE SARAH Gen. 23–25:18
This sidra deals with the life of Abraham and Sarah, his wife, including his purchase of a burial plot in Hebron. It also mentions Rebecca at the well.
6. TOLEDOT Gen. 25:19–28:9
Esau sells his birthright for a bowl of soup and thereby creates a metaphor for repudiating one's potentialities. Jacob acquires his father's blessing.
7. VAYYETZE Gen. 28:10–32:3
Jacob lies down, tired, under the open sky, to sleep. He dreams a remarkable dream. It was a dream that gave Jacob the faith that God is everywhere and cares for the well-being of man. It gave him new hope for his life ahead.
8. VAYYISHLACH Gen. 32:4–36
Jacob wrestled with God's messenger. He is thereupon renamed Israel, "He who has striven with God and with men, and has prevailed."
9. VAYYESHEV Gen. 37–40
Joseph is sold into slavery by his jealous brothers. Despite every adversity, he never deviates from his faith in God.
10. MIKKETZ Gen. 41-44:17
This sidra is a continuation of Joseph's experiences in Egypt. When Joseph's brothers appear before him, Joseph needs time to decide whether to make peace with them or to take vengeance for the past. He plans to test his brothers to see how they feel about their wrongdoing of long ago.
11. VAYYIGGASH Gen. 44:18–47:27
Joseph, by now Prime Minister of Egypt, reveals his true identity to his brothers. Jacob and his sons take up residence in the land of Goshen.

12. VAYYECHI Gen. 47:28-50:26
Jacob blesses his grandsons with words that Jewish parents say to their sons today, "May God make you as Ephraim and as Manasseh."

BOOK OF EXODUS/*SHEMOT*

1. SHEMOT Ex. 1-6:1
In this sidra Moses has a vision while tending his flock one day near Mount Horeb. A voice speaks to him out of a burning bush. Moses is given a mission: He must return to Egypt to liberate the Israelite slaves with the assistance of God.
2. VA-AYRA Ex. 6:2-9
God begins to bring plagues upon the land of Egypt, but Pharoah's heart will not be moved.
3. BO Ex. 10-13:16
Upon suffering the tenth and most destructive plague, ***makat bechorot*** (the smiting of the first born), Pharoah tells Moses and Aaron to take their people forth from Egypt.
4. BESHALLACH Ex. 13:17-17
The Egyptian oppressors drown but "The children of Israel walked upon the dry land in the midst of the sea" reflecting the mighty hand of the Lord. This was the turning point separating the period of slavery from that of freedom.
5. YITHRO Ex. 18-20
The Ten Commandments are revealed at Mt. Sinai amidst thunder and lightning. The Israelites tremble before God's power and majesty.
6. MISHPATIM Ex. 21-24
This portion deals with many specific laws. We may deduce from this that it is inadequate to be a Jew "in general"; Judaism is lived in and through specific application.
7. TERUMAH Ex. 25-27:19
The opening words of the sidra set the stage for our voluntary support of the Jewish community, "The Lord spoke to Moses, saying: 'Tell the Israelite people to bring Me offerings; you shall accept offerings for Me from every person whose heart so moves him.'"
8. TEZAVEH Ex. 27:20-30:10
The *Ner Tamid,* or perpetual lamp, burning before the Ark, is described here. The rabbis interpret the lamp as a symbol of Israel, whose mission it was to become "a light of the nations." (Isaiah 42:6)
9. KI THISSA Ex. 30:11-34
The Israelites forsake their God by worshipping a golden calf. Moses shatters the tablets of the Law when he beholds the people's idolatrous worship.
10. VAYYAKHEL Ex. 35-38:20
The Israelites begin construction of the Tabernacle. Despite its sanctity, Moses admonishes the people that observance of the Sabbath takes precedence over the

building of the Tabernacle, "On six days work may be done, but on the seventh day you shall have a Sabbath of complete rest, holy to the Lord."

11. PEKUDEY Ex. 38:21–40
This sidra describes the final steps in building Israel's first house of worship. This takes place in the wilderness at Sinai while the people are on their long march to the Promised Land. The tabernacle is to be portable so that it can be set up and taken down as the people move from one camping site to another.

BOOK OF LEVITICUS/ *VAYYIKRA*

1. VAYYIKRA Lev. 1–5
This portion details the law concerning sacrifices offered in the Sanctuary. After the times of the First and Second Temple, prayer replaced sacrifices as the form of worship.
2. TZAV Lev. 6–8
This sidra tells the laws for sacrifices brought to the altar of the Sanctuary which was Israel's house of worship during their years of wandering in the wilderness. The idea was that God blesses man with crops and flocks and, in turn, man gives these gifts to God. This portion also describes the event in the sanctuary when Aaron, the first High Priest, and his sons were initiated into their holy assignment as priests, *Kohanim.*
3. SHEMINI Lev. 9–11
This sidra contains laws concerning the purity and holiness of the people of Israel. The sacrifices which they are to bring to the sanctuary are only part of their obligation. They must also, as part of their religious observance, act in every way with a sense of holiness. Here are the beginnings of the religious laws dealing with kosher and nonkosher, as they pertain to eating as well as other areas of human activity.
4. THAZRIA Lev. 12–13
This Torah portion deals with sickness and health, with what was considered clean and unclean. The physical well-being of the community was a sacred concern among the Israelites. Physical cleanliness and health were considered important in order to achieve spiritual well-being. From early in Jewish history, the care and treatment of the sick was considered of greatest importance for the community.
5. METZORA Lev. 14–15
The Kohanim were given the responsibility for healing the sick, including leprosy and other skin ailments. How does this treatment of illness belong to religion? How we live, what we eat, what we think, how we act in our everyday life, according to Judaism, all of these are included in the religious life.
6. ACHAREY MOT Lev. 16–18
Only on Yom Kippur could the High Priest enter the Holy of Holies which contained the Ark of the Covenant which in turn contained the Tablets of the Law. Neither the

High Priest's plea for forgiveness nor other ritual acts could achieve final forgiveness for Israel. Each Israelite was required to fast and atone on this day. Together, the High Priest and Israel, in sincerity, sought to achieve forgiveness for sins.

7. KEDOSHIM Lev. 19–20
   This surveys the foundations of Judaism, summarizing some of the most important ethical teachings of the Torah. This sidra clearly states that Israel must consider life as sacred, "You shall be holy; for I, the Lord, your God, am holy." These ethical teachings are summarized in the proclamation, "You shall love him [the stranger] as yourself, for you were strangers in the land of Egypt."
8. EMOR Lev. 21-24
   This sidra includes the lesson that the weekly Shabbat and the holidays which come at different seasons of the year are intended to teach Israel the holiness of time. On these days, there is opportunity to stop work and business, pause, and consider life's meaning and purpose, and to be refreshed.
9. BEHAR Lev. 25–26:2
   This sidra defines a remarkable approach to the relationship that should exist between man and the earth which gives him sustenance. Balance is to be achieved on the basis of faith that "the earth is the Lord's." Man is only given the privilege of using it to sustain him and therefore must never abuse the land.
10. BECHUKOTAI Lev. 26:3-27
    Moses puts an important challenge before Israel—to choose the way of the Torah. Let Torah's laws be the basis for Israel's life and the people will live well and prosper, and there will be "peace in the land."

BOOK OF NUMBERS/*BAMIDBAR*

1. BAMIDBAR Num. 1–4:20
   This reports in detail the taking of the census of all adult males of Israel in the second year after their exodus from Egypt. It also tells how the large number of men, women, and children were organized for encampment during their years of wandering. The Tabernacle was always placed in the center of the camp.
2. NASO Num. 4:21–7
   Here is introduced the priestly benediction first spoken by Aaron and his sons in the Tabernacle of the wilderness long ago. The *Birchat Kohanim* implores, "May the Lord bless you and keep you. May the Lord make his face to shine upon you and be gracious unto you. May the Lord lift his countenance to you and grant you peace."
3. BEHAALOTECHA Num. 8–12
   Moses needed great faith and courage to carry out his task as Israel's leader in the face of recurring criticism and uprisings. That is the underlying message of this portion.
4. SHELACH Num. 13–15
   Shelach tells the story of the spies sent to survey the land of Canaan in preparation

for its conquest. They reported that it was good agricultural land, but so strongly fortified that the Israelites could not possibly conquer it. Lacking faith, they raised a protest against Moses. Bitterly disappointed, Moses, the great leader, pleaded to God to forgive the people. Moses' plea was accepted, but God decreed that this adult generation would never enter Canaan.

5. KORACH Num. 16–18
   This sidra reports another uprising against Moses due to Korach's envy. Moses prayed to God that justice be done against the rebels, and they were punished with death. It was the only way that the Israelites could be made to understand that Moses was truly the leader of Israel and that Aaron was legitimately *Kohen ha-Gadol.*
6. CHUKKAT Num. 19–22:1
   This portion tells of the death of Miriam and Aaron, Moses' sister and brother. This was a sad time in the life of Israel's great leader. It was a period when the wilderness generation was quickly passing, making way for the younger generation who were to be given the opportunity to enter the Promised Land.
7. BALAK Num. 22:2–25:9
   This sidra tells of Israel's confrontation with the Moabites, a people through whose territory Israel wished to march peacefully on their way to Canaan. Seeking to fight Israel, Balak, the King of Moab, sought to have Israel cursed. Instead of being cursed, the Jews are given a blessing, including the famous words, "How goodly are your tents, oh Jacob, your dwelling places, oh Israel!"
8. PINCHAS Num. 25:10–30:1
   Here, Moses is instructed to go up to Mt. Abarim, to get a good view of the Promised Land, since he was not permitted to cross over into it. Moses is also told to appoint Joshua as his successor to Israel's leadership. The appointment ceremony was to be public, so that when Moses died it would be clear in the people's mind that Joshua was their new leader.
9. MATTOT Num. 30:2–32
   Having arrived east of the Jordan River, two tribes, Reuben and Gad, together with half of the tribe of Manasseh requested that they be permitted to settle there. Moses criticized them. Did they plan to separate themselves from the rest of Israel, who would be settling on the west side of the Jordan? The leaders of these tribes assured Moses that they were fully loyal and would share in every responsibility of Israel.
10. MASSEY Num. 33–36
    This sidra reports on the wanderings of Israel from the time they left Egypt to the time they reached the borders of Canaan. It also gives a detailed description of what were to be the boundaries of the land of Israel.

BOOK OF DEUTERONOMY/*DEVARIM*

1. DEVARIM Deut. 1–3:22
   This consists of Moses' farewell to Israel, delivered at the end of his long period as its leader. He was soon to die and wanted to use his remaining strength to review for Israel its history, its special relationship with God, and its future as a people.
2. VA-ETHCHANAN Deut. 3:23–7:11
   Here, Moses continues his farewell to Israel, with a review of the Ten Commandments and an appeal not to forget what they experienced at Mt. Sinai. Moses then gives to Israel the great *Sh'ma* message. Israel must hear as clearly as possible that there is but one God, have a deep love for Him, study His teachings carefully, and live by them inside and outside their homes. Moses warns Israel, as strongly as possible, that when they enter Canaan, they must live their own sacred way of life. They must not intermarry with any of the pagan people whom they will meet in Canaan. To do so would weaken Israel's covenant with God.
3. EKEV Deut. 7:12–11:25
   What does God require of Israel for all His generosity to us? Nothing that is beyond the reach of each of us: only that we love and serve Him and live by the commandments which He revealed to us.
4. RE'EH Deut. 11:26–16:17
   "Behold, I set before you this day a blessing and a curse: the blessing, if ye shall hearken unto the commandment of the Lord your God, which I command you this day; and the curse, if you shall not hearken . . ." The future depends on our making the right choice. To do right, we must follow the laws, which Moses now spells out in detail.
5. SHOFETIM Deut. 16:18–21:9
   Justice must be carried out in the land which the Israelites will soon settle, "Justice, justice must you follow, that you may live, and inherit the land which the Lord, your God, gives you."
6. KI THETZE Deut. 21:10–25
   Moses reviews a variety of laws which are intended to strengthen family life and human decency in Israel. Parents are responsible for the education of their children. If one finds lost property, it must be returned to the owner. Accident prevention is obligatory for property owners. Kindness to animals is required by law. The community is responsible for the needs of strangers, widows, and orphans. The law requires honest business practices: weights and measures must be absolutely dependable.
7. KI THAVO Deut. 26–29:8
   The people soon would be crossing the Jordan, and their first assignment was to write the code of laws by which they were to live, as a sign that this land was theirs

in consequence of the covenant and on condition of carrying out the law. The second assignment, on entering the land, was to build an altar for public worship on which to bring peace offerings to God.

8. MITZAVIM Deut. 29:9–30
   In Moses' third farewell address to Israel, he points out that all Israel is gathered for the completion of the convenant with God. It is binding upon all the generations of Israel that will follow for all time to come. The Torah and its teachings will be theirs as much as if they personally had received it at Sinai. The covenant is unending.
9. VAYYELECH Deut. 31
   Here, Moses completes the writing of the Torah and entrusts it to the Kohanim and elders of Israel. He instructs them to read the Torah before the people at regular intervals. The Torah was not to remain the special preserve of the priests but was to be heard by and be familiar to all the people.
10. HAAZINU Deut. 32
    At the beginning of his role as Israel's leader, Moses has sung a song of praise to God at the crossing of the Red Sea. Now, though he will soon die, Moses' faith in God is as strong as ever. He sings a final hymn of joy to God on the banks of the Jordan with the Promised Land on the horizon.
11. VEZOTH HA-BERACHAH Deut. 33–34
    Before Moses goes up to the mountain top to have a brief look at Canaan, he blesses the tribes of Israel. He then goes up, dies, and is buried in the Valley of Moab. Israel mourns his passing deeply and turns to his successor, Joshua, for leadership.

If you may request a specific date for your child's ceremony and have reviewed the various Torah portions, here are some ideas to consider: Perhaps your child will want to read the same portion which his father or a favorite relative read at his Bar Mitzvah. Perhaps your youngster would like to read a section which includes his biblical namesake or other material of particular interest to him. But all the portions are valuable. One scholarly rabbi has said that every week he wants to say that this is the best, most important portion in the cycle. This reflects the fact that each section has its own significance, which becomes apparent when one has studied it with care and supervision.

Jewish Holydays with Their Special Festivities

You may wish to check the Jewish holyday schedule during the season of your Bar/Bat Mitzvah. Every Jewish holyday is marked by special religious rituals and is an occasion for joyous celebration. These observances and festivities would enhance any Bar/Bat Mitzvah ceremony happening at that time. At Sukkot, Chanukah, the Shabbat before Purim, and certain other times during the year an extra Torah scroll is taken from the ark as part of the service. This may give you the opportunity to extend additional synagogue honors to your guests. Certain festivals, such as Pesach and Sukkot, may call for chanting the *Hallel,* prayers of praise which embellish the service on that holiday. If it is a Jewish holyday, this may affect the readings at that service as well. To know the rituals observed at your synagogue, it is best to check with your rabbi, cantor, ritual committee chairman, or other congregational leaders. To plan ahead, turn to the Hebrew-Civil Calendar Chart in the back of this book which has the Jewish holiday schedule through the year 2000.

If your child's Bar/Bat Mitzvah falls at a holiday time, you will be able to enhance your celebration with the traditional rituals and foods appropriate to that occasion. At Sukkot, you could have your reception outdoors, either in your own or the synagogue's sukkah, decorated with the fruits, grains, and vegetables of that harvest festival. Several families we know had beautiful Bar Mitzvah receptions during Chanukah. They placed a *Chanukiah* (Chanukah menorah) as the centerpiece at each table, served potato latkes, and sang the songs customary for that season of rejoicing. In this and in many other ways, you can add an extra dimension of holiday joy to your Bar/Bat Mitzvah celebration.

Jewish Days of Remembrance with Certain Limitations

There are certain days of remembrance in the Jewish calendar when you may not want to hold a Bar/Bat Mitzvah. Although you may enhance your Bar/Bat Mitzvah by having it on a festival, it may be inappropriate to select times which commemorate tragic events in our collective Jewish history. Among these is Yom Ha-Shoah, the day when we remember the lives of 6 million of our people who perished in the Holocaust. In the summer, at Tisha b'Av, we recall the destruction of the First and Second Temples. At this and at five other times in the Jewish calendar year, it has been traditional to fast. In addition, during the period from Pesach to Shavuot, during the counting of the Omer, there may be certain restrictions on having a Bar/Bat Mitzvah celebration. At Pesach, while basically a season of gladness, your reception could be affected by the prohibition against eating leavened foods. Consult with your rabbi or ritual leaders as to how these special dates may affect you.

Secular Holidays, Vacation Times, the Weather, and Other Factors

Secular holidays, vacation times, and the weather may influence your request for a specific Bar/Bat Mitzvah date. Keep in mind that these factors will undoubtedly be secondary to other more important criteria.

Secular holidays can be a good time to schedule a Bar/Bat Mitzvah. This can affect your planning in several ways. When a secular holiday is observed on a Monday, this offers you a long weekend. If your child's Bar/Bat Mitzvah is on Shabbat, you then have an extra day for your guests to visit and/or travel home. If you belong to a synagogue where the Torah is read on Mondays and Thursdays, in addition to Saturday morning, this may give you the opportunity to schedule a complete Bar/Bat Mitzvah on a weekday. For more information on these services, please see the end of the chapter.

You should keep in mind that secular and important Christian holidays may also affect your plans. For instance, if your child's Bar/Bat Mitzvah falls on New Year's weekend, you must consider if you will have a difficult time hiring help and scheduling a caterer. Determine if it will be difficult for your guests to plan travel arrangements and accommodations for that period. Ask yourself if there are other problems which may arise because of this Bar/Bat Mitzvah date.

If you have the option to request a specific Bar/Bat Mitzvah date, the time of the year may be a factor. Check with your congregation to see whether they schedule Bar/Bat

Mitzvah ceremonies during July and August. In some congregations, summer services are held on a limited basis since many members as well as synagogue staff may be on vacation at that time. You may find that the Sisterhood is not available during these months to assist with your reception. Some of your guests may have planned summer trips far in advance; these may conflict with your Bar/Bat Mitzvah date. Does your child usually go to overnight camp? Since a Bar/Bat Mitzvah is a community celebration, you should consider these factors in requesting your date.

The weather may be another consideration. If you are likely to worry about what the day may bring, you may not want to request February, if you live in Boston, or August, if you live in Dallas. Elderly grandparents may prefer a date when the local climate is likely to be pleasant. If you can plan a date when you can expect reasonable weather, your anxiety level will drop accordingly. Does your child have allergies every spring which cause his nose to run and his voice to go hoarse? Does your child have a good friend in another congregation who may be requesting the same Bar/Bat Mitzvah date? Are there any other circumstances which may influence your request? However, remember that religious considerations should take priority over convenience.

When more than one child requests the same Bar/Bat Mitzvah date, two children may participate in a ceremony at the same service. In some large congregations, this is commonly done, because the calendar is crowded with children reaching age thirteen at the same time. We have been to services where two youngsters shared the occasion, each leading part of the service and reading sections from the Haftarah and Torah. This can be very satisfactory.

One family in Atlanta chose to have their twins share their ceremony with a newly discovered relative who had recently moved to New York from South Africa. The three young cousins were turning thirteen at the same time. They all gathered in Atlanta for a very special family occasion, the B'nai Mitzvot of their children and a large family reunion.

A Bar/Bat Mitzvah Ceremony as Part of a Regular Synagogue Service

From the very start, Jewish worship was a communal matter. While one may pray in private, there is special merit in praying with a congregation. Traditionally, one needs a *minyan*—ten men—to hold a worship service. In this and other ways, Judaism placed the individual within the support of a communal context. It was here, within his community of fellow Jews, that he would celebrate life's joys and sustain its tragedies. It is within the synagogue service that the formal ceremony of Bar/Bat Mitzvah takes place. The child, his family and friends, his entire congregation rejoice as another young adult commits himself to the community.

In planning your child's Bar/Bat Mitzvah, you may wonder at which service to hold the ceremony. While you may be familiar with the Friday evening and Saturday morning services there may be other options available. Consult your rabbi to learn about the choices at your synagogue.

The Shabbat Morning Service and Kiddush

It is common today and closely follows tradition for the Bar/Bat Mitzvah ceremony to occur at the Saturday morning synagogue service. This is what you probably visualize as the usual Bar/Bat Mitzvah experience. With roots back in the Middle Ages, this has been the setting where the child publicly demonstrates his commitment to fulfill the responsibilities of an adult member of his Jewish community. It is here that he is allowed to participate in the rituals associated with religious maturity. He is called up to the Torah for an aliyah for the first time. To demonstrate his interest and learning, it is customary for the child to read the Maftir (concluding section) from the Torah portion for the week, and the accompanying Haftarah from the prophetic literature. If the child is particularly able and interested, he may lead part or all of the service, or do more of the Torah reading for that week. Your synagogue may prescribe the extent to which a Bar/Bat Mitzvah may participate in leading the service. Check with your rabbi or ritual leaders for that information. They may restrict participation so that the regular Shabbat service maintains precedence over the Bar/Bat Mitzvah ceremony which takes place within it.

In some synagogues, blessings are said over the challah and wine directly after the service. The entire congregation is usually included at this kiddush. Sometimes foods, such as herring, gefilte fish, and cookies, may also be served. The purpose is to break bread together and to share fellowship with other members of the synagogue community.

The Friday Evening Service and Oneg Shabbat

Some congregations offer girls the option of a Friday evening Bat Mitzvah ceremony. Other congregations may insist on Friday evening. At this service, the girl may say the blessing over the candles, chant kiddush, say prayers, and generally assist in leading the congregational service. Usually there is no Torah service at this time. However, we do know of a few synagogues where the Torah readings for the week are divided between the Friday night and Saturday morning service. Be certain to check on this if you are interested in having your child read from the Torah and/or Haftarah as part of the Bar/Bat Mitzvah experience. If this reading is not possible on Friday night, you might inquire about a Saturday morning Bat Mitzvah as more and more synagogues are now offering this opportunity to girls. Typically, the Friday evening service is followed by an oneg Shabbat at the synagogue for the entire congregation. Desserts, coffee, tea, and soft drinks are served at that time. The Friday evening service encompassing a Bat Mitzvah ceremony and the oneg Shabbat usually runs from about 8:30 P.M. to 10:30 P.M.

Mincha and Havdalah

Over a period of time, holding prayer services three times daily became traditional Jewish practice. The schedule of prayer services corresponds to the prescribed order of offerings which had been made in the days of the Temple. When the Temple was no longer standing and the Jews were dispersed, leaders of the Jewish community determined that communal prayer was an appropriate substitute for these earlier sacrifices. In fact, the Hebrew word, *Mincha,* means present or offering, reflecting how this service would now take the place of sacrifices which formerly had been made at that time of day. This is the origin of Mincha, the afternoon service.

Mincha occurs before sunset, around 4:30 P.M., in the winter, and 7:30 P.M., in the spring through fall months, when the days are longer. Typically, the Torah is read at this Shabbat afternoon service. It can be a very nice setting for a Bar/Bat Mitzvah ceremony. It could be a less demanding experience. Perhaps at this time your child might be given the opportunity for more personal or even creative participation.

The Mincha service can be followed directly by the traditional third meal, the *seudah shlishit,* which is eaten just before Shabbat concludes. It is customary for this to be a simple meal served in the synagogue. It is sometimes known as *shalosh seudot* which really means "three meals" and suggests that the religious significance of these Shabbat meals is symbolized by participating in this final one of the day.

You may have heard the phrase, "a Havdalah Bar Mitzvah." Just as the beginning of Shabbat is ushered in with the lighting of candles, so does the ending of this day call for a special ritual, *Havdalah* (separation), which separates Shabbat from the work week. Often a Saturday afternoon Bar/Bat Mitzvah ceremony includes Havdalah along with the earlier Mincha service during which the Torah is read. Wherever you observe this Havdalah ceremony, whether it's at the synagogue or at home, it maintains the religious tone appropriate to the occasion. At the end of Shabbat, the lighting of the braided Havdalah candle with the accompanying blessings for wine, spices, and light, is a very moving moment. In this case, the candlelighting serves as an additional reminder of the beauty of the day, the Shabbat of your child's Bar/Bat Mitzvah.

If you are interested in having a Bar/Bat Mitzvah ceremony at a Saturday afternoon service, check first with your rabbi. While some may encourage or permit this, others may prefer that your child participate in the usually better attended services of Shabbat, Friday evening or Saturday morning.

For those who want a full day of prayer and synagogue involvement, it is possible to take part in both the Saturday morning service and the afternoon service on Shabbat. In this way, you can have an all-day experience, returning to the synagogue for Mincha/ Havdalah and an evening celebration. The emotional pitch and religious connection is maintained throughout the day; the festivities keep the primary focus on communal worship and the synagogue, which is appropriate for a Bar/Bat Mitzvah.

Other Services: A Monday or Thursday Torah Service, Rosh Hodesh, a Festival

In some congregations, the Torah is read on Mondays and Thursdays, as well as at the regular Shabbat services. This tradition goes back to the days of the Temple when the Torah was read on market days—Mondays and Thursdays—so that all could hear the law. It may be possible for your child to be called up to the Torah as a Bar/Bat Mitzvah at one of these weekday services. This may be a good choice. When appropriate, some people plan a Bar/Bat Mitzvah on the Monday of a secular holiday such as Memorial Day or Labor Day. A child we know had a Bar Mitzvah on December 25 when it fell on a Thursday. A Monday or Thursday ceremony can be particularly desirable if you have invited guests who are *Shomer Shabbat.* These strictly observant Jews will not travel on Friday night or Saturday and so a weekday observance is much easier for them to attend. On Monday or Thursday, the regular congregation may be small, so those who are present will be mainly your own guests. This Bar/Bat Mitzvah format can also offer a suitable opportunity for a child who is not well prepared or who has learning limitations, since this can be a less demanding experience. On the other hand, a child who is extremely capable and knowledgeable may be allowed to lead more of the service at this time than he might be permitted to do at a Saturday morning synagogue service.

Some synagogues hold services on Rosh Hodesh, which is the first day of a new Hebrew month. Many congregations throughout the broad spectrum of Judaism have services on the mornings of the Jewish festivals: Sukkot, Pesach, and Shavuot. At these times, the Torah customarily is brought out and read. It may be possible to schedule a Bar/Bat Mitzvah ceremony at these times if this is a good alternative for you and if it meets with the approval of your congregation. Whatever you plan, remember that a Bar/Bat Mitzvah is not a strictly personal event. It is a ritual made possible by a fully developed Jewish community, and you must place your celebration in the context of what is appropriate within your congregation.

Preparing Your Child

Preparing Your Child

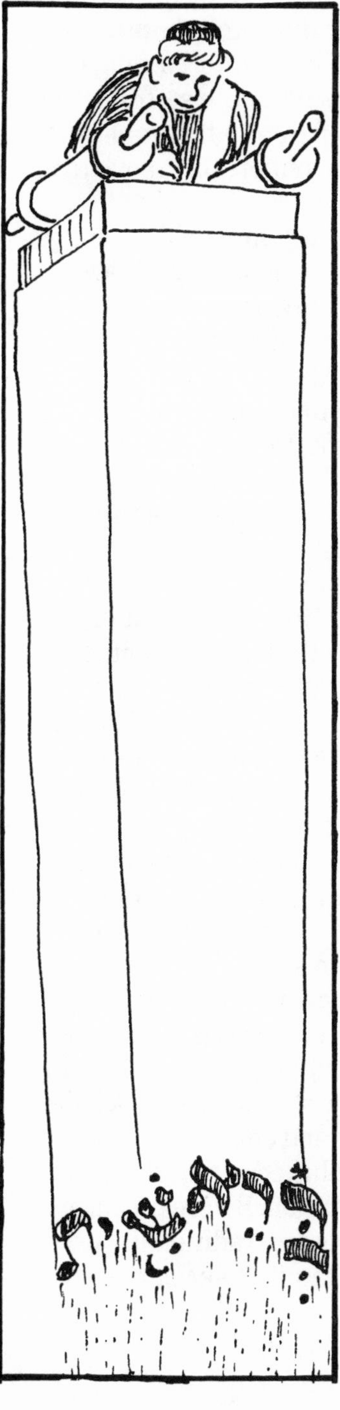

Basic Training

A course of study will prepare your youngster for his part in the Bar/Bat Mitzvah ceremony. The child's role in the service depends on his skills and interest and the customs of the congregation. The child may be called upon to lead part of the service, to read from the Torah, to chant the Haftarah, or to lead prayer.

The public reading of the Torah is a fundamental part of the synagogue service. A different sidra (portion) is read on each Shabbat of the year; so, your child's Bar/Bat Mitzvah date will have its specific Torah portion. A specified Haftarah, a reading from the prophets, follows the Torah reading. In the Charts and Timetables section of this book you'll find a calendar that will let you cross-reference your child's Bar/Bat Mitzvah date and its connected Torah and Haftarah readings.

Arrangements for Bar/Bat Mitzvah training can be made through the synagogue. Sometimes, all pre-Bar/Bat Mitzvah children are taught as a group, so that they can gain the general skills required for this occasion. Together they can learn the blessings said when one is called up to the Torah for an aliyah and those said before and after chanting the Haftarah. Basic synagogue skills can also be taught at this time: the use of the tallit, tefillin; the blowing of a shofar; how to lift and dress the Torah, and other traditional Jewish practices.

As the child prepares for his Bar/Bat Mitzvah, he may be taught the distinctive trope (melodic notations) for the Torah and the one for the Haftarah. Learning to read trope instead of simply memorizing the portion will enable your child to use that skill in years to come. The process is like learning to read music. Understanding the melodic notation will help your child master his portion and feel comfortable and secure when delivering it in public.

Individualized Tutoring

In addition, an individualized tutoring program will prepare each child for his specific role before the congregation on his Bar/Bat Mitzvah date. This training may be provided by your congregation or you may have to hire a private tutor. The cantor, a religious school teacher, a capable post-Bar/Bat Mitzvah student, or someone else from the Jewish community can all be effective. A very rare case is the parent who is able and willing to tutor his own child. This can work well if both can comfortably move to a teacher-student relationship.

Who would serve as a good role model for your child? With whom would he enjoy working? Of course, having a tutor from the synagogue has the added advantage of reinforcing your child's connection to this religious institution. You may find that the major concern for you is the location of the tutorial sessions: at home, at the synagogue, or elsewhere. Make certain that transportation arrangements are sufficiently convenient so that you do not resent the tutorial sessions. That would undermine your child's preparation and attitude. If you prefer to have someone come to your home, your synagogue, a local Jewish bookstore, or a Jewish newspaper may have information about qualified persons seeking this type of work. It is best to work out the cost of the tutorial sessions in advance.

There are two distinct forms of Hebrew pronunciation, Ashkenazic and Sephardic. Ashkenazic was originally used in Eastern Europe. During the Holocaust, most of the European Jews who prayed in Ashkenazic were exterminated by the Nazis. Despite this tragedy, this form of Hebrew still remains as the language of prayer in some congregations. The other pronunciation, Sephardic, originated in Spain and spread to North Africa and other resettlement areas after the Jews were expelled from Spain in 1492. Strengthened by being the Hebrew form spoken in Israel today, the Sephardic pronunciation is the most commonly used. In Sephardic, the Hebrew letter *Taf* is pronounced like a "T," while, in Ashkenazic, it is said as an "S," as in Shabbat as compared to Shabbos. There are many other differences between these two forms of spoken Hebrew and your child should prepare using the pronunciation favored by your synagogue.

One can say the same written but unvoweled Hebrew word in a number of different ways. During the dispersion outside the land of Israel, the Jews lost their familiarity with the correct pronunciation of Hebrew texts. Only the learned were certain that they were reading and pronouncing the writings correctly. A system of vowels evolved in written Hebrew which clarifies pronunciation. With the passage of time, trope (melodic notation) was developed in order to make it easier to remember and chant the words of the Torah and Haftarah. While the marks have not changed or shifted position over the years, there is flexibility in individual expression and interpretation. Before preparing your child, check with your synagogue to see what melodic forms are traditionally used in your congregation. If a melody has been passed down in your family, ask your rabbi if you may follow it during your child's ceremony. It should be noted that in some congregations, the Torah and Haftarah may be recited rather than chanted, then the issue of melodic notations will not apply.

Study Aids

The Torah has been copied meticulously in hand-lettered Hebrew by learned scribes. It has remained unchanged, without vowel or trope signs, for thousands of years until today. In studying the Bar/Bat Mitzvah portion, your child will be helped by using a *Tikkun*. A Tikkun is a book which contains one column with a copy of the hand-lettered Torah printed exactly as it looks on the Sefer Torah in your synagogue Ark. On the adjacent column is the identical passage written in modern Hebrew print with markings indicating vowel sounds and melodic patterns. While your child will be aided by practicing the Torah portion with the Tikkun, he will not be allowed to use it on the bimah (pulpit). When reading his portion at the Bar/Bat Mitzvah, your child will be in front of the congregation, pointing with a *yad* (Torah pointer), chanting from the Sefer Torah written in the traditional hand-lettered manner.

Shilo Publishing House, Inc., has the most comprehensive and readily obtainable study aids for the individual child's Bar/Bat Mitzvah preparation. It distributes four separate series which all contain the Maftir (final section of the Torah portion), Haftarah (readings from the Prophets), and their accompanying blessings. The series of study aids are available as a booklet, book, record, or cassette. There is one for each week of the annual Torah-reading cycle. The booklets, called "Hamaftir" are numbered and named for the Torah portion of the week. Booklet #3, for example, refers to the third week in the yearly cycle and is also identified by the traditional name of the portion, "Lech Lecha." These booklets are printed with vowels and melodic markings. They also contain the Haftarah translation and instructions and prayers for the use of tefillin (phylacteries). Your child can carry his "Hamaftir" around with him and rely on it as a valuable study guide.

בְּרֵאשִׁית

א 2 בְּרֵאשִׁית בָּרָא אֱלֹהִים אֵת הַשָּׁמַיִם וְאֵת הָאָרֶץ: וְהָאָרֶץ
הָיְתָה תֹהוּ וָבֹהוּ וְחֹשֶׁךְ עַל־פְּנֵי תְהוֹם וְרוּחַ אֱלֹהִים
3 מְרַחֶפֶת עַל־פְּנֵי הַמָּיִם: וַיֹּאמֶר אֱלֹהִים יְהִי אוֹר וַיְהִי
4 אוֹר: וַיַּרְא אֱלֹהִים אֶת־הָאוֹר כִּי־טוֹב וַיַּבְדֵּל אֱלֹהִים בֵּין
ה הָאוֹר וּבֵין הַחֹשֶׁךְ: וַיִּקְרָא אֱלֹהִים ׀ לָאוֹר יוֹם וְלַחֹשֶׁךְ
קָרָא לָיְלָה וַיְהִי־עֶרֶב וַיְהִי־בֹקֶר יוֹם אֶחָד: לוי פ
6 וַיֹּאמֶר אֱלֹהִים יְהִי רָקִיעַ בְּתוֹךְ הַמָּיִם וִיהִי מַבְדִּיל בֵּין
7 מַיִם לָמָיִם: וַיַּעַשׂ אֱלֹהִים אֶת־הָרָקִיעַ וַיַּבְדֵּל בֵּין הַמַּיִם
אֲשֶׁר מִתַּחַת לָרָקִיעַ וּבֵין הַמַּיִם אֲשֶׁר מֵעַל לָרָקִיעַ וַיְהִי
8 כֵן: וַיִּקְרָא אֱלֹהִים לָרָקִיעַ שָׁמָיִם וַיְהִי־עֶרֶב וַיְהִי־בֹקֶר
יוֹם שֵׁנִי: ישראל פ
9 וַיֹּאמֶר אֱלֹהִים יִקָּווּ הַמַּיִם מִתַּחַת הַשָּׁמַיִם אֶל־מָקוֹם אֶחָד
י וְתֵרָאֶה הַיַּבָּשָׁה וַיְהִי־כֵן: וַיִּקְרָא אֱלֹהִים ׀ לַיַּבָּשָׁה אֶרֶץ
11 וּלְמִקְוֵה הַמַּיִם קָרָא יַמִּים וַיַּרְא אֱלֹהִים כִּי־טוֹב: וַיֹּאמֶר
אֱלֹהִים תַּדְשֵׁא הָאָרֶץ דֶּשֶׁא עֵשֶׂב מַזְרִיעַ זֶרַע עֵץ פְּרִי
עֹשֶׂה פְּרִי לְמִינוֹ אֲשֶׁר זַרְעוֹ־בוֹ עַל־הָאָרֶץ וַיְהִי־כֵן:
12 וַתּוֹצֵא הָאָרֶץ דֶּשֶׁא עֵשֶׂב מַזְרִיעַ זֶרַע לְמִינֵהוּ וְעֵץ עֹשֶׂה
13 פְּרִי אֲשֶׁר זַרְעוֹ־בוֹ לְמִינֵהוּ וַיַּרְא אֱלֹהִים כִּי־טוֹב: וַיְהִי
עֶרֶב וַיְהִי־בֹקֶר יוֹם שְׁלִישִׁי: פ

14 וַיֹּאמֶר אֱלֹהִים יְהִי מְאֹרֹת בִּרְקִיעַ הַשָּׁמַיִם לְהַבְדִּיל בֵּין
הַיּוֹם וּבֵין הַלָּיְלָה וְהָיוּ לְאֹתֹת וּלְמוֹעֲדִים וּלְיָמִים וְשָׁנִים:
טו וְהָיוּ לִמְאוֹרֹת בִּרְקִיעַ הַשָּׁמַיִם לְהָאִיר עַל־הָאָרֶץ וַיְהִי
16 כֵן: וַיַּעַשׂ אֱלֹהִים אֶת־שְׁנֵי הַמְּאֹרֹת הַגְּדֹלִים אֶת־הַמָּאוֹר
הַגָּדֹל לְמֶמְשֶׁלֶת הַיּוֹם וְאֶת־הַמָּאוֹר הַקָּטֹן לְמֶמְשֶׁלֶת
17 הַלַּיְלָה וְאֵת הַכּוֹכָבִים: וַיִּתֵּן אֹתָם אֱלֹהִים בִּרְקִיעַ
18 הַשָּׁמָיִם לְהָאִיר עַל־הָאָרֶץ: וְלִמְשֹׁל בַּיּוֹם וּבַלַּיְלָה
וּלֲהַבְדִּיל בֵּין הָאוֹר וּבֵין הַחֹשֶׁךְ וַיַּרְא אֱלֹהִים כִּי־טוֹב:
19 וַיְהִי־עֶרֶב וַיְהִי־בֹקֶר יוֹם רְבִיעִי: פ

כ וַיֹּאמֶר אֱלֹהִים יִשְׁרְצוּ הַמַּיִם שֶׁרֶץ נֶפֶשׁ חַיָּה וְעוֹף יְעוֹפֵף
21 עַל־הָאָרֶץ עַל־פְּנֵי רְקִיעַ הַשָּׁמָיִם: וַיִּבְרָא אֱלֹהִים אֶת־
הַתַּנִּינִם הַגְּדֹלִים וְאֵת כָּל־נֶפֶשׁ הַחַיָּה ׀ הָרֹמֶשֶׂת אֲשֶׁר
שָׁרְצוּ הַמַּיִם לְמִינֵהֶם וְאֵת כָּל־עוֹף כָּנָף לְמִינֵהוּ וַיַּרְא
22 אֱלֹהִים כִּי־טוֹב: וַיְבָרֶךְ אֹתָם אֱלֹהִים לֵאמֹר פְּרוּ וּרְבוּ
23 וּמִלְאוּ אֶת־הַמַּיִם בַּיַּמִּים וְהָעוֹף יִרֶב בָּאָרֶץ: וַיְהִי־עֶרֶב
וַיְהִי־בֹקֶר יוֹם חֲמִישִׁי: פ

24 וַיֹּאמֶר אֱלֹהִים תּוֹצֵא הָאָרֶץ נֶפֶשׁ חַיָּה לְמִינָהּ בְּהֵמָה
כה וָרֶמֶשׂ וְחַיְתוֹ־אֶרֶץ לְמִינָהּ וַיְהִי־כֵן: וַיַּעַשׂ אֱלֹהִים אֶת־
חַיַּת הָאָרֶץ לְמִינָהּ וְאֶת־הַבְּהֵמָה לְמִינָהּ

v. 1. [illegible] v. 11. [illegible] v. 18. כא ולהבדיל v. 21. חסר י בתראה

בראשית ברא אלהים את השמים ואת הארץ
והארץ היתה תהו ובהו וחשך על פני תהום ורוח
אלהים מרחפת על פני המים ויאמר אלהים יהי
אור ויהי אור וירא אלהים את האור כי טוב
ויבדל אלהים בין האור ובין החשך ויקרא
אלהים לאור יום ולחשך קרא לילה ויהי ערב
ויהי בקר יום אחד
ויאמר אלהים יהי רקיע בתוך המים ויהי מבדיל
בין מים למים ויעש אלהים את הרקיע ויבדל
בין המים אשר מתחת לרקיע ובין המים אשר
מעל לרקיע ויהי כן ויקרא אלהים לרקיע שמים
ויהי ערב ויהי בקר יום שני
ויאמר אלהים יקוו המים מתחת השמים אל
מקום אחד ותראה היבשה ויהי כן ויקרא אלהים
ליבשה ארץ ולמקוה המים קרא ימים וירא
אלהים כי טוב ויאמר אלהים תדשא הארץ
דשא עשב מזריע זרע עץ פרי עשה פרי למינו
אשר זרעו בו על הארץ ויהי כן ותוצא הארץ
דשא עשב מזריע זרע למינהו ועץ עשה פרי
אשר זרעו בו למינהו וירא אלהים כי טוב ויהי
ערב ויהי בקר יום שלישי
ויאמר אלהים יהי מארת ברקיע השמים להבדיל
בין היום ובין הלילה והיו לאתת ולמועדים ולימים
ושנים והיו למאורת ברקיע השמים להאיר על
הארץ ויהי כן ויעש אלהים את שני המארת
הגדלים את המאור הגדל לממשלת היום ואת
המאור הקטן לממשלת הלילה ואת הכוכבים
ויתן אתם אלהים ברקיע השמים להאיר על
הארץ ולמשל ביום ובלילה ולהבדיל בין האור
ובין החשך וירא אלהים כי טוב ויהי ערב ויהי
בקר יום רביעי
ויאמר אלהים ישרצו המים שרץ נפש חיה
ועוף יעופף על הארץ על פני רקיע השמים
ויברא אלהים את התנינם הגדלים ואת כל נפש
החיה הרמשת אשר שרצו המים למינהם ואת
כל עוף כנף למינהו וירא אלהים כי טוב ויברך
אתם אלהים לאמר פרו ורבו ומלאו את המים
בימים והעוף ירב בארץ ויהי ערב ויהי בקר
יום חמישי
ויאמר אלהים תוצא הארץ נפש חיה למינה
בהמה ורמש וחיתו ארץ למינה ויהי כן ויעש
אלהים את חית הארץ למינה ואת הבהמה למינה

Tikkun page

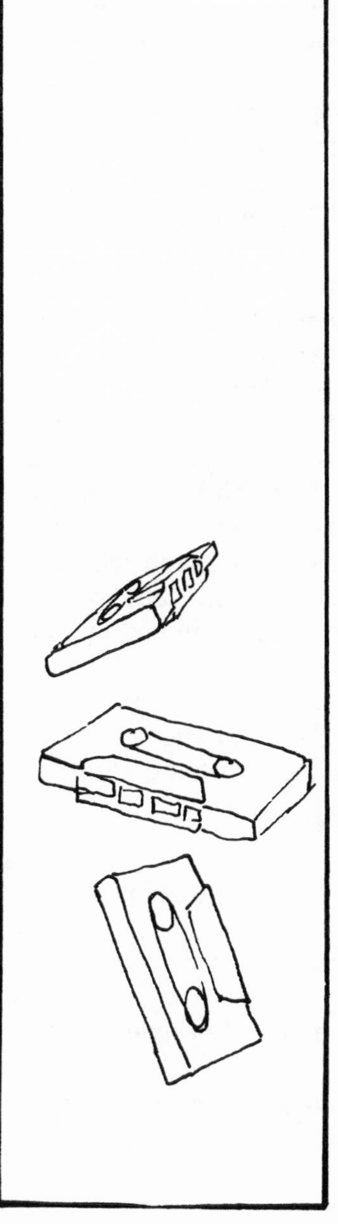

Shilo also publishes a second series called *My Bar Mitzvah Book,* which includes everything in "Hamaftir," plus additional articles on the Torah, Ten Commandments, Prophets, and a discussion of the teachings of that week's Haftarah. This supplemental information may be of interest to your child. Their records and cassettes cover each week of the Jewish calendar year. The tapes use Sephardic pronunciation while the records can be obtained with either Sephardic or Ashkenazic Hebrew. The Shilo series can be found in a local Jewish bookstore, perhaps your synagogue shop, or they can be ordered directly from Shilo Publishing House, Inc., 73 Canal Street, New York, NY 10002, (212) 925-3468.

Another, more informal, learning aid is a cassette prepared by your child's tutor. The Bar/Bat Mitzvah blessings and readings can be recorded phrase by phrase with a space for repetition in between. In this way, the student can copy and practice on his own whenever he wishes. All of these study aids can assist the Bar/Bat Mitzvah student as he prepares for his public ceremony.

D'Rash, Bar/Bat Mitzvah Speech, Personal Prayer

There are many ways in which your child may expand his participation in the service. In medieval Germany it was common for a child to give a public discourse to demonstrate his learning. These words of Torah (d'var Torah) were often given at the feast following the ceremony itself, thus helping to keep a religious tone at the celebration. From this stems the contemporary practice of having a child deliver a d'var Torah, describe the message of his Haftarah, make a speech, and say a prayer before the Ark. If your child is preparing for one of these, he can be assisted by his tutor or rabbi. Here are guidelines for these presentations.

In delivering a description of his Torah or Haftarah portion, a child should be confident that he understands what he is saying and that the message he is giving is clear to the listeners. Some adult supervision may be needed to see that the speech is well organized and of a reasonable length. A junior high-school-age child usually is able to express himself fairly well orally; writing may be more difficult. The parent or tutor can help the child develop his thoughts by talking with the child and then typing or writing down his ideas so he can review and polish his presentation. If the child is making a speech describing his personal religious commitment, feelings, and gratitude on this occasion, be careful that it remains within good taste. Professing too much religious fervor, with cute comments, and thanks for possessions as well as training, could border on the inappropriate. Nor is this the occasion for the mother to stand up and vividly describe her memories of the day this child was born.

If the child—and perhaps the parents—chooses to make a personal prayer before the congregation, these prayers should reflect the thoughts of the child and parent. A prayer, like a gift, is no less precious if it is selected rather than made by hand. Here are some suggestions for writing or selecting a prayer:[1]

- The prayer the child chooses may express a feeling of gratitude upon reaching this milestone in life.
- A child may ask for God's blessings on his family and teachers for having guided him and prepared him for this occasion.
- The child may wish to express aspirations for his future as well as hopes for the welfare of the Jewish people.
- The child may wish to pledge that he will continue studying and remain devoted to the ideals of his faith.

1. Stanley Rabinowitz, *Prayers for the Bar Mitzvah Child* (Washington, D.C.: Adas Israel Congregation).

Many rabbis arrange for a meeting with the Bar/Bat Mitzvah and his parents before the ceremony. In any event, you may wish to give the rabbi some background material about your child and family. You may outline some of your child's interests and/or accomplishments. There is always something positive to say. You may also include information about special relatives and those who have traveled great distances to attend. This will give the rabbi specifics for the personal remarks that he will undoubtedly direct to your child on the Bar/Bat Mitzvah day.

Understanding the Synagogue Service

To give needed support to your child's undertaking, the immediate family should also be familiar with the service at which the Bar Mitzvah is being held. If you do not ordinarily attend services at your synagogue, you should make a point of going regularly before your Bar/Bat Mitzvah so that you are comfortable at this service. The service may seem foreign or unfamiliar, or even without much meaning to you. Those feelings can be overcome by attendance, participation, or guidance from synagogue members who attend regularly. Many congregations run a minicourse on Jewish topics for the Bar/Bat Mitzvah parents. Not only is this a form of adult education, but it also brings together a group with common interests and concerns. If your synagogue does not do this, you may suggest that they run a short series of classes for the Bar/Bat Mitzvah parents.

Tips for Success

Your child can benefit from a few words of advice about what to expect and how to behave throughout the ceremony. This is best discussed in a quiet moment a few days before the Bar/Bat Mitzvah. You may make the following suggestions, taking into consideration the customs of your particular congregation:

- Follow the service with an open book, participating in prayers and songs.
- Do not wave or signal friends and family from the bimah. Sit on the bimah in a dignified manner.
- Be prepared to shake hands with the rabbi, cantor, those presenting gifts (e.g., the Sisterhood president).

The Bar/Bat Mitzvah child will be the center of attention, somewhat overwhelmed at times, but in the back of his mind should be this parental encouragement on how to be friendly, composed, and polite at this, his big moment.

About three weeks before the Bar/Bat Mitzvah date, at least one dress rehearsal should be planned in the sanctuary. This will help set your child at ease as he practices where to stand, how to face the open Ark, volume levels (with a microphone, if one is used), and whatever else needs to be reviewed. If possible, he should practice chanting his portion from the Sefer Torah from which he will be reading at the ceremony. Reassure your child that he will do well. If necessary, remind him that the quality of his chanting voice is not significant. This is a time when some children's voices may be changing and others are simply not that musical. Musical ability is not the issue. The Bar/Bat Mitzvah ceremony marks the culmination of a period of Jewish study with a public religious ceremony acknowledging this commitment. It is this, not the voice, that is important. A reassuring call from the tutor can give an added psychological boost, sometimes very necessary in these last days before the Bar/Bat Mitzvah.

Clearly, a Bar/Bat Mitzvah is an important emotional event for the child and his family. Understandably, there is anxiety beforehand, rejoicing as the ceremony takes place, and often a post-Bar/Bat Mitzvah letdown, when all the excitement is over. The usual little sports accidents take on more meaning and may occur more frequently in the weeks before the Bar/Bat Mitzvah. Active young teenagers are often in slings and casts, and this time is no exception. One Bar Mitzvah boy we know was so aware of his parents' concerns about his health that it led him to write a very amusing short story:

> "Irving, now that Joel is in perfect condition, how are we going to keep him this way for his Bar Mitzvah? We can't have him go up to the bimah with a broken leg or stitches over his eyes," Miriam said.

> "Yes, I know, Miriam. With his past record, he will have something wrong with him, if we don't do something. Why, just last month, he had a broken toe, and he had a terrible case of poison ivy, he stepped on a nail, and got bitten by a rabbit. What more could happen?" Irving said.

The story goes on to describe how Joel was put to bed for two weeks prior to his Bar Mitzvah. Even then, something happened. The story ends when:

> Miriam realized, at last, that Joel wouldn't be his real self, without *some*thing being wrong with him.[2]

If your plans are set ahead of time, you can remain cheerful even when the unexpected occurs right before the Bar/Bat Mitzvah.

Pre-Bar/Bat Mitzvah tension is common the week before the big event. Your child will be sensitive to any anxiety his parents express. Guest lists, family personalities, and seating plans may demand your attention. However, parents should teach their children to differentiate between what is important and what is not. Don't confuse your child by losing sight of the fact that the religious ceremony is the heart of the Bar/Bat Mitzvah experience.

Your twelve- or thirteen-year-old may have waves of cheerful anticipation, alternating with despair about his ability to uphold the central role in this special occasion. Just prior to her Friday night ceremony, one young girl told her rabbi, "I don't think I can do it. I'm going to faint." He reassured her by suggesting that she wait until after the service! Feelings of this sort are normal. So much rests on your child's shoulders as he is called to stand alone before the entire congregation. Therefore, your child needs to be well prepared and given much parental support. Take time to listen to your child's concerns and express your confidence in his ability to do a fine job. The personal sense of achievement and joy of completion come from having mastered a difficult and complex task. With this feeling of accomplishment, the Bar/Bat Mitzvah ceremony will mark a meaningful point in your child's life.

2. David Pomerantz, "The Bar Mitzvah Boy," *Reflections,* Vol. 3 (Rockville, Md., 1978).

The Importance of a Jewish Education

At the Bar/Bat Mitzvah, your child will be called up to the Torah, before the entire congregation, to acknowledge his commitment to lead a responsible, Jewish life. Several years of Jewish education should precede this ceremony as an important foundation on which your child can build in the future. These years should be only the beginning, a time to gather information about our faith, our people, and the basic skills he'll need to practice his Jewish obligations. While the Bar/Bat Mitzvah is an occasion for joy, it can also be a time for concern if your child feels that this is a final ceremony and that now he is finished with his Jewish education. You wouldn't allow your child to terminate his secular school education at age twelve or thirteen. It is contradictory to fundamental Jewish tenets to ever consider education at an end. Studying has always been important to Jews of all ages, for we take to heart the idea that, "this book of the law shall not depart out of your mouth, but you shall meditate therein day and night, that you may observe to do according to all that is written therein." (Joshua 1:8). With adequate parental support and synagogue programming for teenagers, your child can continue his Jewish education through the high school years. Having dealt with the easier material, he can now turn to questions which have no answers, pondering the meanings of biblical and prophetic messages and their relation to his life. Being connected to the synagogue or other Jewish community youth groups can have an important effect on the adolescent seeking his identity by giving him a sense of belonging. Clearly, Jewish education is a lifetime experience.

In his studies, the Bar/Bat Mitzvah child is in a position similar to that of a contractor who worked for a large construction company for many years. One day, he was given plans to build a lovely home in a nice residential area. He was told to spare no expense. As the work progressed, the contractor thought to himself, "Who would know if I don't use the most expensive and best materials and labor? Outwardly, the house will look the same." He began to substitute cheap, poor quality materials and labor, pocketing the difference as his gain.

Shortly after the house was completed, a reception was held to celebrate the occasion. The chairman of the board surprised the contractor by presenting him with the keys to the house as a gift. It was to be a token of their esteem for his long and high-quality service. In the years that followed, the contractor never ceased to regret the way that he had cheated, "If only I had known that I was building the house for myself!"[3] So it is with the Bar/Bat Mitzvah. The child may fulfill his potential and meet his obligations or do less and ultimately weaken himself and the community. Many hopes rest on his shoulders on his Bar/Bat Mitzvah day as the influence of the past and the expectations for the future join together in sharp focus.

3. Morris Mandel, *Thirteen: A Teenage Guide to Judaism* (New York: Jonathan David Publishers, 1961), pp. 26–27.

Education for the Child with Special Needs

The Jewish community generally acknowledges its responsibility to offer a Jewish education to all its members. No child should be denied religious training because he or she cannot function successfully in the regular setting of a congregational or day school. Many cities, such as New York, Miami, Atlanta, Richmond, and others, offer programs for children with physical handicaps and/or learning disabilities. These individual programs are often run within the framework of the synagogue school.

In 1974, the Board of Jewish Education in Washington, D.C. inaugurated a unique separate school to serve the entire metropolitan community by helping its children, whatever their special needs. Supported by funds from the United Jewish Appeal Federation, this coordinated effort is known as Sh'ma V'Ezer, meaning, "Listen and help." It holds eight classes, with more than 75 children in attendance. In addition, it runs an outreach program to residential facilities and to congregational and day schools, giving important assistance to students with special needs. Sara Simon, the director of this program, states that, "the ability to experience a Bar/Bat Mitzvah ceremony is the single-most normalizing factor in these children's lives." This community has had Bar Mitzvahs by deaf children who have signed the service; retarded children who do as much as they are capable of; and children who cannot learn to read but have learned their portion by memory. Bar/Bat Mitzvah need not be limited to age thirteen, therefore, children with special needs may hold their ceremony at a later date, which best insures their sense of accomplishment. Often, both teachers and parents are amazed at how much the child wants to do and is able to achieve, thus marking an important milestone in his life.

More and more is being done to assist the Jewish child with special needs to maximize his individual development. Early detection and an early start is important. A task force, the Coalition for Alternatives in Jewish Education, is seeking to establish more options as well as a comprehensive course guide of different communities' programs. *The Other Child in Jewish Education: A Handbook on Learning Disabilities,* by Reuven Hammer, is a useful source book. To investigate this further, you should first turn to your community's central agency for Jewish education. Sh'ma V'Ezer has been instrumental as a model of Jewish education for the special child. For further information about Washington, D.C.'s Sh'ma V'Ezer program, or how to start one in your own community, contact: The Board of Jewish Education, 9325 Brookville Road, Silver Spring, MD 20910 (301) 589-3180.

Creative Bar/Bat Mitzvah Courses of Study

Recognizing that the year of Bar/Bat Mitzvah is an important one in the lives of its students, many Jewish educators have developed special programs for this age group. By the time of the Bar/Bat Mitzvah, the child is expected to know the basic vocabulary of Jewish life. When a congregation offers the child an opportunity to have a Bar/Bat Mitzvah ceremony, it is also attesting to his knowledge and commitment as a new member of the adult Jewish community.

One approach to the Bar/Bat Mitzvah training was developed by rabbis, educators, and parents at Temple Emanu-El, in Providence, Rhode Island. They felt that their children should be trained to understand the multifaceted life of today's committed Jew. To enrich their program, they went beyond formalized schooling to expose their children to various persons who reflect their Jewishness in their everyday lives and work: a cantor, a kosher butcher, a UJA administrator, a Jewish funeral director, and others. Parents were also involved as participants. This strengthened their personal dedication to Judaism while setting them as role models for their own children. Children came from public, private, and day school backgrounds and formed their own sense of community.

The Temple Emanu-El program was reviewed and praised in *Conservative Judaism,* Vol. III, No. 3, Spring, 1976. It comes as an educational packet with colored cards, covering four general categories: cognitive learning, rituals and life cycle, the synagogue, and the Jewish people. It is a unique and exciting way to create an intensive course of study for the Bar/Bat Mitzvah years. It's a program your synagogue may want to look into. For more information, contact the Temple Emanu-El, 99 Taft Avenue, Providence, RI 02906.

This creative curriculum for pre-Bar/Bat Mitzvah students has been used successfully by many congregations throughout the country. Others are being developed by Jewish educators both in Israel and in the United States.

The Jewish Home Transmitting Jewish Values

The Jewish home should reinforce the child's Jewish education. Throughout the centuries, the individual Jewish home has been the critical link in Jewish survival, for it is there that tradition is transmitted. As parents, we try to pass on to our children a Jewish moral code and a sense of identity with our people. There are many ways to enhance your family's home in a meaningful Jewish way. Lighting candles on Shabbat is another reminder of the cycle in the Jewish week and the uniqueness of this day, a reminder of God's creation and of the Jewish people's exodus from slavery in Egypt. There are various festive holidays whose celebration invites family participation. Whether it be Chanukah, Purim, or Passover, there are many traditional ways of observing these holidays. A Passover seder, a sukkah in the back-yard give important messages to your children.

Many current books describe the traditions, crafts, and special foods customary for each holyday.

We know a growing number of families who regularly study Torah together at the Friday night dinner table. Each week the discussion focuses on a few ideas in the Scriptures. Guided by the many commentaries now available in English, a parent can lead a ten-minute discussion involving children of every age. By using biblical topics to elevate table talk, you will build everyone's knowledge and show that Jewish learning really matters. When the parents participate in Jewish observances they set an example for the children. The familiar saying that, "children learn what they live" is valid. It's difficult for a child to do what he is told if he doesn't see his parents leading the way. Children try to act grown-up, they seek responsibility, they want to do what adults do. If your children see that being Jewish is important to you, it will be important to them, too.

Suggestions for Those Starting Late

There are times when a child has not been fortunate enough to have had a good Jewish background. In some families the parents do not assume the responsibility for giving their children a Jewish education. Despite this, the children, without parental guidance or pressure, have themselves sought to affirm their Jewish identity. They became conscientiously involved in Judaic studies, even motivating their parents to join a synagogue. When the impetus to become a Bar or Bat Mitzvah comes from a committed child, the parents should be sensitive to the child's desires to identify with his people and should encourage him to reach this goal.

Sometimes, as Bar/Bat Mitzvah age approaches, a child from an intermarriage may decide that he wants to acknowledge that he is part of the Jewish people by preparing for a Bar or Bat Mitzvah. If there is family cooperation and support from your synagogue, the expressed interest of the child can be fulfilled. If the mother is the non-Jewish partner, this may also involve a conversion for the child. If you want this to happen, turn to friends and leaders in your Jewish community. They can help make it possible.

We know of a Reform congregation that will not accept children as Bar/Bat Mitzvah unless a specified number of years of study has preceded this occasion, and of an Orthodox congregation where the rabbi says that at thirteen a child automatically becomes a Bar Mitzvah, whether or not he has studied. This rabbi states that if the child only knows the blessings before and after the Torah passage is read or perhaps not even that, he becomes, under Jewish law, a Bar Mitzvah merely by reaching the age of thirteen. However, he does not advocate this for it belittles the significance of the occasion.

A parallel situation would be a child who "completes" his formal secular education, unable to read or write English, ignorant of science, literature, history, and math. To transmit our rich Jewish heritage, in depth, many communities support Jewish day schools which offer an extensive program of both Judaic and general studies. In this way, religious education is treated no less seriously than secular education.

In answering questions about Judaism, two contemporary Jewish thinkers have observed:

> Just as a poor education in chemistry will produce poor chemists or no chemists, so a poor Jewish education will produce poor Jews or no Jews; and the chances of alienation from Jewish identity increase even more in the proportion that secular education surpasses in time and quality Jewish education.[4]

Whatever the depth of your commitment, we urge you, as parents, to give your children the best education available.

4. Dennis Prager and Joseph Telushkin, *Nine Questions People Ask About Judaism* (Simon and Schuster, New York, 1981), p. 136.

Sharing the Honors

Sharing the Honors

The religious service is the heart of the Bar/Bat Mitzvah experience. It is what gives you the opportunity to confirm the spiritual meaning of the occasion. As your guests participate in the religious service, they demonstrate how adult Jews continue to share in synagogue ritual throughout their lives. As you call upon them to honor the Torah, they will be setting an example for the next generation. This will help the Bar/Bat Mitzvah child understand that his participation this day should be only the beginning of a lifelong involvement in the rituals of his people. The Bar/Bat Mitzvah ceremony is just the first public demonstration of this commitment.

It is customary to call individuals from the congregation to be honored by personal participation in the synagogue service. The Bar/Bat Mitzvah family is often given the privilege of designating persons to receive these honors. From the very beginning, you should check with your congregational leaders to see whether women may receive the same honors as men. In addition, there may be dress requirements for those participating in the service. Check all this to plan correctly and avoid any misunderstanding.

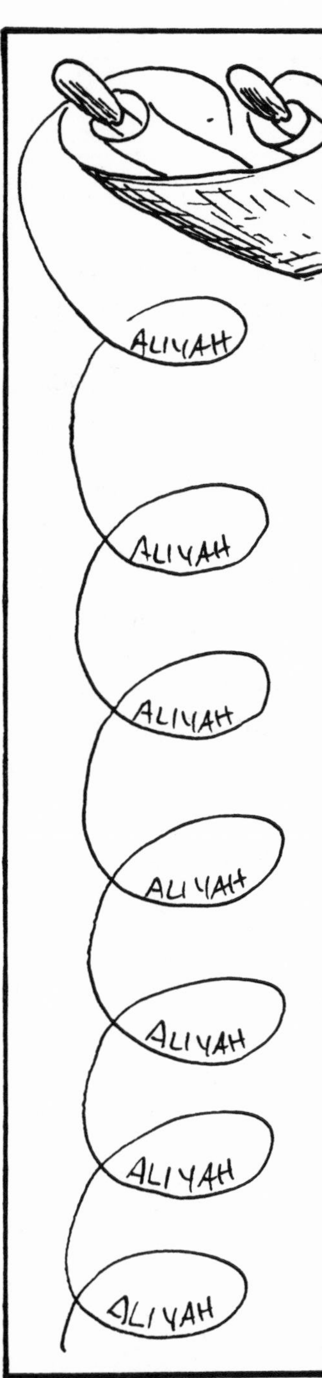

Aliyah—Being Called to the Torah

Being called to recite the blessings before and after the Torah is read is called an *aliyah* (going up). It is a great privilege to be called to the Torah. One goes up literally as one ascends the bimah where the Torah is read and one goes up in a spiritual sense, by participating in this ritual. (The Hebrew word *aliyah* is also used to refer to Jews moving to the land of Israel, which is seen as a spiritual uplifting.)

There are seven aliyot at a Saturday morning service, according to tradition. There may be more, but there may not be fewer. The Maftir (one who concludes) is the person called up to read the Haftarah (Prophets). To maintain the link between the Torah portion and the prophetic reading which follows, the Maftir also chants a few verses from the Torah scroll. The Torah blessings done by the Maftir are an addition to the required number of aliyot.

On Shabbat Rosh Hodesh (celebrating the new Hebrew month) and certain holidays such as Sukkot and Chanukah, more than one Torah scroll are used within the service. As a result, there may be more honors to be distributed by the Bar/Bat Mitzvah family. Check with your synagogue to learn the specific procedures and customs for the service on your child's Bar/Bat Mitzvah day.

The Bar/Bat Mitzvah child is honored with the Maftir (the concluding honor), which involves the usual two Torah blessings and also the blessings which precede and follow the child's reading of the Haftarah. The other seven aliyot may be yours to assign as honors to your guests. Many congregations seek to follow a fixed pattern in assigning aliyot. The first aliyah is traditionally given to a Kohen (one of priestly descent), the second to a Levite (one whose forefathers maintained the ancient temple and helped the priests in its rituals), and the rest to other members of the congregation, or Israelites. The third and sixth are sometimes given to distinguished persons in the community, who are not Kohanim or Levites.

According to differing traditions, the numerical position of an aliyah may have inherent significance. For example, it is generally accepted that there is a "scholar's aliyah," but it is disputed as to which one it is. If you wish to distinguish between the different aliyot, it is best to consult your rabbi or congregational leaders to determine the custom followed in your synagogue.

It is your responsibility to let each honored guest know what is expected of him or her. There is no rehearsal. Your guests will rely on you for the necessary information. It is an awkward moment when someone ascends the bimah and is at a loss about what to do or say. Avoid this by planning ahead and communicating the specific details to those honored with an aliyah, so they will be prepared and comfortable. Here are some suggestions you may wish to convey to your guests:

- Sit where you can easily get to the bimah when called.
- Be certain that men are wearing a tallit if customary in your synagogue.
- Listen for when you are called to the Torah. Sometimes you are called by your English name, but you may be called by your Hebrew name, for example, "Benyamin Meir ben Pinchas ha-Kohen" or "Natan ben Yaakov," or they may just call the number of the aliyah, *Ya-amod shishi* (sixth aliyah).
- Step up to the reading table and stand to the right of the Torah reader.
- Touch the fringe of your tallit to the spot in the Torah text indicated by the reader.
- Then recite the following blessings before reading the Torah:

ONE: Bor-chu et Ado-nai hamevorach.

בָּרְכוּ אֶת יְיָ הַמְבֹרָךְ.

Bless the Lord who is blessed.

TWO: The congregation makes the following response which you repeat:
Boruch Ado-nai hamevorach le-olam va-ed.

בָּרוּךְ יְיָ הַמְבֹרָךְ לְעוֹלָם וָעֶד.

Blessed is the Lord who is forever blessed.

THREE: You continue directly with the following blessing:
Boruch A-tah Ado-nai Elohenu Me-lech
Ha-olam a-sher boechar bo-nu me-call
ha-amin v'notan la-nu et Torah-to
Boruch A-tah Ado-nai no-ten ha-Torah.

בָּרוּךְ אַתָּה, יְיָ אֱלֹהֵינוּ, מֶלֶךְ הָעוֹלָם, אֲשֶׁר בָּחַר בָּנוּ מִכָּל
הָעַמִּים וְנָתַן לָנוּ אֶת תּוֹרָתוֹ. בָּרוּךְ אַתָּה, יְיָ, נוֹתֵן הַתּוֹרָה.

Blessed art Thou, Lord our God, King of the universe, who has chosen us from among the nations and has given us His Torah. Blessed art Thou, Lord, who gives the Torah.

FOUR: After the Torah is read, touch the fringe of your tallit to the Torah as before and recite the concluding blessings:
Boruch A-tah Ado-nai Elo-henu Me-lech
Ha-olam a-sher no-tan la-nu Torat emet
v-cha-yay olam no-tah b'to-chenu
Boruch A-tah Ado-nai no-ten ha-Torah.

בָּרוּךְ אַתָּה, יְיָ אֱלֹהֵינוּ, מֶלֶךְ הָעוֹלָם, אֲשֶׁר נָתַן לָנוּ תּוֹרַת
אֱמֶת וְחַיֵּי עוֹלָם נָטַע בְּתוֹכֵנוּ. בָּרוּךְ אַתָּה, יְיָ, נוֹתֵן הַתּוֹרָה.

Blessed art Thou, Lord our God, King of the universe, who gives the Torah.

It may be necessary to furnish the Hebrew names of those to be honored so that they may be called up accordingly. You should also know who is a Kohen, a Levi, and an Israelite, because the aliyot are not interchangeable. Have one copy of this list on the bimah and another in a capable usher's hands in the congregation to assure that the right person comes up at the specified time. Your guest may be new to your synagogue and may need assistance when his name is called, especially if it is called in Hebrew.

Grandparents and Their Participation

Grandparents and other older relatives should get special consideration at a Bar/Bat Mitzvah, for this is a ceremony which involves handing down the law, a generational concept. At one service, the maternal grandfather and paternal grandmother both chanted Torah portions before their grandson was called up as a Bar Mitzvah. We have also seen a grandfather, father, and son on the bimah, passing the Torah from one generation to another.

Hagbah and Glilah

After the reading is completed, the Torah is returned to the *Aron ha-Kodesh* (Holy Ark). Before this takes place, two persons are given the honor of lifting and dressing the Torah, the *hagbah* and *glilah*, respectively. They are usually called up at the same time. Both of these are significant honors, although neither involves saying blessings aloud.

There is a special technique for lifting and displaying the Torah to the congregation. It involves sliding the Torah partially off the reading table and bending your knees to lever it up while you straighten up. This takes some strength, so do not call on an aged relative for this honor. The scroll is heavy and can be quite unbalanced at the beginning or end of the annual cycle, when most of the parchment rests on one handle. We don't wish to make it sound more complicated than it is, but it may be wise to have someone who has done this before serve as hagbah. Rolling and dressing takes place after the Torah has been held aloft. The gabbai who stands at the reading table will assist the glilah in doing this, according to custom. The Torah must be tied with a sash and the mantle or cover replaced. If there is a silver breastplate, that goes on after the cover. The yad and crown or finials, if there are any, go on last. If acceptable to your congregation, it might be nice to offer this honor to a grandmother or other woman you wish to have participate in the service.

To assist you in keeping track of the honors you distribute, there is an Aliyot and Honors Chart in the Chart and Timetable Section at the end of this book.

Possibilities for lay participation will differ in each congregation. Consult your rabbi or ritual committee to explore these options. Some synagogues have a Torah reader; others may have a Torah reading club which prepares members of the congregation to read each week, and there are other variations. At one Bat Mitzvah, four women, friends of the family, chanted from the Torah before the Bat Mitzvah was called up. They affectionately became known as the "four matriarchs of Israel." In this way, through personal example, the meaning of the service was enriched for the Bat Mitzvah and her family.

Perhaps a friend or relative could deliver a few remarks from the pulpit in honor of the occasion. This could take the form of a d'var Torah (words of Torah) or a personal speech about the meaning of this special moment in time. The speaker must choose his words carefully to fit within the format of this religious service. Sometimes, as a father presents the tallit to his son, he takes this opportunity to say a few words to his son, noting how proud he is as his son acknowledges his religious responsibility to the Jewish community. But any speaker should avoid speaking in an overly sentimental way about childhood episodes and other anecdotes which may embarrass your teenager in this public setting.

An Aliyah in the Name of a Soviet Jew

In some synagogues, especially those which have adopted a prisoner of conscience, we have seen the honor of an aliyah given to a Soviet Jew who is unable to express his religious beliefs on his own. The rabbi will take one of the aliyot in his name. This adds an extra dimension reflecting the unity of all Jews. In addition, with a donation to support Soviet Jewry, your child may be "twinned" with the child of a Soviet "refusenik," a Russian Jew who has been refused permission to emigrate and cannot publicly affirm his Judaism. Though not present in person, the Soviet Jewish child is present in spirit and symbolically shares the ceremony taking place that day. For more information about how to arrange this procedure, please turn to the section "Twinning with a Soviet Jew" in the Gift chapter.

Sharing the Spotlight with Siblings

A Bar/Bat Mitzvah is a very important experience in the life of a child and his immediate family. Focusing the spotlight so clearly on one child sometimes brings out unexpected behavior on the part of the siblings, especially if they are younger and have not had this experience themselves. We have seen a slightly younger sister, obviously seeking attention, spend the entire morning running up and down the aisles of the sanctuary. One younger brother stepped out for a drink and never returned. When the rabbi spoke with pride about that youngster's forthcoming Bar Mitzvah, the child was nowhere to be seen. Another little sister stationed herself in the parking lot, grabbing the attention of those arriving for the Bat Mitzvah service. This type of behavior can be avoided by giving siblings a part in the service and understanding their feelings at a time like this.

Brothers and sisters should be given a role in the Bar/Bat Mitzvah experience if possible. Their personal participation will help them appreciate the meaning of this important Jewish ritual. Naturally, parents must consider the strengths and interests of each child. A clearly more competent older sibling or a cute younger one should not be allowed to overshadow the Bar/Bat Mitzvah child. At one Bar Mitzvah, a much younger, pigtailed little sister led the closing prayer and quite visibly won the hearts of all the congregation. While brothers and sisters should have a share in the Bar/Bat Mitzvah service, planning for their participation takes thought and sensitivity. These plans should be discussed with the Bar/Bat Mitzvah child so he understands how and why his siblings will be involved.

Brothers and sisters should know that they are expected to remain with the congregation. This is a very special day, one which deserves their finest cooperation. In many cases, a sibling had or will have this important opportunity himself, and now is the moment to give the Bar/Bat Mitzvah the center of the stage. If a sibling is very young, a relative or good friend should look after the child during the service, leaving the parents free to give their attention to the Bar/Bat Mitzvah. Their child has prepared long and hard for this ceremony and should not have to deal with distractions from his siblings.

How can brothers and sisters become involved in the Bar/Bat Mitzvah ceremony in a meaningful way? There are a variety of possibilities, depending on your children and the nature of your child's Bar/Bat Mitzvah service. An older sibling can be called up for an aliyah or to read a portion of the Torah. A younger sibling may lead a song or prayer. We have seen youngsters wait patiently and then lead the hamotzi right before the food is served. Some congregations have a custom of throwing candy at the Bar/Bat Mitzvah child on the bimah when he has completed his Haftarah readings. This is a sign of rejoicing as the child has fulfilled his promise. A younger member of the family may be given the responsibility of distributing wrapped candies to those in the congregation, beforehand, so this can take place. Whatever you decide upon, this special participation will be important and help the sibling identify positively with his brother or sister's Bar/Bat Mitzvah experience.

If you want to involve brothers or sisters, or other family members or friends, the Bar/Bat Mitzvah service can offer an opportunity for them to participate. It all depends on the customs of your synagogue and the synagogue skills of your relatives and friends. Be certain to review these options carefully and to give accurate instructions to those sharing the honors. By maximizing your guests' involvement, you will add to the message and meaning of the Bar/Bat Mitzvah ceremony, setting a fine example for all who are there.

Providing the Traditional Ritual Items

Providing the Traditional Ritual Items

While preparing for your child's Bar/Bat Mitzvah, you should be aware of the ritual objects which may be needed for this occasion and for future use. Behind each Jewish symbol lies a long history and tradition. Knowing the background of each of these objects will help you select the ritual items needed. Hamakor Judaica, a store in Chicago, includes in its catalogue a section for ordering "Everything for your Bar/Bat Mitzvah (except the speech)." It lists tallit, tallit clips, tallit bag, kipot or yarmulkes (hats for men), lace chapel caps (for women), tefillin, and tefillin bag.[1] This by no means exhausts the list of objects you may want to obtain.

Head Coverings

Covering one's head is a traditional Jewish sign of respect for God; however, the hat itself has no inherent sanctity. The Torah prescribed that priests cover their heads when engaged in Temple service. And the sages have proclaimed, "Cover your head so that reverence for God be upon you."[2] Covering one's head symbolizes that there is something higher than man. From these roots developed the custom of wearing a head covering, especially when entering a house of study or worship.

Does your congregation expect men and/or women to wear head coverings in the sanctuary? If so, any hat will suffice but typically a man uses a specific lightweight head covering, known by various names: kippah (Hebrew), kipot (plural), yarmulke (Yiddish), and skullcap (English). If customarily worn at your synagogue, standard black kipot are usually available in a bin outside the sanctuary. It is possible to order matching ones to give out on the Bar/Bat Mitzvah day. These caps come in many shapes, fabrics, and designs. If you anticipate more than one Bar/Bat Mitzvah in your family, you might consider imprinting them inside with the family name, for example, "Feldman Bar Mitzvah," so you can use them again for your next child. Some families only provide matching kipot for the men in the immediate family: Bar Mitzvah boy, brothers, father, uncles, grandfathers. This way, they stand out as a recognizable group. You may

1. Hamakor Judaica, Inc., 6112 N. Lincoln Ave., Chicago, IL 60659.
2. Rabbi Hayim Halevy Donin, *To Pray as a Jew* (New York: Basic Books, Inc., 1980).

purchase these caps or perhaps you have a talented friend or relative who would enjoy crocheting or embroidering a set for you. *The Jewish Catalog,* Volume I, pages 49–50, and Joyce Becker's *Jewish Holiday Crafts,* page 40, provide detailed instructions and patterns for making kipot. Remember that providing special kipot for your congregation is an optional expense which you do not have to incur. Though one kippah may be inexpensive, a large number can be costly. Keep in mind that head coverings should not be treated as if they were party favors.

Whether women are expected to wear hats may not be as clearly defined. If married women cover their heads in your synagogue, you should suggest that your female guests wear hats as part of their regular outfit that day. Otherwise, little lace veils with hair pins (chapel caps) are often provided for this purpose in a bin outside the sanctuary. If you feel that more of them may be needed, they can be ordered in quantity through a Judaica shop or a catalogue.

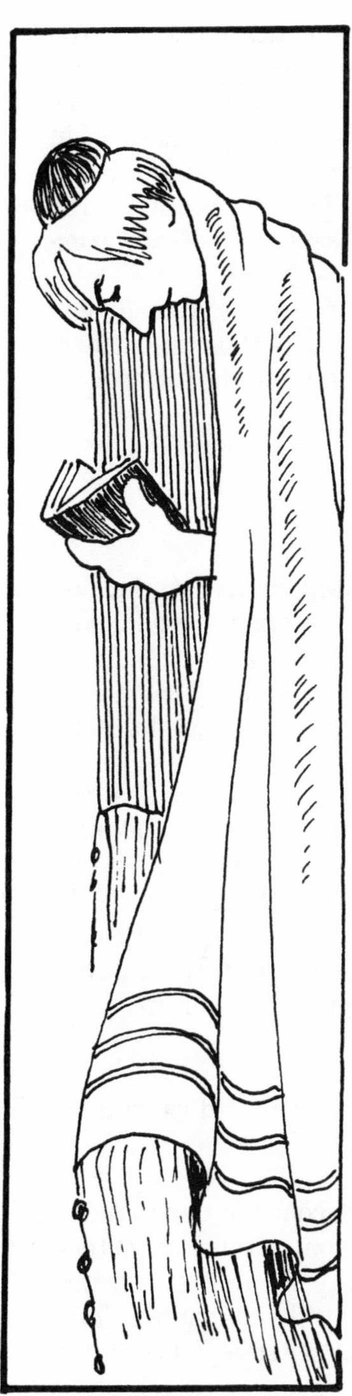

Tallit: A Prayer Shawl with Tzitzit (Fringes)

A *tallit* (prayer shawl) is customarily worn in many synagogues. A tallit is a composite garment made up of a shawl with the essential tzitzit or fringes attached to its corners. The word *tallit* comes from the Aramaic, meaning "to cover." The tradition of wearing a tallit is based on God's command found in Numbers 15:37-40:

> And the Lord spoke unto Moses, saying: "Speak unto the children of Israel and bid them that they make them throughout their generations fringes in the corners of their garments, and that they put with the fringe of each corner a thread of blue. And it shall be unto you for a fringe, that ye may look upon it, and remember all the commandments of the Lord, and do them; and that ye go not about after your own heart and your own eyes, after which ye used to go astray; that ye may remember and do all My commandments, and be holy unto your God."

Thus, the fringes serve as a tangible reminder of God's commandments to the Jewish people.

In ancient days, Jews wore a free-flowing cloak with fringes attached to the corners. In this way, tzitzit were part of their everyday clothing. As time passed and clothing became more elaborate, people no longer attached fringes directly to their outer garments. New garments evolved to allow the observant Jew to fulfill the mitzvah of wearing tzitzit. A *tallit katan* (little covering), with its fringes, is still worn by many Orthodox Jews every day as an undergarment. Another development was to reserve the tallit as a ritual item for use at times of prayer. The sage Maimonides emphasized that the tallit should be worn especially when praying; thus, the prayer shawl became an important ritual object that is used in many synagogues to this day.

The tallit reflects many levels of religious symbolism. Jewish mystics using numerology (determining the numerical value of a word, since Hebrew letters also stand for numbers) have underscored the significance of tzitzit. They calculated that the numerical value of the word *tzitzit* = 600. To this, they add the 5 knots and the 8 threads used in fashioning the fringes, which adds up to 613. This is equivalent to the total number of commandments given by God to the Jewish people in the Torah. They maintain that the wearing of the tzitzit is therefore a visible reminder to observe all of God's commandments.

If prayer shawls are usually worn in your congregation, the synagogue typically will provide extras on racks outside the sanctuary for those coming without their own. Ushers can direct those who need them to take a tallit before entering the service.

Selecting a Tallit for Your Son

Selecting a tallit is one preliminary step in preparing for the Bar Mitzvah ceremony. You may purchase one in a Jewish religious supply shop, through your synagogue gift shop, or you may even buy one in Israel. You may select one to match his father's or a tallit may be handmade by a knowledgeable Jewish craftsperson in the community. Whatever your choice, make certain that your son likes it and that he can wear it comfortably, since he is not likely to be full grown on his thirteenth birthday.

The exact construction of a tallit follows a prescribed pattern based on specifications set down in the Torah (refer to Numbers 15:37–40). Specific instructions for making a prayer shawl and knotting the fringes can be found in the *Jewish Catalog,* Vol. 1, pages 52–57 or in Joyce Becker's *Jewish Holiday Crafts,* pages 41–42 (Bonim Books, NY, 1977).

Often, a father presents his son with a tallit during the Bar Mitzvah service. He may take this occasion to say a prayer and a few words of praise. The Bar Mitzvah boy usually says the blessings for the prayer shawl before wrapping himself in it and ascending to the Torah:

> Blessed are You, Lord our God, King of the universe, who hast sanctified us with His commandments and commanded us to wrap ourselves in tzitzit.

Customs differ about when one may start to wear a tallit. In some congregations a young man is presented with a prayer shawl at his Bar Mitzvah ceremony, to wear from then on as a tangible symbol of his coming of age. In other synagogues, a Bar Mitzvah child may wear the tallit only at his Bar Mitzvah and not again until he is married. This tradition is based on the fact that the commandment concerning tzitzit is followed by a reference to taking a wife (Deut. 22:12–13).

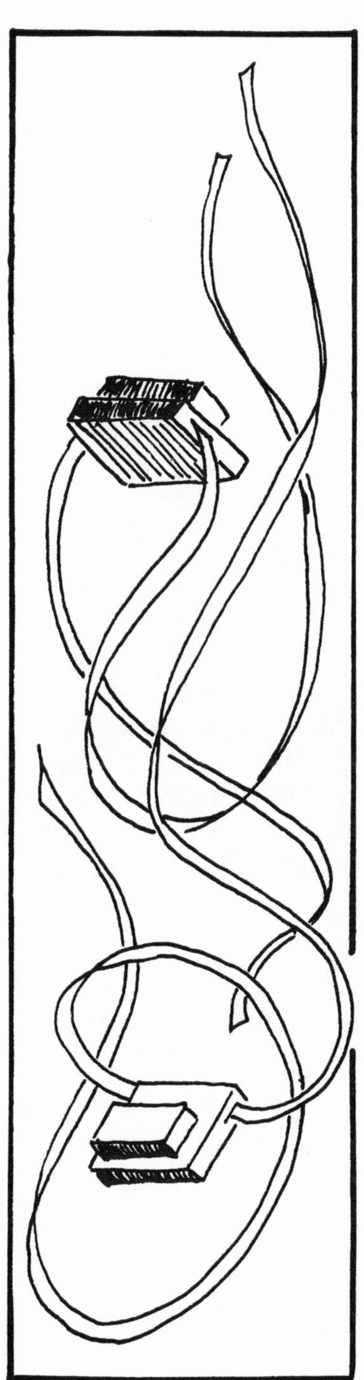

Tefillin

If your child will be wearing a prayer shaw, he may also wear tefillin at weekday morning prayers after his Bar Mitzvah. As a Bar Mitzvah, it is both a privilege and an obligation to perform certain religious rites, and the use of tefillin is usually included as part of Bar Mitzvah instruction. Whether or not you put on tefillin, it is important to support this and other parts of your child's Jewish education. At this point in the history of American Jewry, many children are more interested than their parents were in the symbols of their heritage. Ethnic identity is seen in a positive light. One rabbi we know believes that it is extremely important to perpetuate our distinct religious symbolism so that our children will know the "mystery and magic" of our own faith. Cults and other mind-controlling groups may then have less appeal, for these Jewish youngsters will have a rich ritual heritage of their own with which to identify.

Tefillin give a Bar Mitzvah boy something sacred and specific as a sign of his coming of age in the Jewish community. Tefillin are a symbolic reminder of man's relationship with God and their use is a ritual which is part of the totality of Jewish religious expression.

What are Tefillin?

Tefillin are two cubical leather containers with leather straps attached. One is the *tefillin shel yad* (for the arm and hand) and the other is the *tefillin shel rosh* (for the head). Inside each is a piece of parchment upon which a scribe has written four prescribed biblical passages referring to God's kingship, the unity of God, the deliverance of the Jewish people from Egyptian bondage, and the law commanding the use of tefillin.

Why Are Tefillin Used as Part of Jewish Ritual?

The use of tefillin is commanded four times in the Torah. One time is in the Sh'ma, which holds a central place in all of Jewish prayer, which states (Deut. 6: 4–8):

> Hear, O Israel: The Lord our God, the
> Lord is one.
> And thou shalt love the Lord , thy God
> with all thy heart, and with all thy
> soul, and with all thy might.
> And these words, which I command thee
> this day, shall be upon thy heart;
> and thou shalt teach them diligently
> unto thy children, and shalt talk of
> them when thou sittest in thy house,
> and when thou walkest by the way, and
> when thou liest down, and when thou risest
> up.
> And thou shalt bind them for a sign upon
> thy hand, and they shall be for frontlets
> between thine eyes.

Putting on tefillin interrupts the continuous demands of everyday life by focusing one's attention on God. In fact, the word *tefillin* comes from the same root as the Hebrew word for prayer, *tefillah,* and these two words are closely connected in meaning. Binding one's arm and head is meant not only as a physical act but also as a spiritual experience. The tefillin serve as a symbolic reminder of the entire Torah. Recalling the exodus from Egypt, we are reminded that God freed the Jewish people from physical slavery in Egypt so that they could be bound to the service of God instead.

Why Are Tefillin Connected to the Ritual of Bar Mitzvah?

The use of tefillin begins at the age of religious responsibility, the time of Bar Mitzvah. Boys typically are taught the prayers and customs pertaining to tefillin as part of their preparation for Bar Mitzvah. Traditional practices vary and therefore, it is a good idea to learn the use of tefillin from a teacher belonging to your own congregation. If you need further assistance, you can turn to *The Jewish Catalog,* Vol. I, pages 58–63, or Rabbi Hayim Halevy Donin's *To Pray as a Jew,* pages 33–37, for detailed diagrams, descriptions, and the accompanying prayers. Participating in the ritual of tefillin is the most visible sign of coming of age. The beginning of this religious obligation was seen as an important part of the Bar Mitzvah ceremony. Traditionally, in Eastern Europe, the Bar Mitzvah was held on a Monday or Thursday with the first use of tefillin a public ritual marking that day. Recently, we attended a Bar Mitzvah on a Labor Day Monday, where grandfather, father, and son all laid tefillin together, on the bimah. It was very moving to see this commandment being observed by three generations simultaneously, reflecting the passing on of Jewish ritual from generation to generation.

Tefillin are not used on Shabbat. The reason for this is that Shabbat itself is a reminder of God and his creation; therefore, tefillin, as a sign, become superfluous. Because the majority of Bar Mitzvah ceremonies now take place at Saturday services, the use of tefillin is no longer an integral part of the Bar Mitzvah ceremony. But, having reached the age of religious responsibility, a thirteen-year-old can participate in the ritual of tefillin starting the day after his Bar Mitzvah service.

How Do You Buy Tefillin?

Selecting tefillin should be done with great care. You may wish to consult your congregational teachers, *The Jewish Catalog,* Vol. I, or Donin's *To Pray as a Jew,* so that you will know what to look for when making this purchase. Tefillin are usually constructed in Israel and can be found in a reliable local Jewish bookstore, Jewish religious supply shop, or through a Jewish mail-order catalogue. Prices vary greatly.

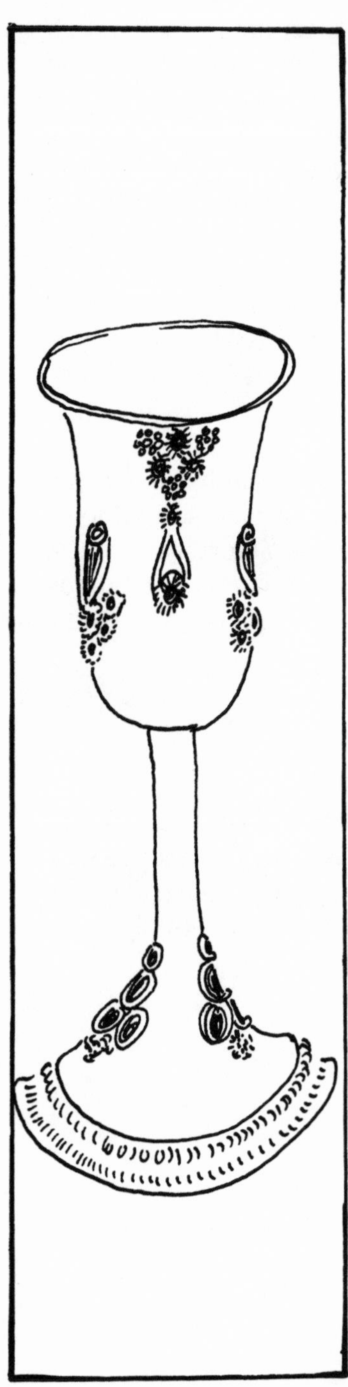

Other Ritual Items: Candlesticks, Kiddush Cup, Challah Cover

Other Jewish ritual items are used at the time of Bar/Bat Mitzvah. Shabbat candlesticks, a kiddush cup, and a challah cover will probably be needed either at the synagogue or at your own home. The Friday evening synagogue service typically includes the blessings for Shabbat candles, wine, and challah. On Saturday morning, the kiddush for wine and the motzi for challah are said before drink and food are tasted. Your congregation will undoubtedly provide the ritual objects for these blessings. However, you may want to use your own personal ones instead. In a family we know, a talented relative embroidered a magnificent challah cover as a gift for the Bat Mitzvah. She was delighted and honored to see it used as part of the actual Bat Mitzvah ceremony.

If you will be serving Friday night dinner or Saturday lunch at home, you will want to maintain the religious nature of this occasion, a Shabbat meal. To participate in the traditional Jewish rituals, you may want to use Shabbat candlesticks, a kiddush cup, and a challah cover. Your celebration at home should convey to your guests that this is not just a Friday night dinner party or Saturday luncheon, but rather a meal shared by family and friends to rejoice at a religious passage. Participating in the traditional Jewish rituals will set this celebration apart from an ordinary social event and convey the appropriate tone for Shabbat and this special occasion.

The Invitation

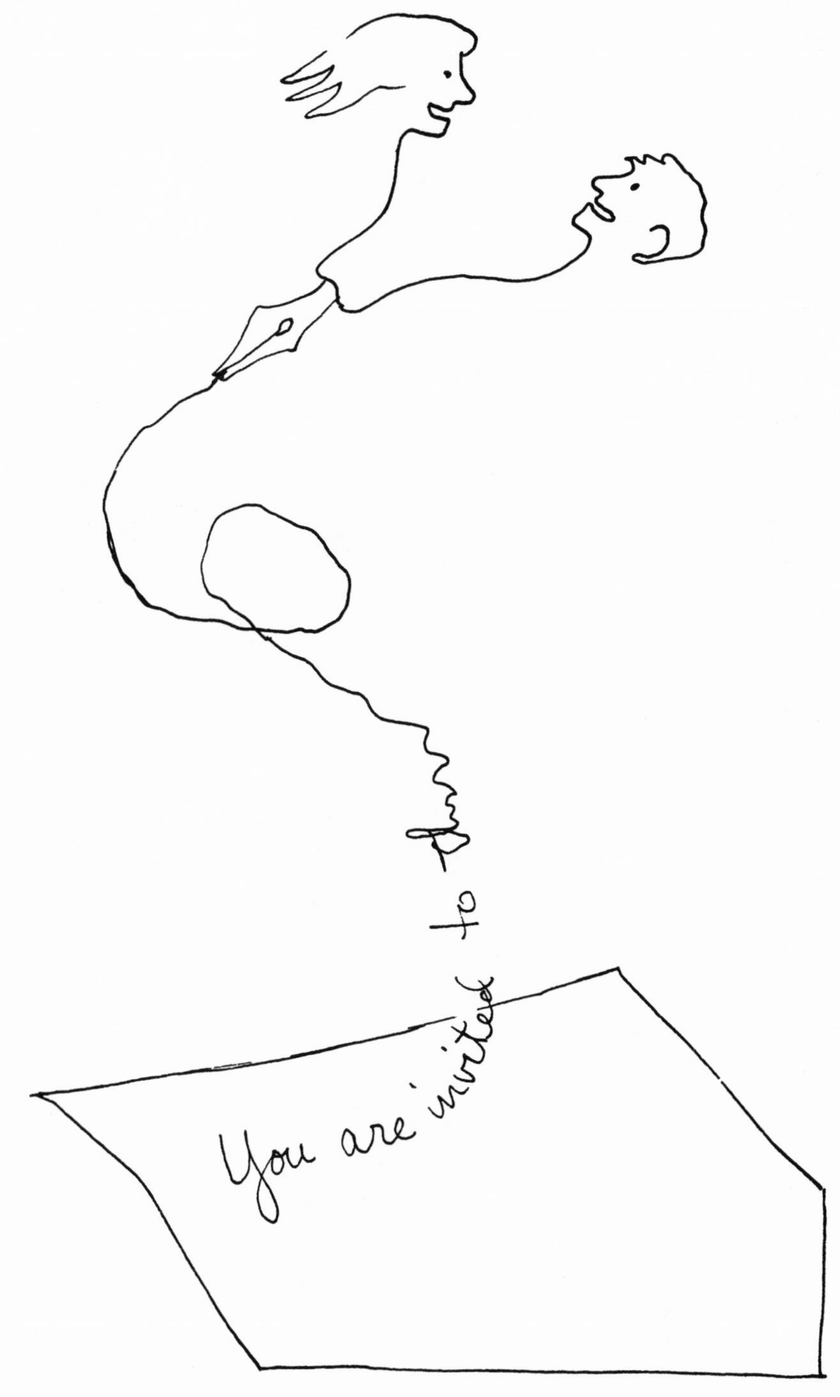

The Invitation

About six months prior to your child's Bar/Bat Mitzvah date, you should begin selecting or designing the invitation. Allow sufficient time, whether you choose and order them from a commercial printer's samples, or design and print them on your own. Decide beforehand what you want to convey, for the invitation can help set the tone for the occasion. With a little planning, the entire process need not be complicated.

One good idea is to save Bar/Bat Mitzvah invitations you've received over the years. They may serve as models when you plan your own child's invitation. Friends may help you by sharing details on where and how they got their invitations.

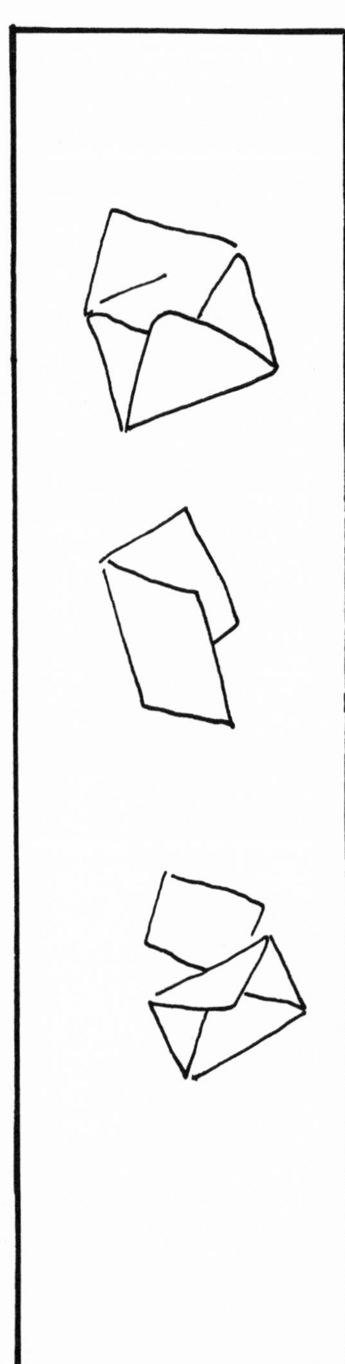

Standard Printed Invitations

Using standard printed invitations is an easy way to handle this part of your preparations. These invitations vary widely in style, message, and cost. After some comparison shopping, you should be able to find one which expresses your personal message well while fitting your budget. Depending on where you live, you probably can order this type of invitation from your Jewish bookstore or synagogue shop. They also may be found in display binders containing sample invitations of different types at a gift shop or the stationery section of a department store. Before you order, study the available samples to refine your ideas for wording and format, then specify how your individual selection should appear. Make certain that you allow enough time for the order to be handled, even with some unexpected delay. When placing the final order, find out if it's possible to take the envelopes home before the invitations are printed. This will allow you extra time to begin addressing the envelopes.

Designing Your Own Invitation

If you prefer, you can design your own invitation. It can take one of many forms depending on your personal talents, the assistance you can get from friends and professionals, and how simple or complex you want the end product to be. With the following guidelines, you should be able to design and duplicate your own composition. The entire invitation can be printed on the front side of a sturdy card. If you wish a more elaborate format, you may want to work with a folded note. The printing can still be done in one operation, but folding the paper will allow you to have a design on the front as well as a message inside. The front may carry a quotation from the Torah or Haftarah portion for the Bar/Bat Mitzvah or a quote from the rabbis or Jewish wisdom literature. This may be written in Hebrew with the translation or in English, depending on your taste. An original design on the front, whether done professionally or by the parent or child, may also be inspired by the Torah/Haftarah readings for that week. If the ceremony falls during a holiday season, your graphic might reflect, for example, the harvest of Sukkot or the candles of Chanukah. Here are a few examples of original Bar/Bat Mitzvah invitations to give you an idea.

Because of joy, the heart opens.
Rabbi Nachman of Brazlav

מתנאל

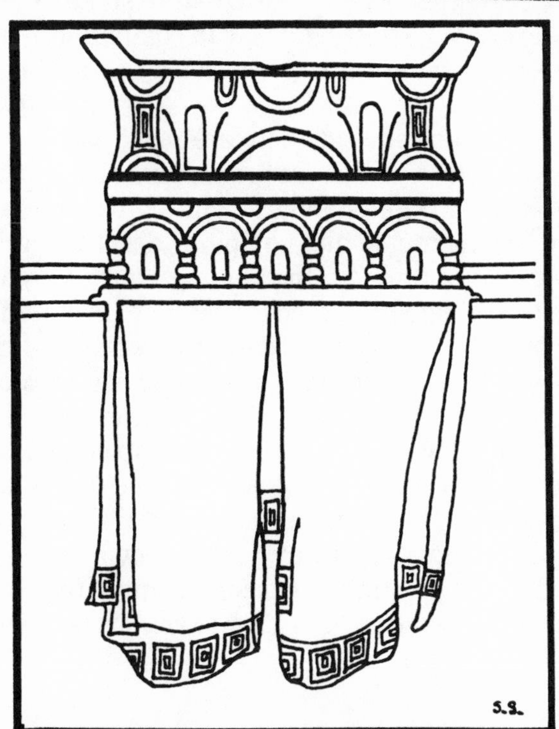

ב"ה

בנו היקר, בן-ציון, יעלה לתורה
בהגיעו לגיל מצוות ביום שבת קודש,
שבת וישלח, ט"ז בכסלו תשמ"ב,
בשעה תשע וחצי בבקר בבית הכנסת
עדת ישראל בעיר ווסינגטון הבירה.

אנו מתכבדים להזמינכם להתפלל
אתנו ולהשתתף בשמחתנו.

טוביה ויהודית

בעזה"ת

פסח ואליעור סגל
שמחים להזמין את כבודכם
להשתתף בשמחת הבר מצוה
של בנם היקר
יקיר הלוי נ"י
שיתפלל לפני התיבה ויעלה לתורה
אי"ה בשבת פרשת בלק י"ב תמוז תשל"ט
שנת ל"ב למדינת ישראל
בשעה שבע וחצי בבקר
על יד הכותל המערבי
בעיר הקודש ירושלים

קבלת פנים וכיבוד
לאחר התפילה

סעודת בר מצוה
תתקיים במוצאי שבת

In any case, such a sketch or quotation will add a distinctively Jewish tone to the invitation. Inside one originally designed invitation, it read, "As my father and grandfathers before me, it is now I who will be privileged as a Bar Mitzvah to stand at the pulpit and chant my Haftorah . . ." Whatever your selection, you can communicate to those invited that your Bar/Bat Mitzvah is much more than an occasion for a party: it is a special Jewish religious ceremony.

When designing your own invitation, keep in mind that there are many factors to consider when dealing with printers. There are many different processes which can be used to reproduce invitations: Xeroxing, instant print, standard printing techniques, engraving, and silk screening. With new photographic and computer developments, these processes are continually changing and improving. In deciding which way to duplicate your invitations, you will have to evaluate the expense, the time involved in developing a finished product, and the technical expertise needed to prepare the original for duplication. You'll be wise to speak with a local printer to examine the various options so that you understand exactly what is involved. Some printers can be extremely helpful in outlining what needs to be done and by giving you instructions on how to do it. It is important to find someone who is willing to give the time to answer your questions. Since some techniques are simple, quick, and inexpensive, it is possible for a person without printing experience to prepare and duplicate his own original Bar/Bat Mitzvah invitations. Note also that the printing business is competitive and prices can vary widely within the same city. Therefore, it is best to ask for personal recommendations and to get more than one proposal.

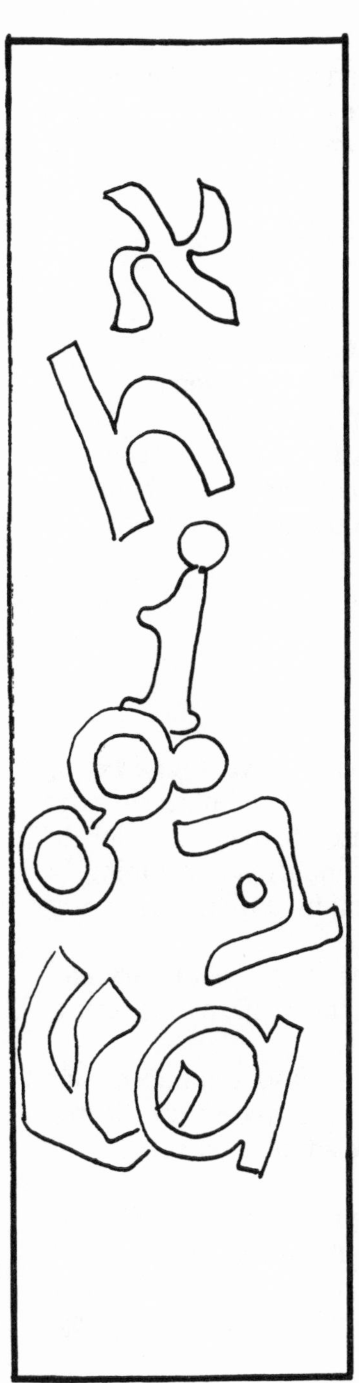

Whatever process you use, you will have to consider some or all of the following: type style, paper weight, ink colors, envelope size to match the invitation, and how the design and writing will look when reproduced. You must work within the technical guidelines specified by the individual printer. We know someone who did a detailed drawing in blue ink and then found out that it could only be duplicated from a black ink original. Preparing an oversized original or master artwork may be desirable if the printer is able to reduce it for the copies. Using a broad, felt-tip pen on a large sheet of poster board will allow you to make an original large enough for reduction, a process which makes for a finer finished product. Instead of plain lettering, you may prefer to use calligraphy. If you are not able to do this yourself, check the bulletin board at your Jewish community center or Jewish bookstore and the classified section of your local Jewish newspaper. You're very likely to find a calligrapher looking for work. We stress these sources for you may want someone who can hand letter in Hebrew as well as English.

An inexpensive way to invite guests is to write the invitations on notecards specifically designed as Bar or Bat Mitzvah invitations. These may be found in a Judaica shop or store featuring party goods. We also know of one girl, with a small number of guests at her Bat Mitzvah, who personally send a hand-written invitation, on plain stationery, to each. This is gracious but works well only when the child or parent has only a few to do by hand.

In the newsletter of some synagogues, it is customary either to announce the forthcoming Bar/Bat Mitzvah or to issue a general invitation to the congregation. Note how this is done at your synagogue so that you can follow the standard procedure.

It is important to remember that 100 or even 50 invitations can be a sizeable expense. However, you need not spend a lot on your invitations in order to have them convey the sentiments you feel.

Parents Who Are Separated or Divorced

If the parents are separated or divorced, the basic invitation can be worded the same as that of a child whose parents are married. The only difference is that the parents may want to list their names on two different lines at the bottom of the invitation. For example:

Barbara Stein		Barbara Goldberg
	or	
Joseph Stein		Joseph Stein

In this way, both parents are acknowledged on the invitation. It's a good idea to enclose return cards and envelopes for guests to use for RSVP's since some of those invited may know one parent and not the other. If desirable, the return envelopes can be addressed to the Bar/Bat Mitzvah child, thereby avoiding the use of one parent's name and not the other. In fact, some families choose to word the invitation in a more casual manner where the Bar/Bat Mitzvah child extends the invitation to the ceremony.

Additional Inserts and the RSVP

You may want to print and mail extra cards with the invitations. An evening gathering at home that Saturday night or a family brunch on that Sunday may require an extra card in the invitation envelope. Sending invitations for these auxiliary parts of the weekend and enclosing them with the primary invitation can simplify your planning. Be certain to decide on these possibilities before placing your final invitation order.

- Will you be including inserts for hotel accommodations, maps, rental cars, etc., for your out-of-town guests? For more information on this topic, please refer to the chapter entitled "Guests."
- How are you going to handle responses? You may enclose a stamped, self-addressed envelope with an RSVP card. This simplifies the process, costs extra, and conveys a certain image which may or may not be suitable for you.

On the bottom of the invitation itself, you may simply request a reply: "RSVP" or "Kindly respond." If you include your telephone number here in addition to your return address, you should be prepared for the series of phone responses which will occur. Although you hope for a timely response from those you've invited, that's not always possible.

Mailing the Invitations

Out-of-town invitations may be mailed as early as eight weeks before the Bar/Bat Mitzvah to allow guests ample time to make travel arrangements; local invitations should be sent six weeks ahead. This difference in the mailing schedule may give you a little extra time to assist your out-of-town guests with their plans. Remember that if some of your relatives who live far away have moved recently, it may take some advance work through the family grapevine to locate their current addresses. Mail all groups of invitations together to avoid possible hurt feelings that may occur if invitations arrive at markedly different times. Include a return address on each envelope so that, if addressed incorrectly, it will be returned to you. At this time, it may be handy to purchase a return-address stamp or embosser which can be used on the invitations and thank-you notes. No matter how carefully you plan, some misunderstandings may occur—an invitation can get lost in the mail or on the recipient's desk. If you do not receive a response in a reasonable time, perhaps the message never arrived. To reach an exact head count and to follow up on your unanswered invitations, you may want to contact those who have not replied.

Guests

Guests

The Guest List

Once the date has been selected, you must decide which guests to invite to join you in the celebration of this joyous occasion. This is a difficult decision to make and you probably will find that the most difficult part is deciding where to draw the line. As a friend said, "I know that they are wonderful people, but do I have to invite them to the Bat Mitzvah?"

To prepare adequately, you should start thinking about your guest list about six months before the Bar/Bat Mitzvah date. A systematic approach, with certain clear guidelines, can help you make a complete list, avoid overlooking anyone, and simplify your decision making. If you plan ahead thoughtfully, you will remain content with your choices because you'll avoid making impulsive decisions under the strain of last minute pressures.

Whom to Invite

As you begin your list, turn to the "Charts and Timetables" section at the end of this book. These charts will help you organize your list efficiently. Begin by filling in the sheets labeled *Preliminary List* with the following categories:

- Family
- Friends of the parents
- Neighbors
- Child's friends, teachers, and the Bar/Bat Mitzvah tutor
- Professional/business associates
- Members of the congregation, its lay and religious leaders

List names by category to help you recall everyone in the same circle. Ultimately you'll not be able to invite everyone, but now is the time to write the names of all those who should be considered.

You may want to ask the Bar/Bat Mitzvah child if there are any special people he would like to include. List all possible names for inclusion, as if no constraints on numbers existed. Finer distinctions can be made later.

After you've listed all possible guests by category, take a moment to reflect on the group as a whole. A Bar/Bat Mitzvah is a religious ceremony which has meaning for guests of all ages. As an important milestone in your child's life, its significance is enhanced by the presence of young and old alike. Most synagogues welcome children to their services. You may be inviting guests who usually spend Shabbat together as a family, and their interests should be respected. Of course a celebration which includes all members of the guest's family, including children, may be very joyful, but it will be less formal. If you decide to limit your invitations mainly to adults you will have a different type of celebration.

When composing your guest list avoid any temptation to use the Bar/Bat Mitzvah as an opportunity to fulfill social obligations. If too many guests are neither familiar with your child nor with the service, the significance of the Bar/Bat Mitzvah can become lost behind a facade of worldly matters which these people represent to you. One child said that at her Bat Mitzvah she did not want to look out upon a sea of unfamiliar faces sharing this special moment with her. It's better to have an appropriately selective Bar/Bat Mitzvah celebration and, when sufficient time has passed, the parents can take care of their business and social obligations by hosting some other kind of party. To make the Bar/Bat Mitzvah party do double duty would subvert the religious significance of the occasion.

Completing the Guest List

WITH YOUR PRELIMINARY GUEST LIST DONE, YOU'LL HAVE TO REFINE IT AND MAKE YOUR FINAL CHOICES.

First, count the total number of adults and children separately to get an idea of the composition of the group. Second, in the categories of family, friends, and neighbors, see if you've included adults only or all members of each nuclear family. Then, you must decide if you want this day to be mainly for adults or a multigenerational family affair. Whether you include all ages, inviting families not just individuals, is an important decision which will shape the tone of your child's Bar/Bat Mitzvah.

The capacity of your synagogue sanctuary may limit the length of your final guest list. In addition, your budget may put restraints on the expenses you could incur for the Bar/Bat Mitzvah. The size of your home and other factors may influence your list as well. You may want to check with your synagogue to see if the Bar/Bat Mitzvah family is expected to sponsor the Friday night oneg Shabbat and/or the Saturday morning kiddush. Remember that it is usually possible to modify the festivities to suit the size and scope of your guest list. This is undoubtedly better than restricting your choice of guests because of a fixed reception style. If more people are to be included, a reception can be planned which is less elaborate and less expensive per person. A simple spread will be well received. Good fellowship is far more important than elaborate eating. The primary consideration is to share the joy of the occasion with those who are close to you and your child. Their presence will enhance the meaning of your child's Bar/Bat Mitzvah.

As you see the broad outlines of your guest list taking shape, you will have to begin planning the festivities. Sufficient lead time is needed for making those arrangements, so don't put off the final difficult decisions. Begin developing general plans for a celebration to accommodate your invited guests. The chapter "Extending the Festivities with a Party" gives useful guidance in this area.

After a few weeks you should review each preliminary guest category to see if any names should be omitted or relegated to "optional" status. Some previously overlooked names may come to mind after that bit of time has elapsed. In a few weeks you'll be reviewing the lists for the third and final time. Make decisions on those marked "optional," realizing that a line must be drawn somewhere. Everyone in your club, school, or social circle cannot be there or your celebration will lose form entirely. These are hard limits to set, ones which the Bar/Bat Mitzvah parents must do with thought and care. You must have the inner strength and conviction to realize that not everyone you know can be invited.

Without a doubt, uninvited friends and neighbors will be talking to you about the Bar/Bat Mitzvah. Inevitably, someone you did not invite will bump into you in the hardware store. This is not the time to tell her that you somehow accidentally overlooked her name and would she and her husband please come to this Saturday's service. Your tennis partner may ask how everything is going. If she does not know your child, you must remember that there is a great gap between the tennis court and the bimah. Only a limited number of people can be invited and that decision is under your control. There is no need to be uncomfortable or embarrassed when meeting someone who is not on your list.

Make your final guest list decisions no later than ten weeks before the date, which will give you time to learn to live with your choices. You will inevitably have argued with yourself over those on the questionable list right up to this deadline. At this final moment, it is better to err on the side of including extras rather than drawing the line too tight. At this point, if one parent still feels that a certain person should be included, he should be invited. There always seems to be enough room and food for a *few* more. If your reception does not involve being seated with placecards, a few extra will not matter. If you complete your choices ten weeks beforehand, you will have no regrets for there is enough time to handle any changes before any of the invitations are mailed.

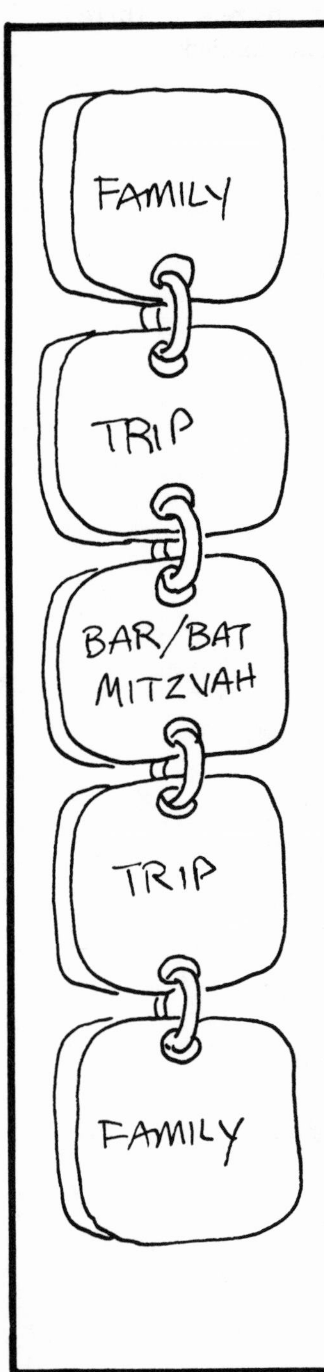

Out-of-Towners

It is true that a Bar/Bat Mitzvah often becomes the setting for a family to convene from far and wide. In past generations, the extended family—aunts, uncles, sisters, brothers, and cousins—often lived within a few miles of each other and may even have belonged to the same congregation. Today, with children leaving home for college or job transfers, and with grandparents often retiring to the Sun Belt, many families are scattered all over the country.

Since out-of-town guests must travel to the Bar/Bat Mitzvah, they'll benefit from your anticipation of their specific needs. It is this group of guests which adds an entire new dimension to your planning. They have come to town specifically to be with you on this important occasion. At Bar/Bat Mitzvah ceremonies we have attended, the rabbi often extends a personal word of welcome to guests who've come from afar. He mentions their respective homes because the distance they've traveled reflects the importance of this occasion.

Lodging: Home Hospitality or Hotel Reservations

WHAT CAN BE DONE TO MAKE OUT-OF-TOWNERS FEEL WELCOME AND COMFORTABLE FOR THE DURATION OF THEIR VISIT?

You can help by providing convenient and suitable accommodations. The Bar/Bat Mitzvah weekend will be very busy for your immediate family and, therefore, not a convenient time for you to have many house guests. Perhaps grandparents, some other relatives, or a close friend could stay with you. The other out-of-towners will also need lodging and meals. Your in-town friends, relatives, and some members of the congregation who live near the synagogue may be eager to share more fully in the joy of this special weekend by offering home hospitality. This can be a positive experience for all, as your local and distant friends and family are afforded the opportunity to get to know each other better. If it's available, be certain to include information about home hospitality along with the basic Bar/Bat Mitzvah invitation.

Perhaps, in your situation, it would be preferable to use a conveniently located hotel or motel. Your out-of-town guests may enjoy staying together for the weekend. If you need a large number of rooms, you should choose these accommodations approximately three months prior to the Bar/Bat Mitzvah. Estimate how many out-of-town guests you expect, and reserve a block of rooms together. Check to see if a discount is offered for this size group, or for senior citizens, which may pertain to some of your guests. Some hotels offer a hospitality suite for the private use of a group booking a large number of rooms. This can be a convenience as a gathering place or as a location for serving family-style meals.

Along with the Bar/Bat Mitzvah invitation sent to out-of-town guests, you may wish to include a brochure from the selected hotel/motel or a Xeroxed sheet describing other possible accommodations. Include specific instructions, telling your guests how they can reserve directly, so that you can stay out of the middle of this time-consuming process. If you choose a national hotel/motel chain, your guests may be assisted by telling them the "800" telephone number to book and confirm reservations. Although you may take the initial step by setting aside a block of rooms, you should expect your out-of-town guests to confirm their reservations and pay for their rooms. However, you may want to provide a warm welcome by leaving a fruit basket, cheese and crackers, or some sweets in each guest's room.

An extremely capable and hospitable Bat Mitzvah mother in Boston did something unusual. She paired each out-of-town family with a local host family. The local host did some or all of the following:

- Met the arriving family at the airport and took them to their motel room.
- Invited them for Friday night dinner.
- Transported the out-of-towners to the Bat Mitzvah events so that they would not have to rent a car.
- Looked after the visiting family during the service and celebration to make certain they were comfortable.
- Returned the traveling family to the airport at the end of the weekend.

Providing for Guests Who Observe Kashrut

Do any of your guests coming from afar observe kashrut (the dietary laws)? How can you help provide for their needs? This is a factor you may need to consider in your Bar/Bat Mitzvah planning. If any of your invited guests keep kosher, while you personally do not, this circumstance may influence the meals you serve over the weekend. You may wish to have available paper plates, plastic utensils, and some basic foods marked with the Ⓤ

or *K* designation. These special provisions will be needed and greatly appreciated. You can also check ahead of time to find out if there are any conveniently located kosher restaurants. Or, if you use the host-family idea, pair up your kosher guests with kosher friends, if possible.

Friday Night Dinner and Sunday Brunch

Besides the celebration following the Bar/Bat Mitzvah ceremony, will you be serving your out-of-town guests other meals? Do you want to offer Friday night dinner for your arriving guests? This decision may be influenced by whether you plan to attend and participate in the Friday evening services at your synagogue. If you plan to go to services, you may combine this with a dinner at the synagogue. Alternatively, you may simply include a more limited number of guests for a meal at your home.

A friend of ours informally gathered everyone together for a delicatessen platter served in her large kitchen. Upon arrival in town, it was nice to feel immediately welcomed and a part of this special weekend. Otherwise, your local friends or family might be delighted to invite an out-of-town family for Friday night dinner at their home. For any of these plans, you must consider whether your guests will arrive early enough and whether you can handle this extra phase of the weekend. If you can arrange it, Friday night dinner can be a lovely opening celebration.

A Sunday brunch at your home is another hospitable touch. This more intimate gathering is a nice way to continue your celebration throughout the weekend. It may include those coming from afar, as well as your local family and special friends. A brunch can be simple and quite informal, with self-service and paper plates. It can consist of some of the leftovers from your Saturday party, along with food that you have prepared in advance and frozen. A basic cold brunch buffet may be ordered from a local delicatessen, caterer, or the supermarket. Or you may want to do something a little unusual. This may be a good time to hire a local firm which comes to the house to cook omelets or crepes. This idea is usually well received by guests and especially by the Bar/Bat Mitzvah child. Any of these possible brunch plans should work well. Carefully evaluate how much you can do ahead, how much you can do when the time comes, how much you can spend, and then make your decision about these meals.

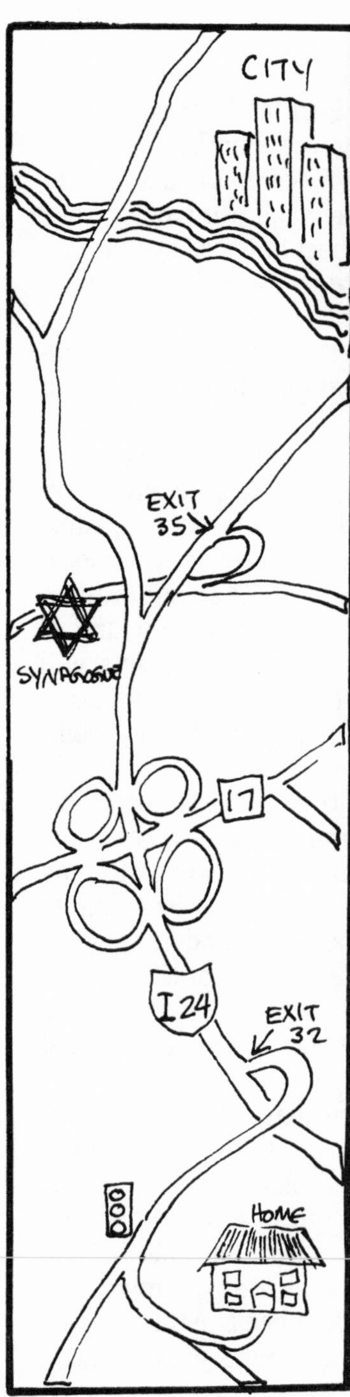

Maps, Directions, and Schedules for the Weekend

When your out-of-town guests have responded that they're coming, it's time to send them directions. There is no need for them to get lost, or have to study gas station maps or ask directions of pedestrians, when you can plan ahead and avoid that problem altogether. Make sure your directions are clear and correct. At a suburban New Jersey Bar Mitzvah, one turn was mistakenly omitted from the directions and two carloads of out-of-town cousins became hopelessly lost on a street with the right name but in the wrong place. Their unexpected delay severely disrupted the service while people already there nervously looked for them. This confusion was totally unnecessary.

As the host, you should write simple but accurate directions covering three locations: the synagogue, the guest's lodging, and your home. Photocopy a section of the local map that includes these three places and, in three distinct colors, mark routes from lodging to synagogue, synagogue to home, and home to lodging. Add directions to the reception if that is held in a different place. You may also want to prepare directions for those coming into town by car or from the airport. Even a taxi driver may need to be directed to your specific area, and guests feel more comfortable when they have a general idea of the route they are to follow.

The care and thought that you put into the directions will assist everyone. Keep copies of all these instructions for some guest inevitably will misplace his and contact you for duplicates at the last moment. (You can also save them for use at your next Bar/Bat Mitzvah.)

Our Boston friend, who arranged for host families, left an information packet at each guest's place of lodging. In this packet the Bat Mitzvah family extended a personal welcome and described the schedule of services and festivities for the weekend. The packet may also include data or newspaper clippings about nearby places of interest, possible walking tours, and events happening locally. If there is some leisure time, visitors might enjoy exploring the unique sights of your community. Another family who lived just outside Washington, DC, arranged for a chartered bus and guide to take out-of-towners on a guided tour of historical sights in lieu of a Saturday night party.

Whatever assistance you choose to offer your visitors, remember that all of them, especially the elderly and those with small children, will appreciate your efforts. The fewer arrangements they have to make for themselves, the easier and more enjoyable their trip to the Bar/Bat Mitzvah will be.

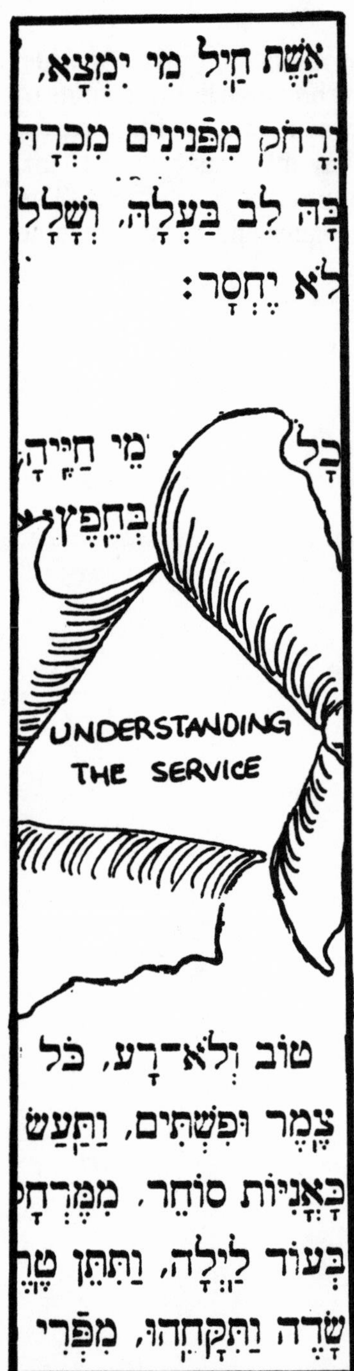

Explaining the Service

Some of your guests may not know your synagogue and its customs. Of course, written prayer books serve as a guide for communal worship; all are welcome to participate regardless of background, experience, and learning. However, as some of your guests may be unfamiliar with the ritual of Jewish worship, it may be helpful to send a personal letter describing the religious service and the Bar/Bat Mitzvah's part in it. This can be particularly useful if you belong to a Conservative or Orthodox congregation, where most of the service will be in Hebrew. Here is a sample of a letter that was sent by a Bat Mitzvah family:

> We are delighted that you are making the effort to be with us at Deborah's Bat Mitzvah. Being together as a family is very important to us at this special moment. To enhance your understanding of the service, we would like to share some information with you.
>
> Our synagogue has a traditional worship service Saturday morning, Shacharit, which includes blessings and songs which praise, petition, and thank God. After this part, the Torah is read, a different portion for every week of the year. This week's sidra (portion) is "Lech Lecha." Here, God calls upon Abraham to leave his father's home, reject idolatry, and enter into a covenant with God. Thus does Abraham become the first Jew and the father of our people.
>
> Deborah will be called to the Torah as a Bat Mitzvah, a ceremony which recognizes her reaching the age of responsibility as a Jew. To celebrate her new position in the congregation, she will be given the honor of chanting from the Torah. She will chant Genesis 17:24–27 the Maftir, or last portion of the Torah reading, as well as the Haftarah, or accompanying section from the prophet Isaiah 40:27–41:16.
>
> While it is optional for women, it is customary in our synagogue for men to wear a head covering or kippah (yarmulke or hat). A tallit (prayer shawl) is traditionally worn by Jewish men over Bar Mitzvah age. As you enter, you will see these in the lobby for your use. The Torah service begins at 10 A.M. promptly. We hope you will arrive on time. Services conclude at noon.
>
> Looking forward to being with you.

Other Questions to Ask—and Answers

HOW CAN WE HELP OUR NON-JEWISH FRIENDS FEEL COMFORTABLE AT THE BAR/BAT MITZVAH SERVICE?

These guests come primarily to be with the Bar/Bat Mitzvah family and are most welcome. They do not worship as Jews and, therefore, they participate in the services in a limited way or not at all. A Christian guest may or may not be expected to wear a kippah depending upon the custom of your synagogue. To cover one's head follows an ancient Jewish tradition as a sign of respect for God, especially in a house of worship. The tallit (prayer shawl) with its tzitzit (fringes) is a ritual garment of religious significance for Jews, since wearing it is commanded by God. Some non-Jews may put on a tallit, if unknowingly given one by an usher, though this is not really appropriate since they are not subject to Jewish law. Keep in mind however that, as the host, your underlying concern is to make all your guests feel at ease.

If you have the time and inclination, you can send a note or speak with your non-Jewish guests and describe the structure and meaning of the religious service and the Bar/Bat Mitzvah ceremony. If you are inviting guests to a traditional Saturday morning service, you can describe it briefly using the following as an outline for your explanation:

1. Shacharit, or the morning worship service.
2. The Torah reading and Rabbi's sermon, or d'var Torah, (literally, "words discussing the Torah"). At this point, the Bar/Bat Mitzvah ceremony will take place, as our child is called up and given the honor of chanting from the Torah (Five Books of Moses) and Haftarah (Prophets). In this way, he acknowledges his new role and responsibility to the Jewish community.
3. The Musaf, or additional service, which is in honor of the Sabbath or a holyday.

HOW CAN WE ASSIST PARENTS WHO BRING SMALL CHILDREN TO THE BAR/BAT MITZVAH?

When the whole family is invited, you may have to deal with infants and toddlers, since it is hard to draw a line once children are included. By providing baby-sitting, it becomes easy to welcome families with young children at your ceremony. A word beforehand or a sign at the synagogue will let parents know about the baby-sitting option, and they will appreciate this special assistance.

Many synagogues regularly hire baby-sitters to look after young children during services. If there is a nursery school at the synagogue during the week, these facilities are an ideal location for baby-sitting. This is something to consider so you can make the necessary arrangements at your specific congregation. Keep in mind that if many young children are invited you may need to engage more than one sitter. In selecting sitters, remember that managing a group of children in a new setting is a big responsibility which demands more competence than taking care of two sleeping children at their own home. You should be certain that toys and books are available. Provide a sufficient amount of juice and cookies for the children since they may be with the sitters for a long time. In some congregations, it is customary for the young children to return to the sanctuary or even to sit on the bimah for the concluding songs. By providing a baby-sitter you will be at ease knowing that the service will not be interrupted by restless young guests.

ARE ANY OF YOUR GUESTS SHOMER SHABBAT (STRICT SABBATH OBSERVERS)?

Some of your guests may be Shomer Shabbat. To make their visit as comfortable as possible, you should take into consideration where they will be staying, either with a host family or at a hotel. Does the host family keep kosher? If the hosts are not Shomer Shabbat, will your guests feel awkward staying with them? Are they within walking distance of your synagogue, or would the walk be a hardship in 85 degree heat or a foot of snow? Might the baby-sitter you've provided ask the children to draw, paste, cut, or watch television? Are you asking these guests to attend a reception outside the synagogue to which they cannot walk? Are you serving only hot, unkosher food which they will not eat? Asking your guests about their particular level of observance will enable you to make them feel at home and will avoid embarrassing situations.

ARE THERE CERTAIN PRACTICES AT YOUR SYNAGOGUE WHICH YOUR GUESTS SHOULD KNOW ABOUT?

If you belong to an Orthodox or Conservative congregation, some of the following concerns must be addressed:

Are married women required to cover their heads?

Is it acceptable for a woman guest to wear a pantsuit?

Would someone using a pay telephone or a soda machine offend members of your congregation?

Would your rabbi or other congregants find it unacceptable to use a camera or tape recorder during the service and reception?

Would someone smoking on the Sabbath cause heads to turn?

We realize that no one seeks to offend, but some people do so out of ignorance. Making your guests aware of the *minhagim* (customs) at your synagogue can prevent some awkward and embarrassing situations.

Extending the Festivities With a Party

Extending the Festivities With a Party

The Bar/Bat Mitzvah Party

Hospitality is fundamental to the Jewish way of life. Its importance is emphasized in the first book of the Torah (Genesis 18:1–8) where three strangers arrived at Abraham's tent. His first thought was to offer them refreshment. Five times there are references to how swiftly he carried out this task so that his guests received proper hospitality before continuing on their journey.

The celebration which follows the religious service and ceremony is a natural extension of the Bar/Bat Mitzvah experience. It is appropriate although not strictly necessary to rejoice with a party afterward. Jewish religious observance typically includes the sharing of food after a *simcha* (a joyous event), whether it be a *brit milah,* a wedding, or a Bar Mitzvah. The party derives from the custom of serving a *seudah mitzvah* (feast) celebrating the performance of a mitzvah.

As the Bar Mitzvah ceremony assumed greater importance in fourteenth and fifteenth century Germany and Poland, a festive meal was usually included as an extension of the celebration. Some traditional sources such as the *Shulhan Arukh* even stated that it was the duty of the father to provide this Bar Mitzvah feast just as he would provide a feast on a wedding day. Therefore, you are helping to preserve an important Jewish custom, fulfilling a mitzvah, by giving a party after your child's Bar/Bat Mitzvah ceremony.

The Party as a Celebration of a Religious Occasion: The necessity for good judgment and good taste

At the heart of a meaningful celebration is the ability to subordinate the social aspects of the gathering to the overriding significance of the day—your child has been called to join his religious community. There is good reason to rejoice, but in planning, it is important to avoid extremes; good judgment must not be sacrificed. Although a Bar or Bat Mitzvah date is often chosen more than one or even two years in advance, it doesn't mean that having all this time to plan should encourage one to have an overly elaborate affair. This is not just a modern concern. For hundreds of years, local Jewish communities were concerned that the feast with its elaborate and possibly wasteful entertainment would detract from the religious significance of the day. Ostentation would undermine the very values which the Bar/Bat Mitzvah seeks to affirm. To avoid this problem, the community developed sumptuary laws to control the style of the celebration after the religious ceremony. In Poland in 1659, it was decreed that no more than ten strangers might be invited to a Bar Mitzvah feast, among whom there must be one poor man to share in the rejoicing. In Germany, the Jewish communities' regulations to control extravagance were very detailed. In the eighteenth century, the Bar Mitzvah boy was formally forbidden to wear a wig, an aristocratic fashion of the time.[1] Today there are no sumptuary laws and only your good judgment can serve as your guide when planning the Bar/Bat Mitzvah party. Within this framework, there are many paths to a joyous and gracious event.

1. Abraham Katsh, ed., *Bar Mitzvah, Illustrated* (New York: Shengold Publishers, 1955), pg. 20.

The Type of Celebration: Number of guests, children, and other variables

In thinking about a party to extend the festivities, the first question is where and how to begin planning. Every seudah mitzvah will bear the personal imprint of the host family. In trying to develop a helpful timetable, we have come to realize that planning the reception is a three-dimensional puzzle with multiple variables. Different people begin planning their celebration from different starting points. For some, the most important aspect is that all guests be seated; others start by first planning the menu. For some families, the time of sundown and the dietary laws are the critical factors. As with any project, one must decide where to begin developing a solution. One approach is to start by reviewing the size and nature of your guest list; then decide where you will hold the celebration; next plan how food will be served; and finally select the menu. How to serve the meal and what the menu will be should be planned simultaneously, since one has a direct influence on the other.

If your budget will allow it, we feel it best to include all those with whom you wish to share this special occasion, rather than limiting numbers to fit a preconceived party plan. You can reasonably expect that most invited guests will come. Knowing the composition of your group will be a very important factor in determining the type of reception you will have. You should consider how many very young children will be among the guests and how many friends your child wishes to invite. Having counted all these, you will have a clear idea of who will be with you to celebrate that day.

The time of day the party will be held is another important factor. Are you planning for Friday evening, Saturday afternoon, Saturday evening, or some other time? When is sundown (the beginning or end of Shabbat) that day, and how will that affect your schedule? The season of the year will also influence your decisions. Of course, the foundation of all realistic planning is a budget. Whatever yours is, you can plan for a lovely celebration. This chapter has many suggestions for enhancing your party without great expense.

Facilities Where the Reception May Be Held: Synagogue, home, hotel, club, or restaurant

Knowing the guest list, time framework, and your budget, you can decide where it will be best to hold the reception. Obviously, the synagogue itself is a very suitable place for a Bar/Bat Mitzvah reception. Some synagogues have the facilities necessary for preparing and/or serving food to a large number of guests. This setting is particularly appropriate for it helps maintain the tone of a religious celebration. It simplifies matters because guests won't have to travel elsewhere in a fleet of cars; they simply can walk into your reception area.

The use of a synagogue social hall for the reception can enhance every guest's sense of participation in the event as a Jewish community function, not just as a private family party. Your synagogue undoubtedly has an established system for handling Bar/Bat Mitzvah receptions and you can easily find out how things are done in that setting. You simply need to get in touch with the right person, the executive director, the president of the Sisterhood, or another member who has just held a similar Bar or Bat Mitzvah party.

The synagogue is not the only suitable place to hold a reception. But even if you plan to have a private party elsewhere, it is usually appropriate to have kiddush or an oneg Shabbat at the synagogue immediately after services. It gives the congregation an opportunity to share refreshments and to congratulate your child and family. If your group of invited guests is to go to another location, it is necessary that this be made clear on the invitation. In most cases, it will help if you've included a detailed set of directions to guide the guests from the synagogue to the reception location.

The party following the ceremony may be held at your home if you've sufficient space to accommodate all the guests. There is something especially nice about a reception at home, or in your garden, but be certain that you have enough space inside in case the weather doesn't cooperate. The use of a tent can make more space available, providing protection against unpredictable weather conditions. If you hold the post-Bar/Bat Mitzvah reception at the synagogue or another location, it is still possible to have a smaller gathering of friends and family at home later during the weekend.

Hotels, clubs, party rooms in an apartment building, and social halls are often selected for Bar/Bat Mitzvah receptions. Even if you do not belong, you may find that a local club will allow use of their facilities for a fee. If the reception is held in a commercial facility, it is important to keep this event from overshadowing the Bar/Bat Mitzvah service and undermining its tone. Less emphasis should be placed on the "Bar" and more on the "Mitzvah," for the party is truly an adjunct to the religious passage which has just occurred. At this time in life, parents and synagogue are trying to help the child "discriminate between what is important and what is trivial, between the good and the merely glittering. Then comes the Bar Mitzvah party, and so often it neutralizes all that . . ."[2]

2. Stanley Rabinowitz, *Helpful Hints for Your Bar/Bat Mitzvah Ceremony*, Adas Israel Congregation (Washington D.C., n.d.).

Serving the Food: A buffet versus a served meal, or how are you going to feed all those invited guests and still enjoy the celebration?

It is important to remember that wine for kiddush and a challah for the *motzi* (the blessing over bread) is all that is needed for congregational fellowship after a service. Platters of challah and thimble shaped wine glasses are basic and adequate. This usually is served on tables in the synagogue social hall, and congregants stand up and help themselves to these traditional foods. Whatever you do to expand this at your Bar/Bat Mitzvah reception is your choice.

If you are planning to offer more, you must decide how the food is to be served. This decision affects your choice of menu and vice versa. Deciding on the style of serving will help you plan the menu. Here are three suggestions:

- A buffet or self-service meal. Using this form, guests may either stand up and eat or return to place settings at tables.
- A served meal.
- Individual tables with place settings and platters of food.

A mix of two styles may involve a served main course, with waiters clearing dishes, and a buffet dessert table. It all depends on where you are, how much space you have, the number of guests, budget, and tone you wish to maintain. More people can be served at a lower cost if you choose a buffet and it is less formal. This works well if there are many children, for it allows some coming and going. If you use this style, it is important to have enough serving centers so all guests can be fed within a reasonable amount of time. Long buffet lines are unpleasant and should be avoided.

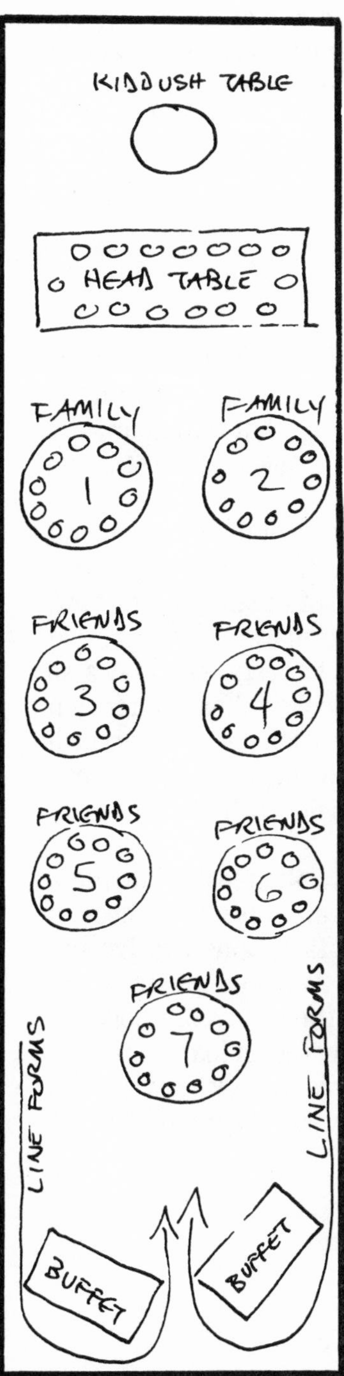

Determine whether you need two, three, or more serving stations to avoid bottlenecks. Consider the shape of the room, and then plan where to place the serving tables and how the lines should flow. Consider an "X" in the middle of the room, which provides four separate serving legs; a "U-shaped" table perhaps with some helpers standing behind to serve portions; or long straight buffet tables on opposite ends of the room, perhaps with separate lines on both sides.

A variation on the self-service theme is to have individual platters on each table so that guests can be seated and still serve themselves. This is one option enabling you to have large numbers of guests while serving them conveniently. A smoked fish or a delicatessen platter are among the menu selections suitable for this kind of setting. If you find that there is not enough room for all to be seated, reserve some of the available seating for the comfort of any elderly guests.

A served meal is more formal, with a large part of the expense due to labor costs. To have a served meal may involve calling an established caterer who can handle most of the party details in addition to providing waiters, waitresses, kitchen help, and the like. If you want to be relieved of direct responsibility and the need to coordinate many details, you can call on a complete caterer who will have menu choices, rental equipment, and a price list for everything from flowers to tablecloths. They are in business to coordinate such an affair and using such a service is certainly one option, but an expensive one. It is important to remember that a caterer's idea about how things are to be done may differ from your vision of the Bar/Bat Mitzvah celebration. To avoid misunderstanding, you may want to write detailed instructions to specify how and when food is to be served and cleared. This leaves little to chance. You may have in mind an order of events such as prayers, speeches, songs, or toasts during the party, and your caterer should know about this well ahead of time. Those helping will know not to serve dessert before your child has had an opportunity to deliver a d'var Torah or Bar/Bat Mitzvah speech to your guests.

A served meal need not be completely catered. Perhaps members of the synagogue maintenance staff or available college students can help serve, and there are many other ways to hire help. Once you've made these decisions, your party will begin to reflect your personal taste and style.

Planning the Menu

Planning the menu is basically a matter of personal preference. It is influenced by those things that are unique about your child's Bar/Bat Mitzvah: your guest list, your date, relative costs, where and how your meal will be prepared. Realizing that the choices are endless and the combinations infinite, we are simply going to suggest some starting points.

There are many excellent Jewish cookbooks available with ideas for planning a menu which fits the nature of your celebration and your pocketbook. If you choose to work with a caterer, remember that it is usually part of his service to offer suggestions for a well-rounded meal. Local delicatessens and even some local supermarkets have printed lists of party platters and other ideas for feeding a large group of guests. You may also want to consider casseroles or something similar which can be cooked ahead and frozen in quantity. There will not be time for last minute food preparations, so plan accordingly. Of course, there is an interaction between planning the meal and serving the meal. Soup, for instance, may be difficult to serve from a buffet. So consider whether the meal will be buffet style or served when deciding on the menu.

Kiddush over wine is traditionally said at a seudah mitzvah, the meal following a joyful religious occasion. In selecting wine for the reception, it is appropriate to choose a kosher brand, whether it is from the United States or Israel. In fact, Conservative and Orthodox synagogues will insist that only kosher wine be used. Many liquor stores are willing to deliver an overestimated amount of wine and allow the return of unopened bottles. Sometimes they will provide you with a free case of glasses on loan as part of their service. Your synagogue may be able to supply wine glasses, too. Otherwise, you may rent glasses or buy plastic wine glasses. The latter are readily available from a party goods store.

The Synagogue and Its Kitchen: Kashrut and a Mashgiach

Planning a meal at the synagogue will be influenced by whether it has a kosher kitchen. The need to respect the congregation's commitment to this basic and traditional Jewish practice makes it necessary to serve a meal which adheres to the dietary laws. It will be wise to get a list of approved kosher caterers who may bring food in and serve at your synagogue. Prepared food usually may not be brought in from other sources. On the other hand, food may be cooked in the synagogue's own kitchen to be served at your reception. It may be necessary to secure the services of a *mashgiach* (overseer or inspector) to supervise the cooking. He is there to insure that food preparation complies with the requirements of the dietary laws. He is entrusted by the rabbinate of the community to perform that function. Be sure to find out if there is a fee for his services.

Another consideration is whether your congregation allows its ovens to be heated during the time of your reception. This question is especially relevant for a Saturday afternoon party, which is during Shabbat. This may influence your choice of menu. If it maintains kashrut, is your synagogue equipped to handle both meat and dairy meals? We know of one party consultant, entrusted with the details of a Bar Mitzvah, who was proceeding nicely until she realized that a meat meal had been planned for a synagogue which only had a dairy kitchen. Check this ahead of time to avoid problems.

Basic Checklist

You're going to need a lot of equipment to help serve your party guests. The list may include:

- Tables and chairs
- Tablecloths and napkins
- Plates
- Silverware
- Glasses

Your synagogue may be able to provide these items if you hold the party there, or you may secure them from a rental service, caterer, or a party goods store. Here, it is just a matter of personal taste and budget whether you select traditional china and silverware or disposable paper and plastic goods. If your synagogue or Sisterhood can provide most of these items, that probably will be the most economical solution. It would be appropriate and gracious to offer a donation to the congregation or the Sisterhood in appreciation for the use of those items. If you elect one of the other options, you probably will find that the charges for renting dishes and the like come to only a bit more than using paper and plastic. If you do use disposable products, a few unobtrusive but strategically placed trash receptacles will simplify the table clearing process. If you choose to go with china and glasses not only will you have a rental fee to pay, but also you may need to hire help to clear away and wash the dishes at the end of the meal unless the rental service does its own washing.

Tables and chairs can be rented if necessary. To simplify matters try to rent everything from one place. It is not necessary to go as far as one woman who rented tables and chairs in Connecticut and tablecloths in New Jersey. Keeping rentals local and simple will avoid unnecessary driving and the extra difficulty of dealing with more than one company. While lovely table settings are nice, remember that the gathering of your guests to celebrate together is more important than any other concern.

Whether you are setting up things yourself or having someone else do it for you, it is handy to have a master sheet of instructions so nothing is overlooked.

- First you may need an overall blueprint of the room.

  If your living room furniture needs to be moved and replaced by a rented buffet table, where does everything go?

  If you are using a social hall, where are the tables to be placed?

  Will there be a head table?

- Second, there should be specifics detailing what goes on each individual table.

  Tablecloth, napkins

  Dishes, silverware, glasses for wine and water

  Bottles of wine

  Flowers or other centerpiece

  Basket with rolls

  Condiments

  Birkat ha-Mazon booklets for reciting grace after the meal

  Other items

- Other possible tables for the following:

  Drinks

  Buffet dinner or dessert service

  Placecards

It's a good idea to duplicate these overall charts so that everyone who needs a copy can have one. On the day of the Bar/Bat Mitzvah, it will be helpful for a friend to have this information so that she can oversee, and make sure that things have been done correctly. If a friend is willing to take on that responsibility you'll be free from those distracting concerns during the ceremony and celebration.

Flowers and Centerpieces

On its Bar/Bat Mitzvah weekend, the family may be expected to provide flowers for the synagogue bimah or platform. There may be a regular procedure for ordering flowers, a certain florist, and a set amount of expenditure. The Sisterhood may be in charge of that function and may ask you for a donation so that the flowers are your gift in honor of the occasion. If you are interested and there is time, you may be able to specify the floral design. If your reception is at the synagogue, you may wish to order some coordinating flowers for the party area. Afterward, if you can move the sanctuary flowers to the reception, it will all look well planned.

Individual floral centerpieces quickly add up in cost. If you are providing tables for all your guests, you may want to consider other centerpiece options. These may reflect either the season of the year or a Jewish holiday that is near. In the fall near Sukkot, you may want to fill individual baskets with fruits of the season. At Chanukah, one could use a simple Chanukiah on each table. Sometimes a footed cake plate is used as a centerpiece with a colorful display of assorted desserts. Let your imagination and your budget dictate what can be done. Remember that something you plan and do yourself will be an original expression of your taste and will cost less than something done where others' labor is involved. Perhaps some friends or members of the congregation will be pleased to help you.

Music and Singing

The first step is to consult the ritual leaders of your congregation to learn your own synagogue's customs relating to playing music at the time your reception will be held. The answer may range from the prohibition of playing music on Shabbat, until sundown, to a completely open range of choices for you. Knowing what is considered appropriate, you can then work out the details.

Above all, music at your Bar/Bat Mitzvah party should enhance the occasion, helping to express your joy at being Jewish and your happiness that your child has just fulfilled the mitzvah of being called to the Torah for the first time.

What is Jewish music? In the *Encyclopedia Judaica,* Curt Sachs says, "Jewish music is that music which is made by Jews, for Jews, as Jews."[3] This broad definition reflects that the evolution of Jewish music parallels the history of our people. In the Diaspora, Jews came in contact with various musical styles, many of which have had a welcome influence. While maintaining a Jewish aspect, the music at your Bar/Bat Mitzvah party may take many different forms and will give your party a special Jewish imprint.

If your synagogue does not permit musical instruments on Shabbat, there are many vocalists who are eager to teach Jewish songs and Israeli dancing to your guests as part of their presentation. This participation adds a warm Jewish dimension to the celebration and is always appropriate. Even without additional musical background, it is possible to include group singing as part of the festivities. It will be helpful to provide song sheets which have words in Hebrew and Yiddish, as appropriate, and in transliteration where needed, to give everyone a chance to be part of the group singing. In any of these ways, this form of Jewish music can enhance the atmosphere of your Bar/Bat Mitzvah party.

3. *Encyclopedia Judaica,* Volume 12 (Jerusalem, Israel: Keter Publishing, 1972), p. 555.

If permitted in your synagogue on Shabbat, Jewish music can be recorded or live depending on the availability of musicians, your preference, and budget. Some reception facilities have a sound system, which easily allows you to play selected records and tapes. If you and your guests are not Shomer Shabbat, and the party is held at your home, you may elect to play music there. Be certain to organize the recorded music ahead of time, perhaps borrowing from friends or making a composite tape which presents the musical background you desire. If you wish to hire musicians with a repertory of Yiddish, Israeli, and older Jewish melodies, you may find advertisements for them in your local Jewish newspaper or bookstore. When deciding which group to engage, you'll be wise to hear them audition beforehand. Some even provide a small recording for you to get a feeling for their music. Both style and volume are important to consider, since overly loud music can destroy the very atmosphere which you are seeking to create. This situation requires your good judgment and good taste.

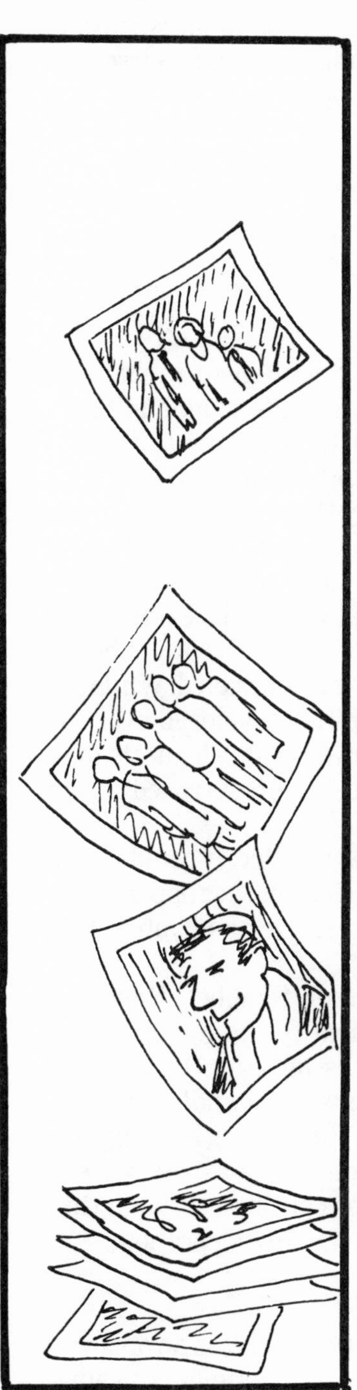

Photography, and other ways to preserve memories

Photographs help preserve memories of the Bar/Bat Mitzvah. First it is necessary to check your synagogue's policy about photography at the ceremony and reception. Most likely, photography is not permitted during the ceremony for it would disturb the service. Therefore, to capture this important moment on film, a better course is to stage photos on the bimah ahead of the actual date. If you know certain guests are avid amateur photographers, you'll want to mention this prohibition in advance to avoid any awkward moments on the Bar/Bat Mitzvah day. To put matters in a more positive light, you could ask such a guest to bring his equipment to record events that take place after the synagogue ceremony and at a time when it is appropriate to photograph. If this person is primarily responsible for the photographic record of the Bar/Bat Mitzvah, encourage him to include others in the pictures, besides those guests he knows. Otherwise, as has happened, you may be overwhelmed with snapshots of his side of the family to the exclusion of the rest of your Bar/Bat Mitzvah party. By calling on a guest to be the photographer, you are gaining a permanent record of the occasion without the expense of hiring a professional. Undoubtedly, you have a friend or relative who would be delighted with the honor of being chosen as your photographer.

With today's technology, there are other ways to capture the Bar/Bat Mitzvah experience for posterity. Some families, whose personal degree of observance permits, use a video-cassette recorder at their reception. Another option is to use a recording device at the synagogue service if this is permitted. If your synagogue uses a microphone and amplification at the ceremony, it may be possible to tap into the public address system with a recording device. Having the service recorded on tape gives you a vivid and meaningful remembrance of that day's experiences. If you are not particularly capable in this field, a friend or audio consultant may be able to help you set up an unobtrusive recording arrangement. Of course, it is essential to ask your rabbi if this will be acceptable.

Suggestions for Enhancing Your Celebration, In Religious and Personal Ways

In Jewish tradition, prayers and blessings certainly are not limited to rabbis and synagogue services. Indeed they can be suitably incorporated into the seudah mitzvah following the completion of the Bar/Bat Mitzvah ceremony. Before starting to drink or eat, one says the kiddush over wine, the motzi over challah, and the blessings for washing one's hands. Reciting these prayers serves to sanctify the day and adds to the religious significance of the meal to be served. By beginning a meal with blessings and prayers, you are indicating your focus, fusing the spiritual with the material.

The Torah commands, "And you shall eat and be satisfied and you shall bless the Lord your God for the goodly land which he gave you." (Deut. 8:10) This is the origin of the *birkat ha-mazon* (grace after meals) which is chanted after eating is completed. While the mitzvah of reciting the Birkat ha-Mazon is specified, its form has developed over the ages into different versions of varying length. At your Bar/Bat Mitzvah, all guests may participate in this traditional ritual if you provide them with booklets or Xeroxed sheets with the Birkat ha-Mazon.

In chanting the grace after eating, there must be a competent leader. It could be the Bar/Bat Mitzvah child, a parent, or a guest. This setting provides another opportunity to share an honor. Perhaps you can ask someone who did not receive an aliyah to lead this blessing.

It is a mitzvah to recite Havdalah after the sun goes down on Shabbat. Havdalah means "separation" in Hebrew and this prayer serves to identify the Sabbath as a unique day, separate and distinct from the weekdays. Just as lighting the Sabbath candles on Friday evening ushers in Shabbat, so lighting the Havdalah candle marks its end, thus bracketing the seventh day from the rest of the week. Containing blessings for wine, spices, and light, the Havdalah ceremony touches all the senses as a new week begins. If your reception will start at sundown on Saturday or continue through that time, reciting these blessings will heighten the religious tone of your celebration.

Here are some additional things you can do:

- The child can give a d'var Torah or Bar/Bat Mitzvah speech. This is an opportunity for some remarks of religious content, perhaps including comments on what it means to be a Jewish thirteen-year-old experiencing this ceremony. This could also include words of thanks to family, teachers, and guests gathered together to celebrate this occasion.

- One child took the time to examine thirteen different persons in Jewish history and to relate information about their lives and times.
- Parents could say some public words of greeting to their guests and speak of their joy on this dav.
- Song sheets, Birkat ha-Mazon booklets, or special "playbills" can include personal data about the Bar/Bat Mitzvah child and family. When duplicating material for each guest, some old family photos, a family tree, and other information can be reprinted as a memento of the day.
- If your child has an enthusiastic group at his table, they could help lead singing at the reception.
- Doing some of the cooking yourself gives a personal touch to the party. Baking challah is an especially nice idea. Recipes can be found in *the Jewish Catalog,* pages 38–39, and many other Jewish cookbooks.

Perceptions of good taste vary with individuals, but few will want to duplicate the following three Bar/Bat Mitzvah "enhancements" which actually happened:

> A 6′ x 3′ chocolate bar into which were frozen photographs of the Bat Mitzvah girl and her sisters.
>
> Renting the Miami stadium, where cheerleaders were hired to spell out the child's name on the occasion of his Bar Mitzvah.
>
> A reception where guests were told to dress in monster costumes and were fed green turtle soup and other ghoulish foods since the Bat Mitzvah fell near Halloween.

Cost-Cutting Hints

- You will save money if food is ordered in bulk, and later arranged on platters.
- If friends volunteer to prepare something for your reception, accept their offers. That will leave less for you to handle yourself.
- Friends and other Bar/Bat Mitzvah parents may join together to help you cook and bake for your simcha. This can be done in small batches at home and put into individual freezers.
- Some Sisterhoods are organized to help with every Bar/Bat Mitzvah by cooperative efforts of their members and the parents of that year's Bar/Bat Mitzvah group. It

may be possible to institute such a cooperative schedule within your own synagogue if none exists.

- Kosher catering is usually expensive. One family we know gathered friends to cook in large quantities in their own synagogue's kitchen. This was done, under supervision, in accordance with the dietary laws of kashrut.
- If wine is served, check whether the liquor store offers the free use of wine glasses as a service. Free delivery and pick-up may be included, saving you both time and effort.
- Help may be needed for serving, clearing dishes, and cleaning up. Some friends, college students, or members of the synagogue maintenance staff may be able to assist you, at lower expense than hiring professional help.
- In lieu of renting plates, silverware, and other party accessories, consider paper and plastic goods. They may cost less when all factors are considered, including rental charges, breakage, and fees for help.
- One family holding an outdoor reception avoided the whole issue of serving platters and place settings. Instead, they prepared individual meals inside corsage boxes which were distributed to guests.
- If you want colorful tablecloths, rather than renting them, it may be possible to buy yards of inexpensive, easy-care, bright fabric or sheets which you can make into tablecloths yourself. Afterward you may keep them for your own use or you may donate them to the synagogue for use by others.
- Making your own centerpieces can let you realize savings. You may create centerpieces which also serve as part of the meal, such as bowls of fruit or trays of petit fours.
- It may be possible to order flowers in bulk and for you and your friends to do the individual arrangements. This allows quite a savings in labor costs.
- Holding your reception at the synagogue is not only in keeping with the tone of the day, but also will be less expensive than renting a commercial facility.

Ideas for Providing for Your Youngest Guests

- Some families offer children a separate menu; others elect to offer children basically the same meal as adults. Consider the ages and usual tastes of younger guests before deciding what to offer them. This can help you avoid waste.
- At a seated reception, it may be wise to have guests sit as families so that parents are at each table to supervise their own young children. Older, well-behaved children may have a table of their own.
- If you hire a baby-sitter, it may be a good idea to have the sitter available during the reception as well as the service. Remember that the sitter will need a meal if she stays this long.
- Buffet service allows some mobility and is less formal than a served meal. This self-service style may be more suitable if you are inviting a large number of children.
- Children sometimes like to have a party for their own friends. This may be done at a later date, perhaps in cooperation with other Bar/Bat Mitzvah children. In this way, you can share expenses.

Following these ideas, you can plan a tasteful party to suit both your guest list and budget. Your child's Bar/Bat Mitzvah will be enhanced as you extend the festivities with a lovely celebration.

Gifts: Giving and Receiving

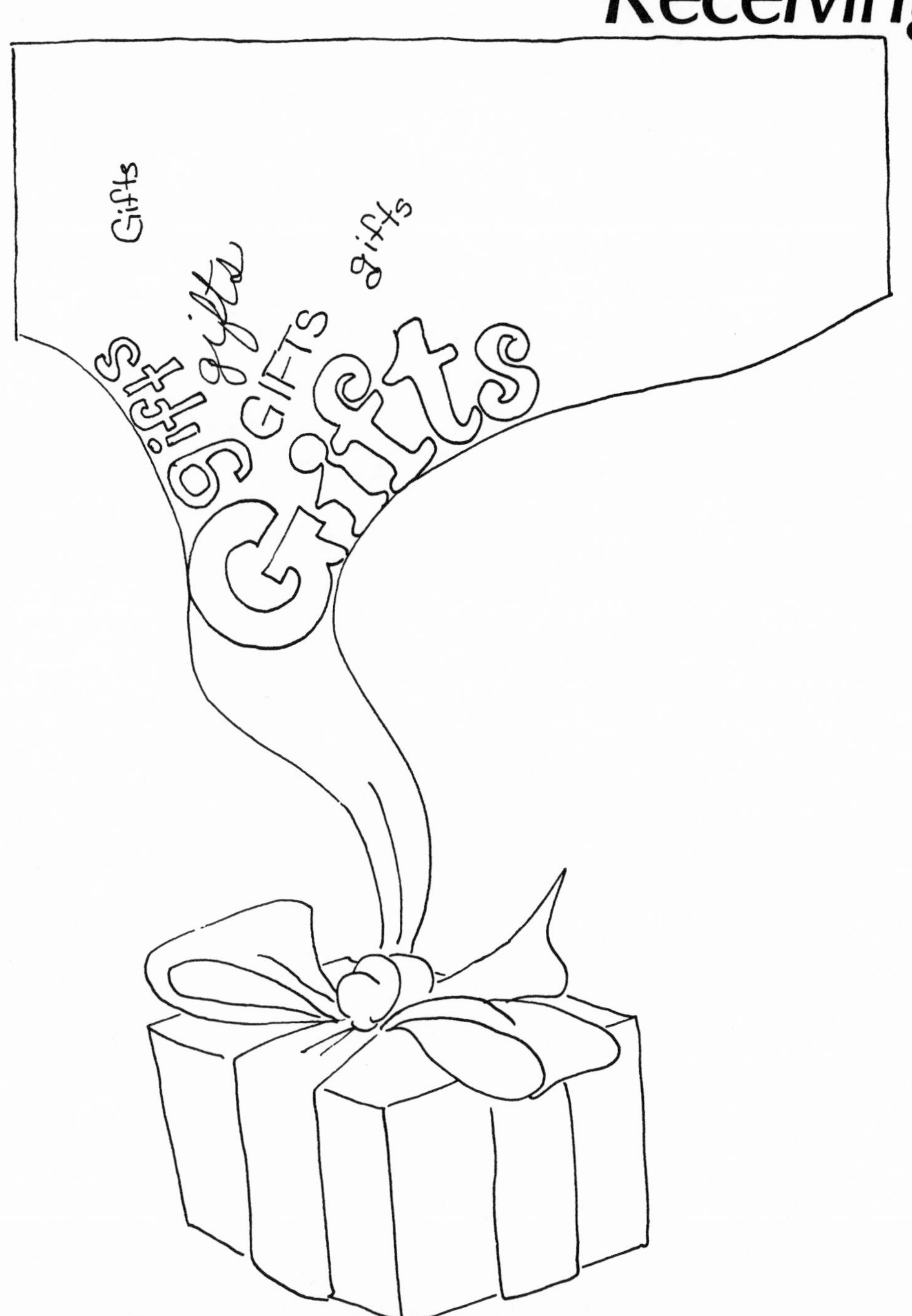

Gifts: Giving and Receiving

Gifts given to a Bar/Bat Mitzvah child should be selected with the understanding that a Bar/Bat Mitzvah is not the same as a birthday party for a thirteen-year-old. It is a religious occasion marking a passage in the Jewish life cycle. So, one should not think just in terms of a suitable birthday present, but rather of something which will reflect the special character of the day. As a parent, you may be asked to make suggestions. What are appropriate gifts with Jewish meaning? The list is long and with a little effort these gifts can be obtained.

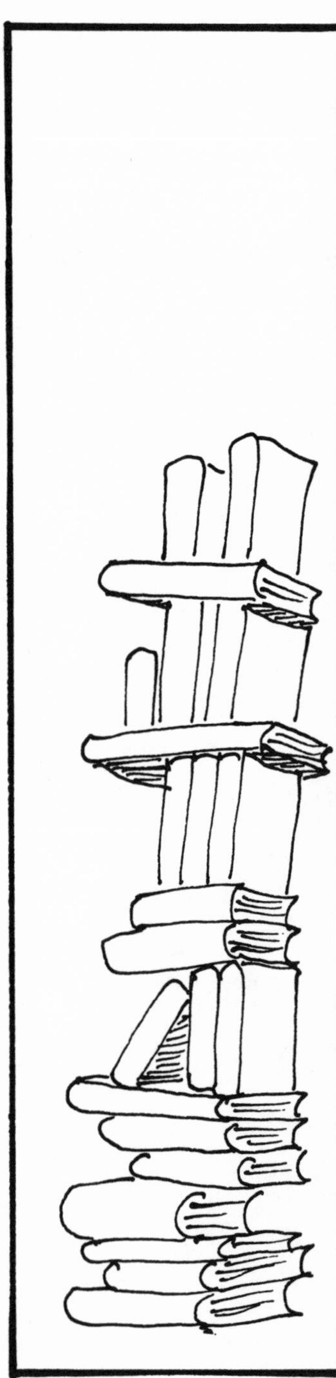

Gifts with Jewish Meaning

• Books on Jewish Topics

Having a personal Jewish library has always been a priority in our tradition, whether one has only a few volumes or considerably more. Jews long have been known as "the people of the book," oriented to the written records of our heritage. Thus, a book makes a most appropriate gift for a Bar/Bat Mitzvah child. What specific books make good Bar/Bat Mitzvah presents?

A prayer book, referred to as a siddur.

A Bible or Chumash, which is the Torah printed in book form. This comes in various translations, with or without commentaries and parallel Hebrew verses.

Other primary Jewish sources such as individual volumes of books of Samuel, Isaiah, Ecclesiastes, or Job.

Scholarly commentaries that analyze Jewish writings. For example, Maimonides, Rashi, Nehama Leibowitz, and many, many others.

Books on Jewish history, ethics, and traditions. There are single and multivolume encyclopedias written on a level suitable for a Bar/Bat Mitzvah child. For example, *The Junior Judaica,* c/o Maccabee Publishing Co., 14 W. Forest Ave., Englewood, N.J. 07631.

Biographies of famous Jews.

Books about the state of Israel—history, archaeology, natural history, some which emphasize a pictorial approach.

Always popular gifts are *The Jewish Catalog,* Volumes I, II, and III; *Jewish Chronicles,* a three volume set; and Martin Gilbert's *Jewish History Atlas* and *Jerusalem History Atlas.*

An easy way to select some of these books is from the mail-order offerings of Jewish book clubs and from the catalogues of some of the publishing houses that specialize in Judaica. A subscription to the magazine *Judaica Book News,* published twice yearly by Book News, Inc., 303 West Tenth Street, New York, N.Y. 10014, can help suggest a list of the publishing houses who have offerings you can consider. The following brief list is by no means all-inclusive.

CCAR PRESS
Central Conference of American Rabbis
790 Madison Avenue
New York, NY 10021
(212) 734-7166

Children-of-the-Book Club
25 Lawrence Avenue
Lawrence, NY 11559
(516) 239-2095

Jewish Book Club
111 Eighth Avenue
New York, NY 10011
(212) 924-6663

Jewish Publication Society of America
1528 Walnut Street
Philadelphia, PA 19102
(215) 564-5925

Judaica Book Club
Div. of Jonathan David Publishers
68-22 Eliot Avenue
Middle Village, NY 11379
(212) 456-8611

Tara Publications
29 Derby Avenue
Cedarhurst, NY 11516
(516) 569-1709 or (516) 295-1061
This house specializes in Jewish music books and recordings.

• Jewish Ritual Items
Ritual objects have a timeless quality, and they make wonderful gifts. They can be used

in religious ceremonies throughout the week and yearly cycle of Jewish holidays. The following items should not be difficult to locate:

Tallit with tallit bag
Kiddush cup
Tefillin and tefillin bag
Shabbat candlesticks
Seder plate
Menorah
Spice box

Your Jewish bookstore, Judaica shop, or synagogue shop should be able to supply most of these items and may be willing to fill telephone or mail-in orders.

You may also be able to secure these items, and others, through newly developed mail-order catalogues devoted strictly to items of Judaica. As the fall 1980 Chanukah catalogue of the Mail Order Maven, Inc. states:

> Judaism has survived in many different lands and circumstances. And in every place and time, our people passed on the laws, the culture, the stories, the ceremonies, the hopes of Judaism. In this time and place we must do the same. But where do we get the things that we need to share our heritage with our children, especially those of us who have moved away from the large cities which have been the sources of American Judaism? . . .

Jewish mail-order catalogues fulfill a specific need. Here are the addresses of such businesses:

Hamakor Judaica, Inc.
The Source of Everything Jewish
6112 North Lincoln Avenue
Chicago, IL 60659
(312) 463-6186

Mail Order Maven, Inc.
RFD Box 375
Norwich, VT 05055
(802) 785-2659

The Source
11106 Whisper Ridge
San Antonio, TX 78230
(512) 492-1432

You may also check in *The Second Jewish Catalog*, under the heading "Gift Services & Mail Order."

- State of Israel Bonds

This gift gives a message to the Bar/Bat Mitzvah child and creates a physical link with the state of Israel. A bond is a continual reminder that coming of age includes responsibilities for our fellow Jews in Zion.

Unusual Jewish Gifts

- For something out of the ordinary:

You can order a Bar Mitzvah Scroll with the child's Haftarah portion in Hebrew and English. This comes rolled inside a wooden case and can be ordered from Jerusalem Products Corp., Dept. B, Center Fayston Road, Waitsfield, VT 05673.

Your local Jewish community center or YMHA-YWHA may have a special membership for teens. This youth membership could be a fine Bar/Bat Mitzvah present. It offers a Jewish community connection to the child while helping support a local Jewish institution.

Another possibility is to offer to take the Bar/Bat Mitzvah child on a tour of American-Jewish historic interest. A trip to New York's Lower East Side and the Chasidic and other Orthodox communities in Brooklyn may leave a lasting impression on the youngster. These are places where Yiddish is still the everyday language, and hearing it on the lips of children no older than he is certain to put him in quick touch with his roots.

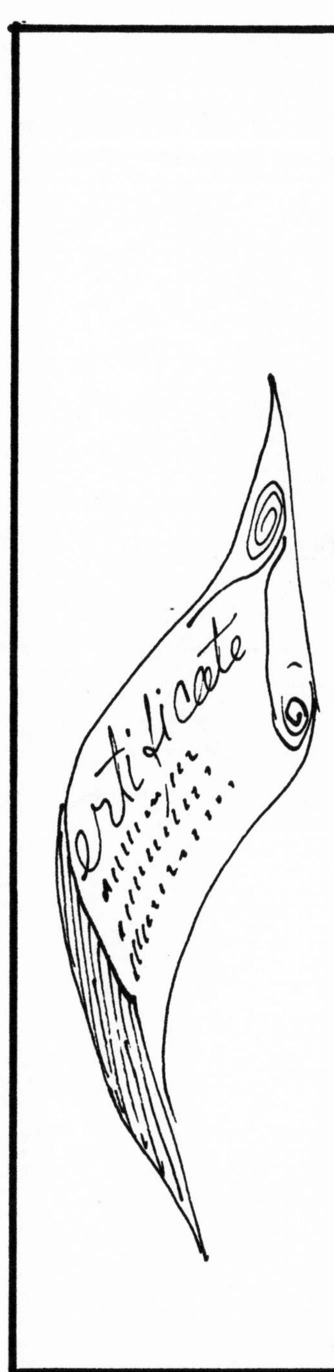

Tzedakah

The obligation to help the poor and needy is stated in the Bible and has been considered basic by Jewish leaders throughout the ages. Becoming a Bar/Bat Mitzvah, a young Jewish person has reached the age of responsibility for the *mitzvot* (commandments). Primary among these is *tzedakah,* a word difficult to translate for it means much more than charity. Rather it has a connotation of righteousness, the root being the same as in the Hebrew word *tzaddik* (a righteous person). Within the context of gifts, how can this idea of tzedakah be transmitted to the Bar/Bat Mitzvah child?

Danny Siegel, an author, suggests how the Bar/Bat Mitzvah experience can include an exposure to the value of tzedakah. He feels that a child should be encouraged to donate a portion of the money he receives as gifts on this occasion. He may need instruction and guidance in selecting a worthy cause for this purpose. Now that the child has demonstrated his intention to take on adult religious responsibilities, giving tzedakah enables him to act upon this.

It is in the best Jewish tradition to make an offering to a community organization in honor of a simcha or joyous event. In lieu of a present for the child, guests may make charitable contributions in the child's name. Occasionally a family may decide that it prefers to receive no personal Bar/Bat Mitzvah gifts. The giving of tzedakah acknowledges that even while rejoicing, a Jew must keep in mind a concern for others. A charity of one's own choosing is perfectly appropriate. Usually the organization receiving the donation sends a card to the Bar/Bat Mitzvah child stating that a contribution was made in the child's honor. Here are some suggestions for a contribution:

- One can plant trees in Israel as a living gift. The Jewish National Fund and B'nai B'rith support reforestation projects. Trees can be planted in the American Bicentennial, John F. Kennedy, Martin Luther King, or Hubert Humphrey forests, if you wish to specify. In addition, the Jewish National Fund also has a Bar/Bat Mitzvah Book in Israel where the child's name and photograph can be permanently recorded in recognition of a donation in honor of this occasion.
- Contributions are welcomed by the various institutions and organizations that underlie the Jewish community: United Jewish Appeal, Hadassah, Organization through Rehabilitation Training, the synagogue with its auxiliaries, Jewish camps, rabbinical schools, and many other worthy causes.
- Twinning with a Soviet Jew. In order to support Soviet Jewry, the Union of Councils for Soviet Jews has developed a special Bar/Bat Mitzvah gift. For a donation, the child having a Bar/Bat Mitzvah ceremony will be paired with a Jewish child in the Soviet Union whose family has been refused permission to emigrate to Israel. The Bar/Bat Mitzvah child receives a biography and the address of this Soviet "twin," a children's handbook on Russian Jews, and a certificate acknowledging his participation in this program. He is thus afforded the opportunity to share responsibility for a fellow Jew, one his own age, as his first act of religious maturity. Though holding a Bar/Bat Mitzvah ceremony is not allowed in the Soviet Union, some "refuseniks" do what they can to approximate the experience. In any event, the Soviet Jewish youngster is symbolically included in the religious ceremony taking place in freedom. Your community may already have this program under the auspices of the Union of Councils for Soviet Jews, or you can contact the Washington Committee for Soviet Jewry, 8402 Freyman Drive, Chevy Chase, MD 20815, (301) 587-4455, and they will make arrangements for you no matter where you live.
- Helping sponsor an Israeli's Bar/Bat Mitzvah. Mizrachi is a multi-faceted organization. One branch provides institutional homes for Israeli youngsters who are on their own whether as a result of war deaths or family deterioration. With a donation, a person can sponsor a Bar/Bat Mitzvah for a Mizrachi child who has no family to do this. For $100 the American child will receive a certificate, a tallit, and a kippah made in Israel. For an $18 donation to the Bar Mitzvah Fund the child will receive a certificate of participation. Knowing that a less fortunate fellow Jew was thus enabled to experience this ceremony stands as an example of responsibility and a graphic reminder of the worldwide bond between the Jewish people. For more information, contact the American Mizrachi Women's Organization, 817 Broadway, NY, 10003, (212) 477-4720.

Underscoring the importance of tzedakah, Danny Siegel offers a novel thought. He suggests that a parent estimate the cost of the Bar/Bat Mitzvah including the party.

Using this as the basis, calculate an amount of tzedakah to be given at this time. One can give either a percentage above the estimated expense or cut back on some anticipated expenditure, for example, flowers or food, and allocate that sum as a donation. This expression serves as a critical example at a time when the Bar/Bat Mitzvah child is influenced by adult models, especially his parents.

Remembering Your Synagogue

It is considered customary to mark a Bar/Bat Mitzvah by offering a contribution to the synagogue in honor of the occasion. This gift connects the celebration of a personal, time-related passage with an enduring Jewish community institution. Thus it helps perpetuate your specific congregation which provided the support necessary to enable you to hold the Bar/Bat Mitzvah. At this time, it also may be fitting to offer an honorarium to your rabbi, cantor, or other professionals on the synagogue staff who gave you special assistance.

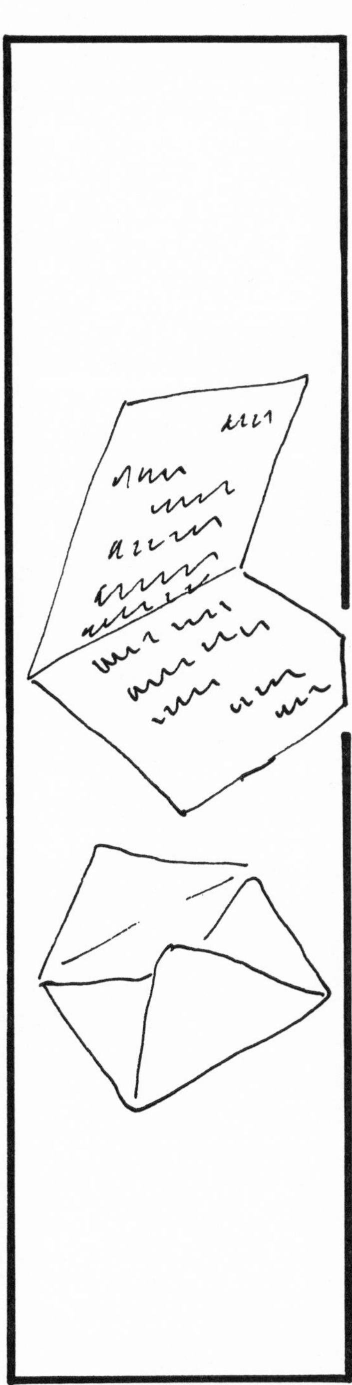

The Thank You Note: Taking the time to respond properly and promptly

A Bar or Bat Mitzvah gift is an expression of caring. This is a significant event, important enough to be marked by a present which has been carefully selected. The Bar/Bat Mitzvah child must respond accordingly. The process of handling the gifts and thank you notes often involves some parental guidance and supervision. Children of age twelve and thirteen are still learning and parents can help them.

It is useful to keep records of all gifts. The gift should be listed with the name of the person who gave it, the date of arrival, and the date of acknowledgment. In the "Charts and Timetables Section," there is a sample chart for recording this information. Obviously, appropriate note paper must be available for the child's use. Thanking people is the responsibility of the child, part of growing up through the Bar/Bat Mitzvah process. Different children will need varying levels of supervision depending on their motivation, personal standards, and spelling ability. A thank you note need not be a masterpiece, but it should demonstrate care in its preparation.

General guidelines for your child:

- Address the people appropriately. Whether he's writing to Aunt Sarah or Mr. and Mrs. Feldman, the name should be written in the proper form and spelled correctly.
- Be quite specific about the gift. A mimeographed note is unacceptable and so is "thank you for the gift."
- The thank you note should be sent within a few weeks. It is embarrassing to receive a call asking if the gift ever arrived. Avoid this by making sure that notes go out in a timely fashion.

Every child is pleased to receive gifts which are a tangible recognition of the significance of this occasion. Above all, help your child keep in mind that gifts are a subordinate part of the total Bar/Bat Mitzvah experience.

Alternatives for the Ceremony and Celebration

Alternatives for the Ceremony and Celebration

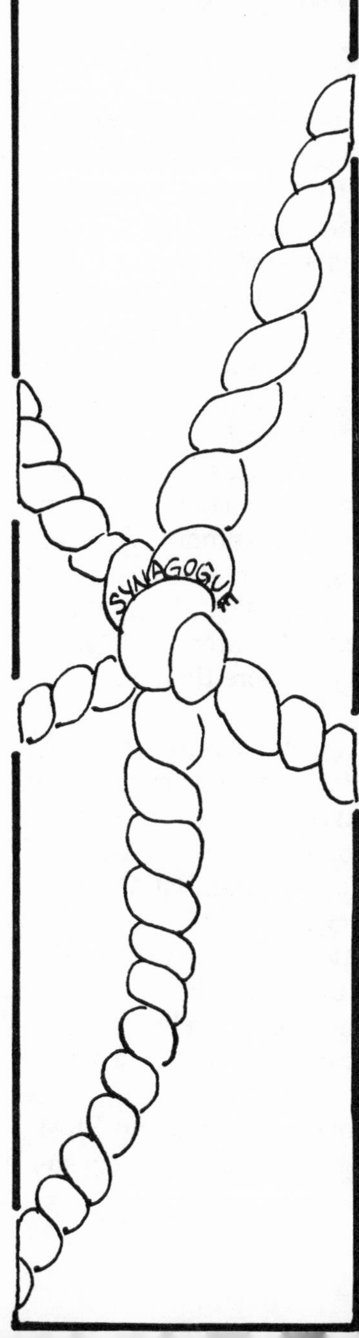

The Synagogue as the Traditional Setting

Judaism is a community based religion. Many of its commandments deal with man's relation to his fellow man. The concept of the Jews as a people is fundamental, for a person leads a Jewish life in relation to others. Judaism is not a religion of withdrawal nor of isolated spirituality. Therefore, it follows that at a Bar/Bat Mitzvah, a child stands before his congregation to proclaim his intention to lead a responsible Jewish life.

Since the Temple in Jerusalem is no longer standing and Jews have been scattered throughout the world in the Diaspora, the local synagogue has become the institutional setting where the religious community gathers. In fact, the word *synagogue* is derived from two Greek words meaning "bring" and "together" or "assembly." Since a Bar/Bat Mitzvah marks a young person's entering the community, it is fitting that this ceremony take place in the synagogue, which is the contemporary center for Jewish religious observance.

Holding the Ceremony in Israel: The Kotel (Western Wall), Atop Masada, or Elsewhere

Since the establishment of the state of Israel, some people have chosen to travel to Israel with close family and friends to hold the Bar or Bat Mitzvah there. Having the ceremony in Israel links two underlying strands in Jewish tradition, identification with one's people and love of Zion. For some families, a trip to Israel is a dream which they realize at the time of their child's Bar/Bat Mitzvah. With the reunification of Jerusalem in 1967, a boy may now have his Bar Mitzvah at the Kotel, the Western Wall of the Temple Mount. Another popular setting is Masada, a symbol of freedom and hope for the Jewish people since the time of the Romans. On a Monday or Thursday morning, a group departs for Masada and ascends to its summit. A Sefer Torah is brought along with the group as it leaves from Jerusalem. The Bar Mitzvah service takes place there amidst the ruins of an ancient synagogue atop the citadel. After the ceremony (and there may be more than one), the day of touring continues.

To make arrangements, the best approach is to work with a competent travel agent who has had sufficient experience in planning a Bar or Bat Mitzvah in Israel. The travel agent can make plans for your hotel accommodations, ceremony, reception, and for your child to receive a Bar/Bat Mitzvah certificate from the Israeli Ministry of Tourism. A knowledgeable agent will make suggestions to fit your specific needs. Whatever you have in mind for an Israeli Bar Mizvah you should start planning this event at least twelve to eighteen months in advance. Remember that international mails are often slow and unreliable.

To get additional information, one can contact an El Al representative; the office of the Israeli Embassy or consulate; or the Government of Israel Tourist Office, 350 Fifth Avenue, New York, NY 10118—(212) 560-0650. This government tourist office will send you relevant information if you request it.

We strongly suggest that if at all possible, you locate a contact person in Israel who will act as your go-between for any arrangements which you or your travel agent cannot handle on your own. If this person is not a good friend or relative, you may be asked to pay a small fee for these services. People offering this assistance usually can be found by word-of-mouth. In any event, certain details will have to be handled after your arrival. However, we must emphasize that your child should be prepared for his part in the service well ahead of time as for any Bar/Bat Mitzvah ceremony. Be sure to verify the Torah portion (sidra) since there are several times a year when the portion being read in Israel differs from the one being read in the Diaspora.

We should also point out that in certain locations in Israel, it may not be possible to hold a service for a daughter. For example, this is true at the Western Wall. However, there are other possible settings for a Bat Mitzvah, such as the Center for Conservative Judaism in Jerusalem, or individual synagogues such as Ramat Zion, Bar Kochba Street 68, French Hill, Jerusalem. You can contact the Jewish Theological Seminary, 3080 Broadway, New York, NY 10027 for further suggestions for a Bat Mitzvah in Israel.

Israelis welcome children coming to celebrate in their land. Sometimes it is even possible to attend a reception at the home of the president of Israel specifically for those youngsters who have come to Israel to celebrate their coming of age. So you can expect to find a cooperative attitude as you seek to plan an Israeli Bar/Bat Mitzvah. This strengthens the link between our people and gives a boost to tourism, an important industry there.

Although a Bar/Bat Mitzvah ceremony is symbolic of acceptance into the worldwide Jewish community, special consideration should be given to your own particular congregation. Family, friends, and synagogue provide the Jewish setting in which you live. Having a Bar or Bat Mitzvah in Israel can be a beautiful and moving experience, but in addition, you may wish to hold a small ceremony at your own synagogue.

D'var Torah/Bat Torah

Some synagogues do not offer the Bat Mitzvah ceremony at all; it is not included in their interpretation of Jewish law or tradition. So, in some cases, a Jewish girl simply does not experience a service marking this point in her life. On the other hand, some Jewish families who wish to acknowledge the religious achievements of their daughters have developed alternative ceremonies for this purpose. Perhaps the girl will give a meaningful speech or lead a learned discussion on the week's Torah portion. This discourse is called a d'var Torah. Or a girl may read Ecclesiastes during Sukkot, the Megillah of Esther during Purim, or the Book of Ruth at Shavuot, portions of the Ketuvim, the sacred writings, not from the Torah itself. The ceremony may be held at home, at a Jewish community center, or in a sukkah at that festive season if the synagogue is not a feasible setting for this religious event. Even though held outside the synagogue, this rite of passage is sometimes termed a Bat Mitzvah. Other times, it is referred to as a Bat Torah, suggesting that the girl has now publicly affirmed that she is a "daughter of the Torah." This has slightly different connotations from the term Bat Mitzvah and reflects that the girl has demonstrated her intention to follow the teachings of her Jewish heritage but avoids the suggestion that she is subject to exactly the same commandments as her brothers.

Nontraditional Settings

Judaism has always been a religion with great variety in its beliefs and its practices. In surveying alternatives to the usual synagogue-based Bar/Bat Mitzvah ceremony, it is important to note that other forms have developed that do without the synagogue entirely. In many instances, the atmosphere is strictly informal, whether it be at the Jewish community center or on a retreat. Here the emphasis is on an innovative and personalized experience. The intention is to be nontraditional, often with the parents structuring the ritual without the involvement of a rabbi. Prayers and songs may be done in a folk-rock idiom. We know of instances where readings included poetry written by the child, selections from Albert Einstein or Kahlil Gibran, along with portions from standard Jewish prayer. The Bar/Bat Mitzvah child may express his achievements by playing the flute or violin. Another new, although limited trend in American Judaism is to celebrate a child's coming of age at his own home. Those wishing to hold the Bar/Bat Mitzvah at home point out that nothing in Jewish tradition forbids this. They regard the Jewish wedding at home as a parallel experience.

To hold such a nontraditional service, one would need a minyan of ten persons for the prayer service and a Torah scroll from which to read. Securing a Torah for your purposes may take some effort but it can be done. Some synagogues may be willing to loan a Torah, with a donation expected as a thank you. In lieu of borrowing large numbers of prayer books, many families prefer to create and print their own booklet for the service. With these basic elements in place, one is ready to hold a personalized ceremony with one's own limited group of invited guests. For further information about alternative Bar/Bat Mitzvah celebrations, consult *The Second Jewish Catalog,* pages 68–75.

Of the families seeking a nontraditional format for their child's Bar/Bat Mitzvah, many may not belong to a synagogue or may be members of an unaffiliated congregation, which is not part of the Reform, Conservative, Reconstructionist, or Orthodox movements. Others may belong to an institution which simply provides a school for the children, but no sanctuary for common worship. The Bar/Bat Mitzvah ceremony is viewed as an event which expresses personal feelings about coming of age within Judaism. They seek to create a celebration to convey this message. It becomes an event outside the traditional framework of American Judaism. However, within the structure of the affiliated congregations, the Bar/Bat Mitzvah ceremony is usually regarded as a community celebration occurring at a synagogue service.

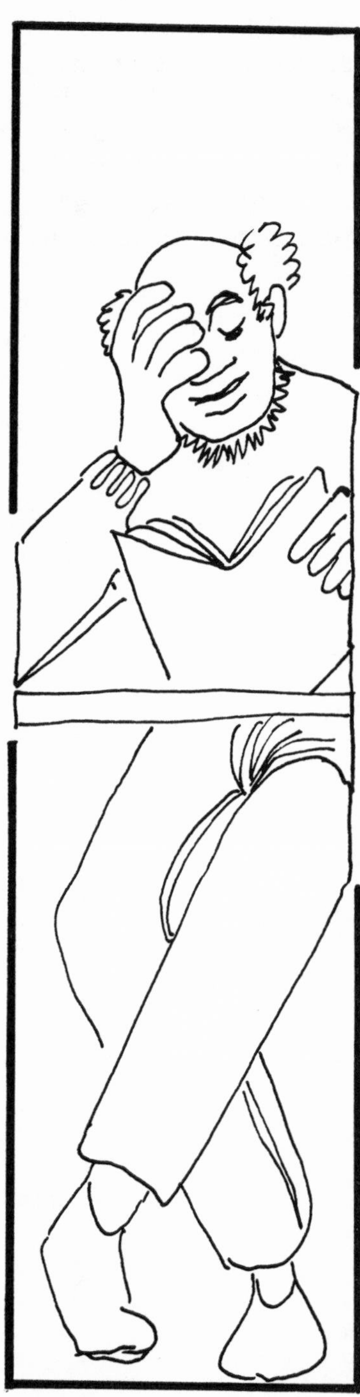

The Adult Bar/Bat Mitzvah

While this book is directed to preparing a child for a Bar or Bat Mitzvah, this ceremony need not occur at age thirteen. For those who have not had the opportunity, it is never too late to affirm publicly one's commitment to Judaism. Thousands and thousands of Jewish boys have passed age thirteen without experiencing a Bar Mitzvah ceremony to mark the occasion. Often inspired by their own children's Jewish studies, men are participating in a belated ceremony. One boy in New York just began his quest for his Jewish identity at age thirteen after his nonobservant parents completely ignored his religious education. This particular child, who had been so uncomfortable with Jewish ritual that he had not attended a friend's Bar Mitzvah, sought to learn more about his own background. Beginning a two-year course of study at a synagogue, he chose to have a Bar Mitzvah ceremony at the age of fifteen.

Some women who did not study and prepare for this occasion may feel that something is lacking in their Jewish background. Some saw their brothers learn and grow through the Bar Mitzvah process and wished they could have had a similar experience. Seeking a firm identification with their Jewish heritage, these adult women today are preparing for a delayed Bat Mitzvah ceremony. Women of all ages, young professionals as well as grandmothers, have worked together and attained a strong sense of pride through this symbolic act.

Many congregations now are conducting an extended study program of Hebrew, rituals, Jewish history, and ethics, culminating in an adult Bar/Bat Mitzvah. Often this is a group experience with participation in the service shared by those completing the course of study. The Torah and Haftarah readings may be divided among those being honored as "sons and daughters of the commandments." If you are interested in starting an adult Bar/Bat Mitzvah program at your synagogue, you probably can find a like-minded group of adults with whom to study. Another possibility is for young adults, often of college age, to reach this goal with the guidance of a Hillel House, chavurah group, or the like.

If this is something which appeals to you, we're confident that you will find the necessary support to achieve this goal.

Some people are fortunate enough to have a second Bar Mitzvah. In some congregations, it is customary to recognize a person of age eighty-three as a Bar Mitzvah, calling him to the Torah for an aliyah and possibly having him chant the Haftarah. Having reached age eighty-three, he is understood to have lived his normal, biblically appointed life span of seventy years and now is marking age thirteen again. Thus, appropriately, there is a second Bar Mitzvah ceremony.

In Conclusion

In the course of this book, we have mentioned ways to enhance the religious meaning of the total Bar/Bat Mitzvah experience. When discussing the Bar/Bat Mitzvah ceremony with your rabbi and educational director, it would be valuable to ask them for personal ideas in this regard. By speaking with your own religious leaders and perhaps delving into relevant books on Jewish prayer and ritual, you can help focus the day in a manner that reflects the joy of being Jewish.

Charts and Timetables

Bar/Bat Mitzvah Timetable: Countdown to a Simcha*

Date Completed	EIGHTEEN MONTHS
	• Select a DATE • Find out your child's TORAH and HAFTARAH PORTION • Determine TUTORIAL arrangements to begin about nine months ahead
	ONE YEAR: PLAN THE BROAD OUTLINES OF YOUR CELEBRATION.
	• RECEPTION FACILITY—if not at the synagogue, reserve elsewhere. • FOOD—caterer, homemade, synagogue kitchen, or a combination. • MUSIC for a Jewish celebration.

*We have left sufficient space in the countdown so that you may fill in any additional factors pertaining to your occasion.

Date Completed	NINE MONTHS: PREPARE FOR THE CEREMONY
	• Find out what the child may do at BAR/BAT MITZVAH CEREMONY. • Child begins preparation for BAR/BAT MITZVAH PORTION.
	SIX MONTHS
	• Begin planning your GUEST LIST, using the charts at the back of this book. • If you will have a HAND-DESIGNED INVITATION, start planning for this. • Select TALLIT and TEFILLIN for your son.

BAR/BAT MITZVAH TIMETABLE: (cont'd)

Date Completed	FOUR MONTHS
	• ORDER INVITATIONS for delivery within four weeks. Take envelopes home, if possible. • Make hotel/motel RESERVATIONS for out-of-town guests or arrange for HOST FAMILIES. • Order YARMULKES (skullcaps) and/or SONG and PRAYER BOOKLETS.
	THREE MONTHS
	• Check availability of PARTY EQUIPMENT: chairs, tables, linens, silverware, dishes. Arrange rental, if necessary. • Review GUEST LISTS.

BAR/BAT MITZVAH TIMETABLE: (cont'd)

Date Completed	TEN WEEKS
	• Determine your final GUEST LIST. • ADDRESS ENVELOPES.
	TWO MONTHS
	• Mail OUT-OF-TOWN INVITATIONS, including inserts for hotel or host-family arrangements and directions. • Complete plans for MEALS, either with caterer, your own cooking, or the assistance of friends. • Order FLORAL ARRANGEMENTS for synagogue service and reception. • Engage ADDITIONAL HELP, if needed. • Prepare list of ALIYOT (those called to honor the Torah). Give instructions to those being honored.

BAR/BAT MITZVAH TIMETABLE: (cont'd)

Date Completed	SIX WEEKS
	• Mail LOCAL INVITATIONS. • Think about SEATING ARRANGEMENTS. • Make PLACECARDS.
	THREE WEEKS
	• Arrange for a dress REHEARSAL in your synagogue for your child. • Make up packet of LOCAL INFORMATION for out-of-town guests.

BAR/BAT MITZVAH TIMETABLE: (cont'd)

Date Completed	THE LAST WEEK
	• Complete ALIYOT list and give copy to synagogue. • Time for FINAL REVIEW, if needed: —Hotel/motel or host families —Musician —Florist —Sufficient party equipment to accommodate guests —Food and wine —Additional help • Prepare a FRUIT BASKET, cheese platter, or sweets for hotel guests.

Preliminary Family List*

Date ____________

	Father's Side	Mother's Side
Grandparents		
Great-aunts and Great-uncles		
Aunts and Uncles		

*Think of both local and out-of-town relatives. If you list one aunt, then all persons of a similar relationship should probably be included. Parents and even the grandparents should contribute the names of relatives from each side.

Preliminary Family List

Date ______________________

	Father's Side	Mother's Side
Parents' First Cousins		
Children of Parents' First Cousins		
Steprelatives		
Other Relatives		

Preliminary List of Friends of the Parents*

Date ____________________

Father's Friends	
Mother's Friends	
Grandparents' Friends	

*Local friends will know about the Bar/Bat Mitzvah through the grapevine. Groups of friends who know each other should be considered together. Think of close out-of-town friends who may want to make the effort to come or who would be offended if not invited. Think also of friends who know your child and would be proud to share this moment.

Preliminary List of Your Child's Friends*

Date ______________

Children:
From school, the neighborhood, religious school, camp, sports, scouting, etc.

Adults:
Teachers and others.

*Think of your child's good friends. Will they understand and appreciate the importance of the occasion? Give your child the opportunity to mention adults whom he wishes to include. He may want his piano teacher, some people for whom he baby-sits, or other adults he knows in special ways. It is his Bar/Bat Mitzvah and his suggestions should be seriously considered as you develop your final list.

Preliminary List of Members of Your Congregation*

Date ________________

Friends from within the Congregation

Regular Synagogue Attendees

*The size of this list depends on the nature of your congregation and your involvement with it. Through the years, you have come to know certain families through membership in your synagogue. In addition, many congregations have members who come regularly for Shabbat services. They may be at your Bar/Bat Mitzvah in any event. If you know them and numbers permit, you may want to honor them individually with an invitation so each feels welcome to share this day with you as an invited guest.

Preliminary List of Professional and Business Associates*

Date ____________

Father's Business/ Professional Associates	
Mother's Business/ Professional Associates	

*If you wish to include associates, it is important to invite all those who fall into a similar category to avoid offending while you are trying to be gracious. But resist the temptation to turn this into a double-duty affair, thereby making a Bar/Bat Mitzvah celebration a big social gathering for your business friends.

Preliminary List of Neighbors*

Date ____________________

Neighbors	

*Immediate neighbors will certainly know that a Bar Mitzvah is forthcoming. However, you may not be able to invite the entire neighborhood. You should feel comfortable wherever you draw the line.

Final Guest List*

Guests	No.		Invited to:									RSVP	No. Coming				
NAME AND ADDRESS	ADULTS	CHILDREN	FRI. DINNER	FRI. EVENING	SAT. MORNING	SAT. P.M. PARTY	SUNDAY BRUNCH	DATE INVITATION MAILED	HOTEL/HOST	DIRECTIONS	LETTER	YES/NO	ADULTS	CHILDREN	ALIYAH	GIFT	THANK YOU NOTE

*You may need additional copies of this page depending on the size of your guest list.

Aliyot and Honors Chart*

For Bar/Bat Mitzvah of ______________________

Honor	*Name (English)*	*Name (Hebrew)*
1st Aliyah (Rishon)—a kohen	______________	______________
2nd Aliyah (Sheni)—a levi	______________	______________
3rd Aliyah (Shlishi)	______________	______________
4th Aliyah (Revi'i)	______________	______________
5th Aliyah (Hamishi)	______________	______________
6th Aliyah (Shishi)	______________	______________
7th Aliyah (Shvi'i)	______________	______________
Maftir	______________ (The Bar/Bat Mitzvah Child)	______________
Torah Holder (Hagbah)	______________	______________
Torah Dresser (Glilah)	______________	______________

*There are many rules and regulations governing who may get an aliyah and the order of precedence. Some of these rules are steadfast; the others vary from congregation to congregation. Be sure to consult your rabbi for specific information.

A Hebrew-Civil Calendar Chart 1970–2000

Instructions for the Calendar Chart

The following calendar chart cross references the traditional Hebrew calendar with the standard civil equivalent. It is designed to assist Bar/Bat Mitzvah parents in their planning. Please note that the Jewish day begins and ends at sunset rather than at midnight. The calendar denotes the first day of a holiday. For example: Shabbat is noted with the Torah portion marked on Saturday, while in fact it begins Friday evening at sunset. Torah portions and holidays have been omitted in years already past, since this information will not be needed for Bar/Bat Mitzvah planning. This calendar chart gives the following information:

I. KEY TO CALENDAR CHART

NISAN = the name of the new Hebrew month
Mishpatim = identifies a Shabbat by the Torah reading for that day
Shavuot = the name of a Jewish holiday
SHABBAT HA-GADOL = the name of a special Shabbat

Note that different types are used to indicate the Hebrew months, the Torah readings, the Jewish holidays, and special Shabbats.

II. YOUR CHILD'S HEBREW BIRTHDATE (consult Section A of the calendar chart)

How to find this: Locate the civil year, month, and day your child was born. In the column directly below will be listed the day, Hebrew month, and Hebrew year of your child's birth.

Example: My child was born on October 22, 1973. What is his Hebrew birthdate?
Turn to the page which contains the year 1973. Go to the number directly below the civil date October 22, which is 26. Follow that column of numbers

back to the left to find the name of the Hebrew month, Tishri. On the top left corner of the page the Hebrew year is noted, changing from 5733 to 5734 on the first of Tishri when, Rosh Hashanah, the Jewish New Year occurs. October 22, 1973 is 26 Tishri, 5734. Of course if the child was born after sundown on October 22, 1973, the equivalent Hebrew calendar date would be 27 Tishri, 5734.

(III, IV, and V may be found in Section B of the calendar chart)

III. YOUR CHILD'S THIRTEENTH BIRTHDAY ACCORDING TO THE HEBREW CALENDAR

How to find this: Follow step #II and find your child's Hebrew birthdate. Then turn ahead thirteen years to find the civil calendar equivalent of that Hebrew date.

Example: If my child was born on 26 Tishri, 5734, his thirteenth birthday according to the Hebrew calendar is 26 Tishri, 5747. What is the equivalent civil date? Find the 26th day in the month of Tishri, 5747. Look at the number directly above which will give the civil day and month. You will see that 26 Tishri, 5747 is the same as October 29, 1986.

Exception: If your child was born in the month of Adar and the Bar/Bat Mitzvah falls in a Hebrew leap year, it is customary to celebrate the occasion in Adar II of the leap year. Furthermore, the Hebrew month Adar II does not occur every year. If your child was born during that month and there is no Adar II in the year in which he became thirteen , the birthday and Bar/Bat Mitzvah should be celebrated on the same numerical date in the month of Adar. There are certain years when the months of Heshvan, Kislev, and Adar have a 30th day; at all other times they have 29 days. If your child was born on the 30th day of one of these irregular months and 13 years later there are only 29 days in the month, then the birthday should be observed on the first day of the following Hebrew month.

IV. THE JEWISH HOLIDAYS WHICH FALL AT YOUR CHILD'S BAR/BAT MITZVAH TIME

How to find this: Check on the calendar chart for the anticipated date of your child's Bar/Bat Mitzvah. Look for major Jewish holidays listed there in *italic* type.

Example: We are considering a Bar/Bat Mitzvah date on Saturday, September 28, 1985. Will that fall near a Jewish holiday? Yes, it will be right after Yom Kippur and before Sukkot.

Note: Hebrew dates of the Jewish holydays, festivals, and fasts included in this calendar chart.

Rosh Hashanah	1 Tishri	New Year
Yom Kippur	10 Tishri	Day of Atonement
Sukkot	15 Tishri	Harvest Festival
Shemini Atzeret	22 Tishri	8th Day of Assembly
Simchat Torah	23 Tishri	Rejoicing with the Torah
Chanukah	25 Kislev	Festival of Lights
Tu b'Shevat	15 Shevat	New Year of the Trees
Purim	14 Adar	Holiday of Lots

(In a Hebrew year when an extra month, Adar II, is added, Purim occurs on the 14th of Adar II.)

Passover	15 Nisan	Passover
Yom Ha-Shoah	27 Nisan	Holocaust Day
Yom Ha-Atzma'ut	3 or 4 or 5 Iyar	Israeli Independence Day
Lag b'Omer	18 Iyar	33rd Day in Counting of the Omer
Shavuot	6 Sivan	Feast of Weeks
Tisha b'Av	9 Av	Destruction of the Temple (When the 9th of Av falls on a Shabbat, this fast day is moved forward to the 10th of Av.)

The calendar chart includes the major Jewish holidays as listed above. To learn when other fast days and minor holidays fall, consult your rabbi or synagogue library.

V. THE TORAH PORTION TO BE READ ON THE BAR/BAT MITZVAH DATE

How to find this: This calendar chart includes identification of the Torah portion read on each Shabbat of the yearly cycle. These are specified by the name of the portion, e.g., Bereshit, Noach, Lech Lecha *or* by a holiday if it falls on a Shabbat. Each holiday falling on Shabbat has special readings which your rabbi will outline. Remember that if you are considering a Monday or Thursday Bar/Bat Mitzvah, the Torah reading on those days will be from the portion listed on the following Saturday.

Example: If my child's Bar/Bat Mitzvah is on November 17, 1984 (22 Heshvan 5745), what would be the Torah reading? Answer: Chayye Sarah is the Torah portion listed on that date in the calendar chart.

Exception: During the Jewish calendar cycle, there are six special Sabbaths. Five of these occur in the seven weeks preceding Passover. They are called Shabbat Shekalim, Shabbat Zakhor, Shabbat Parah, Shabbat Ha-Hodesh, and Shabbat Ha-Gadol. The other one occurs between Rosh Hashanah and Yom Kippur and is known as Shabbat Shuvah. Some congregations have limitations on who may recite the Maftir and Haftarah on Shabbat Ha-Gadol, Shabbat Zakhor, and Shabbat Parah. In these instances the Bar/Bat Mitzvah will read a section of the weekly reading other than the Maftir. Your rabbi will be able to give you the specifics for these dates.

In addition, any time Shabbat and Rosh Hodesh (the first day of the new Hebrew month) or Shabbat and Machar Hodesh (the day before Rosh Hodesh) coincide, there are special readings. If your child's Bar/Bat Mitzvah date falls on one of these days, you would be well advised to consult the professionals at your synagogue to determine the readings for your date.

A FINAL NOTE: The Hebrew calendar has many fine points, some of which have not been detailed in this calendar chart. For further clarification, be sure to read the chapter entitled "Choosing the Date" and to consult your rabbi.

The Calendar Chart

Determining Your Child's Hebrew Birthdate 1970–1981, 5730–5742

SECTION A: DETERMINING YOUR CHILD'S HEBREW BIRTHDATE
1970–1981, 5730–5742

1970

5730/31

January 1 2 3 4 5 6 7 8 9 10 11 12 13 14 15 16 17 18 19 20 21 22 23 24 25 26 27 28 29 30 31

Tevet 23 24 25 26 27 28 29 SHEVAT 1 2 3 4 5 6 7 8 9 10 11 12 13 14 15 16 17 18 19 20 21 22 23 24
February 1 2 3 4 5 6 7 8 9 10 11 12 13 14 15 16 17 18 19 20 21 22 23 24 25 26 27 28

Shevat 25 26 27 28 29 30 ADAR I 1 2 3 4 5 6 7 8 9 10 11 12 13 14 15 16 17 18 19 20 21 22
March 1 2 3 4 5 6 7 8 9 10 11 12 13 14 15 16 17 18 19 20 21 22 23 24 25 26 27 28 29 30 31

Adar I 23 24 25 26 27 28 29 30 ADAR II 1 2 3 4 5 6 7 8 9 10 11 12 13 14 15 16 17 18 19 20 21 22 23
April 1 2 3 4 5 6 7 8 9 10 11 12 13 14 15 16 17 18 19 20 21 22 23 24 25 26 27 28 29 30

Adar II 24 25 26 27 28 29 NISAN 1 2 3 4 5 6 7 8 9 10 11 12 13 14 15 16 17 18 19 20 21 22 23 24
May 1 2 3 4 5 6 7 8 9 10 11 12 13 14 15 16 17 18 19 20 21 22 23 24 25 26 27 28 29 30 31

Nisan 25 26 27 28 29 30 IYAR 1 2 3 4 5 6 7 8 9 10 11 12 13 14 15 16 17 18 19 20 21 22 23 24 25
June 1 2 3 4 5 6 7 8 9 10 11 12 13 14 15 16 17 18 19 20 21 22 23 24 25 26 27 28 29 30

Iyar 26 27 28 29 SIVAN 1 2 3 4 5 6 7 8 9 10 11 12 13 14 15 16 17 18 19 20 21 22 23 24 25 26

July 1 2 3 4 5 6 7 8 9 10 11 12 13 14 15 16 17 18 19 20 21 22 23 24 25 26 27 28 29 30 31

Sivan 27 28 29 30 TAMMUZ 1 2 3 4 5 6 7 8 9 10 11 12 13 14 15 16 17 18 19 20 21 22 23 24 25 26 27
August 1 2 3 4 5 6 7 8 9 10 11 12 13 14 15 16 17 18 19 20 21 22 23 24 25 26 27 28 29 30 31

Tammuz 28 29 AV 1 2 3 4 5 6 7 8 9 10 11 12 13 14 15 16 17 18 19 20 21 22 23 24 25 26 27 28 29
September 1 2 3 4 5 6 7 8 9 10 11 12 13 14 15 16 17 18 19 20 21 22 23 24 25 26 27 28 29 30

Av/Elul 30 ELUL 1 2 3 4 5 6 7 8 9 10 11 12 13 14 15 16 17 18 19 20 21 22 23 24 25 26 27 28 29
October 1 2 3 4 5 6 7 8 9 10 11 12 13 14 15 16 17 18 19 20 21 22 23 24 25 26 27 28 29 30 31

Tishri 1 2 3 4 5 6 7 8 9 10 11 12 13 14 15 16 17 18 19 20 21 22 23 24 25 26 27 28 29 30 HESHVAN 1
November 1 2 3 4 5 6 7 8 9 10 11 12 13 14 15 16 17 18 19 20 21 22 23 24 25 26 27 28 29 30

Heshvan 2 3 4 5 6 7 8 9 10 11 12 13 14 15 16 17 18 19 20 21 22 23 24 25 26 27 28 29 KISLEV 1 2
December 1 2 3 4 5 6 7 8 9 10 11 12 13 14 15 16 17 18 19 20 21 22 23 24 25 26 27 28 29 30 31

Kislev 3 4 5 6 7 8 9 10 11 12 13 14 15 16 17 18 19 20 21 22 23 24 25 26 27 28 29 30 TEVET 1 2 3

1971

5731/32

January 1 2 3 4 5 6 7 8 9 10 11 12 13 14 15 16 17 18 19 20 21 22 23 24 25 26 27 28 29 30

Tevet 4 5 6 7 8 9 10 11 12 13 14 15 16 17 18 19 20 21 22 23 24 25 26 27 28 29 SHEVAT 1 2 3 4
February 1 2 3 4 5 6 7 8 9 10 11 12 13 14 15 16 17 18 19 20 21 22 23 24 25 26 27 28

Shevat 6 7 8 9 10 11 12 13 14 15 16 17 18 19 20 21 22 23 24 25 26 27 28 29 30 ADAR 1 2 3
March 1 2 3 4 5 6 7 8 9 10 11 12 13 14 15 16 17 18 19 20 21 22 23 24 25 26 27 28 29 30

Adar 4 5 6 7 8 9 10 11 12 13 14 15 16 17 18 19 20 21 22 23 24 25 26 27 28 29 NISAN 1 2 3 4
April 1 2 3 4 5 6 7 8 9 10 11 12 13 14 15 16 17 18 19 20 21 22 23 24 25 26 27 28 29 30

Nisan 6 7 8 9 10 11 12 13 14 15 16 17 18 19 20 21 22 23 24 25 26 27 28 29 30 IYAR 1 2 3 4 5
May 1 2 3 4 5 6 7 8 9 10 11 12 13 14 15 16 17 18 19 20 21 22 23 24 25 26 27 28 29 30

Iyar 6 7 8 9 10 11 12 13 14 15 16 17 18 19 20 21 22 23 24 25 26 27 28 29 SIVAN 1 2 3 4 5 6
June 1 2 3 4 5 6 7 8 9 10 11 12 13 14 15 16 17 18 19 20 21 22 23 24 25 26 27 28 29 30

Sivan 8 9 10 11 12 13 14 15 16 17 18 19 20 21 22 23 24 25 26 27 28 29 30 TAMMUZ 1 2 3 4 5 6 7

July 1 2 3 4 5 6 7 8 9 10 11 12 13 14 15 16 17 18 19 20 21 22 23 24 25 26 27 28 29 30

Tammuz 8 9 10 11 12 13 14 15 16 17 18 19 20 21 22 23 24 25 26 27 28 29 AV 1 2 3 4 5 6 7 8
August 1 2 3 4 5 6 7 8 9 10 11 12 13 14 15 16 17 18 19 20 21 22 23 24 25 26 27 28 29 30

Av 10 11 12 13 14 15 16 17 18 19 20 21 22 23 24 25 26 27 28 29 30 ELUL 1 2 3 4 5 6 7 8 9
September 1 2 3 4 5 6 7 8 9 10 11 12 13 14 15 16 17 18 19 20 21 22 23 24 25 26 27 28 29 30

Elul 11 12 13 14 15 16 17 18 19 20 21 22 23 24 25 26 27 28 29 TISHRI 1 2 3 4 5 6 7 8 9 10 11
October 1 2 3 4 5 6 7 8 9 10 11 12 13 14 15 16 17 18 19 20 21 22 23 24 25 26 27 28 29 30

Tishri 12 13 14 15 16 17 18 19 20 21 22 23 24 25 26 27 28 29 30 HESHVAN 1 2 3 4 5 6 7 8 9 10 11
November 1 2 3 4 5 6 7 8 9 10 11 12 13 14 15 16 17 18 19 20 21 22 23 24 25 26 27 28 29 30

Heshvan 13 14 15 16 17 18 19 20 21 22 23 24 25 26 27 28 29 30 KISLEV 1 2 3 4 5 6 7 8 9 10 11 12
December 1 2 3 4 5 6 7 8 9 10 11 12 13 14 15 16 17 18 19 20 21 22 23 24 25 26 27 28 29 30

Kislev 13 14 15 16 17 18 19 20 21 22 23 24 25 26 27 28 29 30 TEVET 1 2 3 4 5 6 7 8 9 10 11 12

1972

5732/33

January 1 2 3 4 5 6 7 8 9 10 11 12 13 14 15 16 17 18 19 20 21 22 23 24 25 26 27 28 29 30 31

SHEVAT
Tevet 14 15 16 17 18 19 20 21 22 23 24 25 26 27 28 29 1 2 3 4 5 6 7 8 9 10 11 12 13 14 15
February 1 2 3 4 5 6 7 8 9 10 11 12 13 14 15 16 17 18 19 20 21 22 23 24 25 26 27 28 29

ADAR
Shevat 16 17 18 19 20 21 22 23 24 25 26 27 28 29 30 1 2 3 4 5 6 7 8 9 10 11 12 13 14
March 1 2 3 4 5 6 7 8 9 10 11 12 13 14 15 16 17 18 19 20 21 22 23 24 25 26 27 28 29 30 31

NISAN
Adar 15 16 17 18 19 20 21 22 23 24 25 26 27 28 29 1 2 3 4 5 6 7 8 9 10 11 12 13 14 15 16
April 1 2 3 4 5 6 7 8 9 10 11 12 13 14 15 16 17 18 19 20 21 22 23 24 25 26 27 28 29 30

IYAR
Nisan 17 18 19 20 21 22 23 24 25 26 27 28 29 30 1 2 3 4 5 6 7 8 9 10 11 12 13 14 15 16
May 1 2 3 4 5 6 7 8 9 10 11 12 13 14 15 16 17 18 19 20 21 22 23 24 25 26 27 28 29 30 31

SIVAN
Iyar 17 18 19 20 21 22 23 24 25 26 27 28 29 1 2 3 4 5 6 7 8 9 10 11 12 13 14 15 16 17 18
June 1 2 3 4 5 6 7 8 9 10 11 12 13 14 15 16 17 18 19 20 21 22 23 24 25 26 27 28 29 30

TAMMUZ
Sivan 19 20 21 22 23 24 25 26 27 28 29 30 1 2 3 4 5 6 7 8 9 10 11 12 13 14 15 16 17 18

July 1 2 3 4 5 6 7 8 9 10 11 12 13 14 15 16 17 18 19 20 21 22 23 24 25 26 27 28 29 30 31

AV
Tammuz 19 20 21 22 23 24 25 26 27 28 29 1 2 3 4 5 6 7 8 9 10 11 12 13 14 15 16 17 18 19 20
August 1 2 3 4 5 6 7 8 9 10 11 12 13 14 15 16 17 18 19 20 21 22 23 24 25 26 27 28 29 30 31

ELUL
Av 21 22 23 24 25 26 27 28 29 30 1 2 3 4 5 6 7 8 9 10 11 12 13 14 15 16 17 18 19 20 21
September 1 2 3 4 5 6 7 8 9 10 11 12 13 14 15 16 17 18 19 20 21 22 23 24 25 26 27 28 29 30

TISHRI
Elul 22 23 24 25 26 27 28 29 1 2 3 4 5 6 7 8 9 10 11 12 13 14 15 16 17 18 19 20 21 22
October 1 2 3 4 5 6 7 8 9 10 11 12 13 14 15 16 17 18 19 20 21 22 23 24 25 26 27 28 29 30 31

HESHVAN
Tishri 23 24 25 26 27 28 29 30 1 2 3 4 5 6 7 8 9 10 11 12 13 14 15 16 17 18 19 20 21 22 23
November 1 2 3 4 5 6 7 8 9 10 11 12 13 14 15 16 17 18 19 20 21 22 23 24 25 26 27 28 29 30

KISLEV
Heshvan 24 25 26 27 28 29 1 2 3 4 5 6 7 8 9 10 11 12 13 14 15 16 17 18 19 20 21 22 23 24
December 1 2 3 4 5 6 7 8 9 10 11 12 13 14 15 16 17 18 19 20 21 22 23 24 25 26 27 28 29 30 31

TEVET
Kislev 25 26 27 28 29 1 2 3 4 5 6 7 8 9 10 11 12 13 14 15 16 17 18 19 20 21 22 23 24 25 26

1973

5733/34

January 1 2 3 4 5 6 7 8 9 10 11 12 13 14 15 16 17 18 19 20 21 22 23 24 25 26 27 28 29 30 31

SHEVAT
Tevet 27 28 29 1 2 3 4 5 6 7 8 9 10 11 12 13 14 15 16 17 18 19 20 21 22 23 24 25 26 27 28
February 1 2 3 4 5 6 7 8 9 10 11 12 13 14 15 16 17 18 19 20 21 22 23 24 25 26 27 28

ADAR I
Shevat 29 30 1 2 3 4 5 6 7 8 9 10 11 12 13 14 15 16 17 18 19 20 21 22 23 24 25 26
March 1 2 3 4 5 6 7 8 9 10 11 12 13 14 15 16 17 18 19 20 21 22 23 24 25 26 27 28 29 30 31

ADAR II
Adar I 27 28 29 30 1 2 3 4 5 6 7 8 9 10 11 12 13 14 15 16 17 18 19 20 21 22 23 24 25 26 27
April 1 2 3 4 5 6 7 8 9 10 11 12 13 14 15 16 17 18 19 20 21 22 23 24 25 26 27 28 29 30

NISAN
Adar II 28 29 1 2 3 4 5 6 7 8 9 10 11 12 13 14 15 16 17 18 19 20 21 22 23 24 25 26 27 28
May 1 2 3 4 5 6 7 8 9 10 11 12 13 14 15 16 17 18 19 20 21 22 23 24 25 26 27 28 29 30 31

IYAR
Nisan/Iyar 29 30 1 2 3 4 5 6 7 8 9 10 11 12 13 14 15 16 17 18 19 20 21 22 23 24 25 26 27 28 29
June 1 2 3 4 5 6 7 8 9 10 11 12 13 14 15 16 17 18 19 20 21 22 23 24 25 26 27 28 29 30

Sivan 1 2 3 4 5 6 7 8 9 10 11 12 13 14 15 16 17 18 19 20 21 22 23 24 25 26 27 28 29 30

July 1 2 3 4 5 6 7 8 9 10 11 12 13 14 15 16 17 18 19 20 21 22 23 24 25 26 27 28 29 30 31

AV
Tammuz 1 2 3 4 5 6 7 8 9 10 11 12 13 14 15 16 17 18 19 20 21 22 23 24 25 26 27 28 29 1 2
August 1 2 3 4 5 6 7 8 9 10 11 12 13 14 15 16 17 18 19 20 21 22 23 24 25 26 27 28 29 30 31

ELUL
Av 3 4 5 6 7 8 9 10 11 12 13 14 15 16 17 18 19 20 21 22 23 24 25 26 27 28 29 30 1 2 3
September 1 2 3 4 5 6 7 8 9 10 11 12 13 14 15 16 17 18 19 20 21 22 23 24 25 26 27 28 29 30

TISHRI
Elul 4 5 6 7 8 9 10 11 12 13 14 15 16 17 18 19 20 21 22 23 24 25 26 27 28 29 1 2 3 4
October 1 2 3 4 5 6 7 8 9 10 11 12 13 14 15 16 17 18 19 20 21 22 23 24 25 26 27 28 29 30 31

HESHVAN
Tishri 5 6 7 8 9 10 11 12 13 14 15 16 17 18 19 20 21 22 23 24 25 26 27 28 29 30 1 2 3 4 5
November 1 2 3 4 5 6 7 8 9 10 11 12 13 14 15 16 17 18 19 20 21 22 23 24 25 26 27 28 29 30

KISLEV
Heshvan 6 7 8 9 10 11 12 13 14 15 16 17 18 19 20 21 22 23 24 25 26 27 28 29 30 1 2 3 4 5
December 1 2 3 4 5 6 7 8 9 10 11 12 13 14 15 16 17 18 19 20 21 22 23 24 25 26 27 28 29 30 31

TEVET
Kislev 6 7 8 9 10 11 12 13 14 15 16 17 18 19 20 21 22 23 24 25 26 27 28 29 30 1 2 3 4 5 6

1974

5734/35

January 1 2 3 4 5 6 7 8 9 10 11 12 13 14 15 16 17 18 19 20 21 22 23 24 25 26 27 28 29 30 31

Tevet 7 8 9 10 11 12 13 14 15 16 17 18 19 20 21 22 23 24 25 26 27 28 29 SHEVAT 1 2 3 4 5 6 7 8

February 1 2 3 4 5 6 7 8 9 10 11 12 13 14 15 16 17 18 19 20 21 22 23 24 25 26 27 28

Shevat 9 10 11 12 13 14 15 16 17 18 19 20 21 22 23 24 25 26 27 28 29 30 ADAR 1 2 3 4 5 6

March 1 2 3 4 5 6 7 8 9 10 11 12 13 14 15 16 17 18 19 20 21 22 23 24 25 26 27 28 29 30 31

Adar 7 8 9 10 11 12 13 14 15 16 17 18 19 20 21 22 23 24 25 26 27 28 29 NISAN 1 2 3 4 5 6 7 8

April 1 2 3 4 5 6 7 8 9 10 11 12 13 14 15 16 17 18 19 20 21 22 23 24 25 26 27 28 29 30

Nisan 9 10 11 12 13 14 15 16 17 18 19 20 21 22 23 24 25 26 27 28 29 30 IYAR 1 2 3 4 5 6 7 8

May 1 2 3 4 5 6 7 8 9 10 11 12 13 14 15 16 17 18 19 20 21 22 23 24 25 26 27 28 29 30 31

Iyar 9 10 11 12 13 14 15 16 17 18 19 20 21 22 23 24 25 26 27 28 29 SIVAN 1 2 3 4 5 6 7 8 9 10

June 1 2 3 4 5 6 7 8 9 10 11 12 13 14 15 16 17 18 19 20 21 22 23 24 25 26 27 28 29 30

Sivan 11 12 13 14 15 16 17 18 19 20 21 22 23 24 25 26 27 28 29 30 TAMMUZ 1 2 3 4 5 6 7 8 9 10

July 1 2 3 4 5 6 7 8 9 10 11 12 13 14 15 16 17 18 19 20 21 22 23 24 25 26 27 28 29 30 31

Tammuz 11 12 13 14 15 16 17 18 19 20 21 22 23 24 25 26 27 28 29 AV 1 2 3 4 5 6 7 8 9 10 11 12

August 1 2 3 4 5 6 7 8 9 10 11 12 13 14 15 16 17 18 19 20 21 22 23 24 25 26 27 28 29 30 31

Av 13 14 15 16 17 18 19 20 21 22 23 24 25 26 27 28 29 30 ELUL 1 2 3 4 5 6 7 8 9 10 11 12 13

September 1 2 3 4 5 6 7 8 9 10 11 12 13 14 15 16 17 18 19 20 21 22 23 24 25 26 27 28 29 30

Elul 14 15 16 17 18 19 20 21 22 23 24 25 26 27 28 29 TISHRI 1 2 3 4 5 6 7 8 9 10 11 12 13 14

October 1 2 3 4 5 6 7 8 9 10 11 12 13 14 15 16 17 18 19 20 21 22 23 24 25 26 27 28 29 30 31

Tishri 15 16 17 18 19 20 21 22 23 24 25 26 27 28 29 30 HESHVAN 1 2 3 4 5 6 7 8 9 10 11 12 13 14 15

November 1 2 3 4 5 6 7 8 9 10 11 12 13 14 15 16 17 18 19 20 21 22 23 24 25 26 27 28 29 30

Heshvan 16 17 18 19 20 21 22 23 24 25 26 27 28 29 KISLEV 1 2 3 4 5 6 7 8 9 10 11 12 13 14 15 16

December 1 2 3 4 5 6 7 8 9 10 11 12 13 14 15 16 17 18 19 20 21 22 23 24 25 26 27 28 29 30 31

Kislev 17 18 19 20 21 22 23 24 25 26 27 28 29 30 TEVET 1 2 3 4 5 6 7 8 9 10 11 12 13 14 15 16 17

1975

5735/36

January 1 2 3 4 5 6 7 8 9 10 11 12 13 14 15 16 17 18 19 20 21 22 23 24 25 26 27 28 29 30 31

Tevet 18 19 20 21 22 23 24 25 26 27 28 29 SHEVAT 1 2 3 4 5 6 7 8 9 10 11 12 13 14 15 16 17 18 19

February 1 2 3 4 5 6 7 8 9 10 11 12 13 14 15 16 17 18 19 20 21 22 23 24 25 26 27 28

Shevat 20 21 22 23 24 25 26 27 28 29 30 ADAR 1 2 3 4 5 6 7 8 9 10 11 12 13 14 15 16 17

March 1 2 3 4 5 6 7 8 9 10 11 12 13 14 15 16 17 18 19 20 21 22 23 24 25 26 27 28 29 30 31

Adar 18 19 20 21 22 23 24 25 26 27 28 29 NISAN 1 2 3 4 5 6 7 8 9 10 11 12 13 14 15 16 17 18 19

April 1 2 3 4 5 6 7 8 9 10 11 12 13 14 15 16 17 18 19 20 21 22 23 24 25 26 27 28 29 30

Nisan 20 21 22 23 24 25 26 27 28 29 30 IYAR 1 2 3 4 5 6 7 8 9 10 11 12 13 14 15 16 17 18 19

May 1 2 3 4 5 6 7 8 9 10 11 12 13 14 15 16 17 18 19 20 21 22 23 24 25 26 27 28 29 30 31

Iyar 20 21 22 23 24 25 26 27 28 29 SIVAN 1 2 3 4 5 6 7 8 9 10 11 12 13 14 15 16 17 18 19 20 21

June 1 2 3 4 5 6 7 8 9 10 11 12 13 14 15 16 17 18 19 20 21 22 23 24 25 26 27 28 29 30

Sivan 22 23 24 25 26 27 28 29 30 TAMMUZ 1 2 3 4 5 6 7 8 9 10 11 12 13 14 15 16 17 18 19 20 21

July 1 2 3 4 5 6 7 8 9 10 11 12 13 14 15 16 17 18 19 20 21 22 23 24 25 26 27 28 29 30 3

Tammuz 22 23 24 25 26 27 28 29 AV 1 2 3 4 5 6 7 8 9 10 11 12 13 14 15 16 17 18 19 20 21 22 2

August 1 2 3 4 5 6 7 8 9 10 11 12 13 14 15 16 17 18 19 20 21 22 23 24 25 26 27 28 29 30 3

Av 24 25 26 27 28 29 30 ELUL 1 2 3 4 5 6 7 8 9 10 11 12 13 14 15 16 17 18 19 20 21 22 23 2

September 1 2 3 4 5 6 7 8 9 10 11 12 13 14 15 16 17 18 19 20 21 22 23 24 25 26 27 28 29 30

Elul 25 26 27 28 29 TISHRI 1 2 3 4 5 6 7 8 9 10 11 12 13 14 15 16 17 18 19 20 21 22 23 24 25

October 1 2 3 4 5 6 7 8 9 10 11 12 13 14 15 16 17 18 19 20 21 22 23 24 25 26 27 28 29 30 31

Tishri 26 27 28 29 30 HESHVAN 1 2 3 4 5 6 7 8 9 10 11 12 13 14 15 16 17 18 19 20 21 22 23 24 25 26

November 1 2 3 4 5 6 7 8 9 10 11 12 13 14 15 16 17 18 19 20 21 22 23 24 25 26 27 28 29 30

Heshvan 27 28 29 30 KISLEV 1 2 3 4 5 6 7 8 9 10 11 12 13 14 15 16 17 18 19 20 21 22 23 24 25 26

December 1 2 3 4 5 6 7 8 9 10 11 12 13 14 15 16 17 18 19 20 21 22 23 24 25 26 27 28 29 30 31

Kislev 27 28 29 30 TEVET 1 2 3 4 5 6 7 8 9 10 11 12 13 14 15 16 17 18 19 20 21 22 23 24 25 26 27

1976

736/37

anuary 1 2 3 4 5 6 7 8 9 10 11 12 13 14 15 16 17 18 19 20 21 22 23 24 25 26 27 28 29 30 31

SHEVAT
evet 28 29 1 2 3 4 5 6 7 8 9 10 11 12 13 14 15 16 17 18 19 20 21 22 23 24 25 26 27 28 29
ebruary 1 2 3 4 5 6 7 8 9 10 11 12 13 14 15 16 17 18 19 20 21 22 23 24 25 26 27 28 29

ADAR I
vat/Adar I 30 1 2 3 4 5 6 7 8 9 10 11 12 13 14 15 16 17 18 19 20 21 22 23 24 25 26 27 28
larch 1 2 3 4 5 6 7 8 9 10 11 12 13 14 15 16 17 18 19 20 21 22 23 24 25 26 27 28 29 30 31

ADAR II
r I/Adar II 29 30 1 2 3 4 5 6 7 8 9 10 11 12 13 14 15 16 17 18 19 20 21 22 23 24 25 26 27 28 29
pril 1 2 3 4 5 6 7 8 9 10 11 12 13 14 15 16 17 18 19 20 21 22 23 24 25 26 27 28 29 30

Nisan 1 2 3 4 5 6 7 8 9 10 11 12 13 14 15 16 17 18 19 20 21 22 23 24 25 26 27 28 29 30
May 1 2 3 4 5 6 7 8 9 10 11 12 13 14 15 16 17 18 19 20 21 22 23 24 25 26 27 28 29 30 31

SIVAN
yar 1 2 3 4 5 6 7 8 9 10 11 12 13 14 15 16 17 18 19 20 21 22 23 24 25 26 27 28 29 1 2
une 1 2 3 4 5 6 7 8 9 10 11 12 13 14 15 16 17 18 19 20 21 22 23 24 25 26 27 28 29 30

TAMMUZ
ivan 3 4 5 6 7 8 9 10 11 12 13 14 15 16 17 18 19 20 21 22 23 24 25 26 27 28 29 30 1 2

uly 1 2 3 4 5 6 7 8 9 10 11 12 13 14 15 16 17 18 19 20 21 22 23 24 25 26 27 28 29 30 31

AV
Tammuz 3 4 5 6 7 8 9 10 11 12 13 14 15 16 17 18 19 20 21 22 23 24 25 26 27 28 29 1 2 3 4
August 1 2 3 4 5 6 7 8 9 10 11 12 13 14 15 16 17 18 19 20 21 22 23 24 25 26 27 28 29 30 31

ELUL
Av 5 6 7 8 9 10 11 12 13 14 15 16 17 18 19 20 21 22 23 24 25 26 27 28 29 30 1 2 3 4 5
September 1 2 3 4 5 6 7 8 9 10 11 12 13 14 15 16 17 18 19 20 21 22 23 24 25 26 27 28 29 30

TISHRI
Elul 6 7 8 9 10 11 12 13 14 15 16 17 18 19 20 21 22 23 24 25 26 27 28 29 1 2 3 4 5 6
October 1 2 3 4 5 6 7 8 9 10 11 12 13 14 15 16 17 18 19 20 21 22 23 24 25 26 27 28 29 30 31

HESHVAN
Tishri 7 8 9 10 11 12 13 14 15 16 17 18 19 20 21 22 23 24 25 26 27 28 29 30 1 2 3 4 5 6 7
November 1 2 3 4 5 6 7 8 9 10 11 12 13 14 15 16 17 18 19 20 21 22 23 24 25 26 27 28 29 30

KISLEV
Heshvan 8 9 10 11 12 13 14 15 16 17 18 19 20 21 22 23 24 25 26 27 28 29 1 2 3 4 5 6 7 8
December 1 2 3 4 5 6 7 8 9 10 11 12 13 14 15 16 17 18 19 20 21 22 23 24 25 26 27 28 29 30 31

TEVET
Kislev 9 10 11 12 13 14 15 16 17 18 19 20 21 22 23 24 25 26 27 28 29 1 2 3 4 5 6 7 8 9 10

1977

5737/38

January 1 2 3 4 5 6 7 8 9 10 11 12 13 14 15 16 17 18 19 20 21 22 23 24 25 26 27 28 29 30 31

SHEVAT
Tevet 11 12 13 14 15 16 17 18 19 20 21 22 23 24 25 26 27 28 29 1 2 3 4 5 6 7 8 9 10 11 12
February 1 2 3 4 5 6 7 8 9 10 11 12 13 14 15 16 17 18 19 20 21 22 23 24 25 26 27 28

ADAR
Shevat 13 14 15 16 17 18 19 20 21 22 23 24 25 26 27 28 29 30 1 2 3 4 5 6 7 8 9 10
March 1 2 3 4 5 6 7 8 9 10 11 12 13 14 15 16 17 18 19 20 21 22 23 24 25 26 27 28 29 30 31

NISAN
Adar 11 12 13 14 15 16 17 18 19 20 21 22 23 24 25 26 27 28 29 1 2 3 4 5 6 7 8 9 10 11 12
April 1 2 3 4 5 6 7 8 9 10 11 12 13 14 15 16 17 18 19 20 21 22 23 24 25 26 27 28 29 30

IYAR
Nisan 13 14 15 16 17 18 19 20 21 22 23 24 25 26 27 28 29 30 1 2 3 4 5 6 7 8 9 10 11 12
May 1 2 3 4 5 6 7 8 9 10 11 12 13 14 15 16 17 18 19 20 21 22 23 24 25 26 27 28 29 30 31

SIVAN
Iyar 13 14 15 16 17 18 19 20 21 22 23 24 25 26 27 28 29 1 2 3 4 5 6 7 8 9 10 11 12 13 14
June 1 2 3 4 5 6 7 8 9 10 11 12 13 14 15 16 17 18 19 20 21 22 23 24 25 26 27 28 29 30

TAMMUZ
Sivan 15 16 17 18 19 20 21 22 23 24 25 26 27 28 29 30 1 2 3 4 5 6 7 8 9 10 11 12 13 14

July 1 2 3 4 5 6 7 8 9 10 11 12 13 14 15 16 17 18 19 20 21 22 23 24 25 26 27 28 29 30 31

AV
Tammuz 15 16 17 18 19 20 21 22 23 24 25 26 27 28 29 1 2 3 4 5 6 7 8 9 10 11 12 13 14 15 16
August 1 2 3 4 5 6 7 8 9 10 11 12 13 14 15 16 17 18 19 20 21 22 23 24 25 26 27 28 29 30 31

ELUL
Av 17 18 19 20 21 22 23 24 25 26 27 28 29 30 1 2 3 4 5 6 7 8 9 10 11 12 13 14 15 16 17
September 1 2 3 4 5 6 7 8 9 10 11 12 13 14 15 16 17 18 19 20 21 22 23 24 25 26 27 28 29 30

TISHRI
Elul 18 19 20 21 22 23 24 25 26 27 28 29 1 2 3 4 5 6 7 8 9 10 11 12 13 14 15 16 17 18
October 1 2 3 4 5 6 7 8 9 10 11 12 13 14 15 16 17 18 19 20 21 22 23 24 25 26 27 28 29 30 31

HESHVAN
Tishri 19 20 21 22 23 24 25 26 27 28 29 30 1 2 3 4 5 6 7 8 9 10 11 12 13 14 15 16 17 18 19
November 1 2 3 4 5 6 7 8 9 10 11 12 13 14 15 16 17 18 19 20 21 22 23 24 25 26 27 28 29 30

KISLEV
Heshvan 20 21 22 23 24 25 26 27 28 29 1 2 3 4 5 6 7 8 9 10 11 12 13 14 15 16 17 18 19 20
December 1 2 3 4 5 6 7 8 9 10 11 12 13 14 15 16 17 18 19 20 21 22 23 24 25 26 27 28 29 30 31

TEVET
Kislev 21 22 23 24 25 26 27 28 29 30 1 2 3 4 5 6 7 8 9 10 11 12 13 14 15 16 17 18 19 20 21

5738/39 — **1978**

January 1 2 3 4 5 6 7 8 9 10 11 12 13 14 15 16 17 18 19 20 21 22 23 24 25 26 27 28 29 30 31

SHEVAT (begins at 1)
Tevet 22 23 24 25 26 27 28 29 1 2 3 4 5 6 7 8 9 10 11 12 13 14 15 16 17 18 19 20 21 22 23
February 1 2 3 4 5 6 7 8 9 10 11 12 13 14 15 16 17 18 19 20 21 22 23 24 25 26 27 28

ADAR I (begins at 1)
Shevat 24 25 26 27 28 29 30 1 2 3 4 5 6 7 8 9 10 11 12 13 14 15 16 17 18 19 20 21
March 1 2 3 4 5 6 7 8 9 10 11 12 13 14 15 16 17 18 19 20 21 22 23 24 25 26 27 28 29 30 31

ADAR II (begins at 1)
Adar I 22 23 24 25 26 27 28 29 30 1 2 3 4 5 6 7 8 9 10 11 12 13 14 15 16 17 18 19 20 21 22
April 1 2 3 4 5 6 7 8 9 10 11 12 13 14 15 16 17 18 19 20 21 22 23 24 25 26 27 28 29 30

NISAN (begins at 1)
Adar II 23 24 25 26 27 28 29 1 2 3 4 5 6 7 8 9 10 11 12 13 14 15 16 17 18 19 20 21 22 23
May 1 2 3 4 5 6 7 8 9 10 11 12 13 14 15 16 17 18 19 20 21 22 23 24 25 26 27 28 29 30 31

IYAR (begins at 1)
Nisan 24 25 26 27 28 29 30 1 2 3 4 5 6 7 8 9 10 11 12 13 14 15 16 17 18 19 20 21 22 23 24
June 1 2 3 4 5 6 7 8 9 10 11 12 13 14 15 16 17 18 19 20 21 22 23 24 25 26 27 28 29 30

SIVAN (begins at 1)
Iyar 25 26 27 28 29 1 2 3 4 5 6 7 8 9 10 11 12 13 14 15 16 17 18 19 20 21 22 23 24 25

July 1 2 3 4 5 6 7 8 9 10 11 12 13 14 15 16 17 18 19 20 21 22 23 24 25 26 27 28 29 30 31

TAMMUZ (begins at 1)
Sivan 26 27 28 29 30 1 2 3 4 5 6 7 8 9 10 11 12 13 14 15 16 17 18 19 20 21 22 23 24 25 26
August 1 2 3 4 5 6 7 8 9 10 11 12 13 14 15 16 17 18 19 20 21 22 23 24 25 26 27 28 29 30 31

AV (begins at 1)
Tammuz 27 28 29 1 2 3 4 5 6 7 8 9 10 11 12 13 14 15 16 17 18 19 20 21 22 23 24 25 26 27 28
September 1 2 3 4 5 6 7 8 9 10 11 12 13 14 15 16 17 18 19 20 21 22 23 24 25 26 27 28 29 30

ELUL (begins at 1)
Av 29 30 1 2 3 4 5 6 7 8 9 10 11 12 13 14 15 16 17 18 19 20 21 22 23 24 25 26 27 28
October 1 2 3 4 5 6 7 8 9 10 11 12 13 14 15 16 17 18 19 20 21 22 23 24 25 26 27 28 29 30 31

TISHRI (begins at 1)
Elul/Tishri 29 1 2 3 4 5 6 7 8 9 10 11 12 13 14 15 16 17 18 19 20 21 22 23 24 25 26 27 28 29 30
November 1 2 3 4 5 6 7 8 9 10 11 12 13 14 15 16 17 18 19 20 21 22 23 24 25 26 27 28 29 30

Heshvan 1 2 3 4 5 6 7 8 9 10 11 12 13 14 15 16 17 18 19 20 21 22 23 24 25 26 27 28 29 30
December 1 2 3 4 5 6 7 8 9 10 11 12 13 14 15 16 17 18 19 20 21 22 23 24 25 26 27 28 29 30 31

TEVET (begins at 1)
Kislev 1 2 3 4 5 6 7 8 9 10 11 12 13 14 15 16 17 18 19 20 21 22 23 24 25 26 27 28 29 30 1

5739/40 — **1979**

January 1 2 3 4 5 6 7 8 9 10 11 12 13 14 15 16 17 18 19 20 21 22 23 24 25 26 27 28 29 30

SHEVAT (begins at 1)
Tevet 2 3 4 5 6 7 8 9 10 11 12 13 14 15 16 17 18 19 20 21 22 23 24 25 26 27 28 29 1 2
February 1 2 3 4 5 6 7 8 9 10 11 12 13 14 15 16 17 18 19 20 21 22 23 24 25 26 27 28

ADAR (begins at 1)
Shevat 4 5 6 7 8 9 10 11 12 13 14 15 16 17 18 19 20 21 22 23 24 25 26 27 28 29 30 1
March 1 2 3 4 5 6 7 8 9 10 11 12 13 14 15 16 17 18 19 20 21 22 23 24 25 26 27 28 29 30

NISAN (begins at 1)
Adar 2 3 4 5 6 7 8 9 10 11 12 13 14 15 16 17 18 19 20 21 22 23 24 25 26 27 28 29 1 2
April 1 2 3 4 5 6 7 8 9 10 11 12 13 14 15 16 17 18 19 20 21 22 23 24 25 26 27 28 29 30

IYAR (begins at 1)
Nisan 4 5 6 7 8 9 10 11 12 13 14 15 16 17 18 19 20 21 22 23 24 25 26 27 28 29 30 1 2 3
May 1 2 3 4 5 6 7 8 9 10 11 12 13 14 15 16 17 18 19 20 21 22 23 24 25 26 27 28 29 30

SIVAN (begins at 1)
Iyar 4 5 6 7 8 9 10 11 12 13 14 15 16 17 18 19 20 21 22 23 24 25 26 27 28 29 1 2 3 4
June 1 2 3 4 5 6 7 8 9 10 11 12 13 14 15 16 17 18 19 20 21 22 23 24 25 26 27 28 29 30

TAMMUZ (begins at 1)
Sivan 6 7 8 9 10 11 12 13 14 15 16 17 18 19 20 21 22 23 24 25 26 27 28 29 30 1 2 3 4 5

July 1 2 3 4 5 6 7 8 9 10 11 12 13 14 15 16 17 18 19 20 21 22 23 24 25 26 27 28 29 30

AV (begins at 1)
Tammuz 6 7 8 9 10 11 12 13 14 15 16 17 18 19 20 21 22 23 24 25 26 27 28 29 1 2 3 4 5 6
August 1 2 3 4 5 6 7 8 9 10 11 12 13 14 15 16 17 18 19 20 21 22 23 24 25 26 27 28 29 30

ELUL (begins at 1)
Av 8 9 10 11 12 13 14 15 16 17 18 19 20 21 22 23 24 25 26 27 28 29 30 1 2 3 4 5 6 7
September 1 2 3 4 5 6 7 8 9 10 11 12 13 14 15 16 17 18 19 20 21 22 23 24 25 26 27 28 29 30

TISHRI (begins at 1)
Elul 9 10 11 12 13 14 15 16 17 18 19 20 21 22 23 24 25 26 27 28 29 1 2 3 4 5 6 7 8 9
October 1 2 3 4 5 6 7 8 9 10 11 12 13 14 15 16 17 18 19 20 21 22 23 24 25 26 27 28 29 30

HESHVAN (begins at 1)
Tishri 10 11 12 13 14 15 16 17 18 19 20 21 22 23 24 25 26 27 28 29 30 1 2 3 4 5 6 7 8 9
November 1 2 3 4 5 6 7 8 9 10 11 12 13 14 15 16 17 18 19 20 21 22 23 24 25 26 27 28 29 30

KISLEV (begins at 1)
Heshvan 11 12 13 14 15 16 17 18 19 20 21 22 23 24 25 26 27 28 29 30 1 2 3 4 5 6 7 8 9 10
December 1 2 3 4 5 6 7 8 9 10 11 12 13 14 15 16 17 18 19 20 21 22 23 24 25 26 27 28 29 30

TEVET (begins at 1)
Kislev 11 12 13 14 15 16 17 18 19 20 21 22 23 24 25 26 27 28 29 30 1 2 3 4 5 6 7 8 9 10

1980

740/41

nuary 1 2 3 4 5 6 7 8 9 10 11 12 13 14 15 16 17 18 19 20 21 22 23 24 25 26 27 28 29 30 31

SHEVAT
evet 12 13 14 15 16 17 18 19 20 21 22 23 24 25 26 27 28 29 1 2 3 4 5 6 7 8 9 10 11 12 13
ebruary 1 2 3 4 5 6 7 8 9 10 11 12 13 14 15 16 17 18 19 20 21 22 23 24 25 26 27 28 29

ADAR
hevat 14 15 16 17 18 19 20 21 22 23 24 25 26 27 28 29 30 1 2 3 4 5 6 7 8 9 10 11 12
arch 1 2 3 4 5 6 7 8 9 10 11 12 13 14 15 16 17 18 19 20 21 22 23 24 25 26 27 28 29 30 31

NISAN
dar 13 14 15 16 17 18 19 20 21 22 23 24 25 26 27 28 29 1 2 3 4 5 6 7 8 9 10 11 12 13 14
pril 1 2 3 4 5 6 7 8 9 10 11 12 13 14 15 16 17 18 19 20 21 22 23 24 25 26 27 28 29 30

IYAR
isan 15 16 17 18 19 20 21 22 23 24 25 26 27 28 29 30 1 2 3 4 5 6 7 8 9 10 11 12 13 14
ay 1 2 3 4 5 6 7 8 9 10 11 12 13 14 15 16 17 18 19 20 21 22 23 24 25 26 27 28 29 30 31

SIVAN
ar 15 16 17 18 19 20 21 22 23 24 25 26 27 28 29 1 2 3 4 5 6 7 8 9 10 11 12 13 14 15 16
une 1 2 3 4 5 6 7 8 9 10 11 12 13 14 15 16 17 18 19 20 21 22 23 24 25 26 27 28 29 30

TAMMUZ
van 17 18 19 20 21 22 23 24 25 26 27 28 29 30 1 2 3 4 5 6 7 8 9 10 11 12 13 14 15 16

y 1 2 3 4 5 6 7 8 9 10 11 12 13 14 15 16 17 18 19 20 21 22 23 24 25 26 27 28 29 30 31

AV
mmuz 17 18 19 20 21 22 23 24 25 26 27 28 29 1 2 3 4 5 6 7 8 9 10 11 12 13 14 15 16 17 18
ugust 1 2 3 4 5 6 7 8 9 10 11 12 13 14 15 16 17 18 19 20 21 22 23 24 25 26 27 28 29 30 31

ELUL
19 20 21 22 23 24 25 26 27 28 29 30 1 2 3 4 5 6 7 8 9 10 11 12 13 14 15 16 17 18 19
ptember 1 2 3 4 5 6 7 8 9 10 11 12 13 14 15 16 17 18 19 20 21 22 23 24 25 26 27 28 29 30

TISHRI
ul 20 21 22 23 24 25 26 27 28 29 1 2 3 4 5 6 7 8 9 10 11 12 13 14 15 16 17 18 19 20
ctober 1 2 3 4 5 6 7 8 9 10 11 12 13 14 15 16 17 18 19 20 21 22 23 24 25 26 27 28 29 30 31

HESHVAN
hri 21 22 23 24 25 26 27 28 29 30 1 2 3 4 5 6 7 8 9 10 11 12 13 14 15 16 17 18 19 20 21
vember 1 2 3 4 5 6 7 8 9 10 11 12 13 14 15 16 17 18 19 20 21 22 23 24 25 26 27 28 29 30

KISLEV
shvan 22 23 24 25 26 27 28 29 1 2 3 4 5 6 7 8 9 10 11 12 13 14 15 16 17 18 19 20 21 22
cember 1 2 3 4 5 6 7 8 9 10 11 12 13 14 15 16 17 18 19 20 21 22 23 24 25 26 27 28 29 30 31

TEVET
lev 23 24 25 26 27 28 29 1 2 3 4 5 6 7 8 9 10 11 12 13 14 15 16 17 18 19 20 21 22 23 24

1981

5741/42

January 1 2 3 4 5 6 7 8 9 10 11 12 13 14 15 16 17 18 19 20 21 22 23 24 25 26 27 28 29 30 31

SHEVAT
Tevet 25 26 27 28 29 1 2 3 4 5 6 7 8 9 10 11 12 13 14 15 16 17 18 19 10 21 22 23 24 25 26
February 1 2 3 4 5 6 7 8 9 10 11 12 13 14 15 16 17 18 19 20 21 22 23 24 25 26 27 28

ADAR I
Shevat 27 28 29 30 1 2 3 4 5 6 7 8 9 10 11 12 13 14 15 16 17 18 19 20 21 22 23 24
March 1 2 3 4 5 6 7 8 9 10 11 12 13 14 15 16 17 18 19 20 21 22 23 24 25 26 27 28 29 30 31

ADAR II
Adar I 25 26 27 28 29 30 1 2 3 4 5 6 7 8 9 10 11 12 13 14 15 16 17 18 19 20 21 22 23 24 25
April 1 2 3 4 5 6 7 8 9 10 11 12 13 14 15 16 17 18 19 20 21 22 23 24 25 26 27 28 29 30

NISAN
Adar II 26 27 28 29 1 2 3 4 5 6 7 8 9 10 11 12 13 14 15 16 17 18 19 20 21 22 23 24 25 26
May 1 2 3 4 5 6 7 8 9 10 11 12 13 14 15 16 17 18 19 20 21 22 23 24 25 26 27 28 29 30 31

IYAR
Nisan 27 28 29 30 1 2 3 4 5 6 7 8 9 10 11 12 13 14 15 16 17 18 19 20 21 22 23 24 25 26 27
June 1 2 3 4 5 6 7 8 9 10 11 12 13 14 15 16 17 18 19 20 21 22 23 24 25 26 27 28 29 30

SIVAN
Iyar/Sivan 28 29 1 2 3 4 5 6 7 8 9 10 11 12 13 14 15 16 17 18 19 20 21 22 23 24 25 26 27 28

July 1 2 3 4 5 6 7 8 9 10 11 12 13 14 15 16 17 18 19 20 21 22 23 24 25 26 27 28 29 30 31

TAMMUZ
Sivan/Tammuz 29 30 1 2 3 4 5 6 7 8 9 10 11 12 13 14 15 16 17 18 19 20 21 22 23 24 25 26 27 28 29
August 1 2 3 4 5 6 7 8 9 10 11 12 13 14 15 16 17 18 19 20 21 22 23 24 25 26 27 28 29 30 31

ELUL
Av 1 2 3 4 5 6 7 8 9 10 11 12 13 14 15 16 17 18 19 20 21 22 23 24 25 26 27 28 29 30 1
September 1 2 3 4 5 6 7 8 9 10 11 12 13 14 15 16 17 18 19 20 21 22 23 24 25 26 27 28 29 30

TISHRI
Elul 2 3 4 5 6 7 8 9 10 11 12 13 14 15 16 17 18 19 20 21 22 23 24 25 26 27 28 29 1 2
October 1 2 3 4 5 6 7 8 9 10 11 12 13 14 15 16 17 18 19 20 21 22 23 24 25 26 27 28 29 30 31

HESHVAN
Tishri 3 4 5 6 7 8 9 10 11 12 13 14 15 16 17 18 19 20 21 22 23 24 25 26 27 28 29 30 1 2 3
November 1 2 3 4 5 6 7 8 9 10 11 12 13 14 15 16 17 18 19 20 21 22 23 24 25 26 27 28 29 30

KISLEV
Heshvan 4 5 6 7 8 9 10 11 12 13 14 15 16 17 18 19 20 21 22 23 24 25 26 27 28 29 1 2 3 4
December 1 2 3 4 5 6 7 8 9 10 11 12 13 14 15 16 17 18 19 20 21 22 23 24 25 26 27 28 29 30 31

TEVET
Kislev 5 6 7 8 9 10 11 12 13 14 15 16 17 18 19 20 21 22 23 24 25 26 27 28 29 30 1 2 3 4 5

SECTION B: DETERMINING YOUR CHILD'S BAR/BAT MITZVAH DATE
1982–2000, 5742–5761

1982

5742/43

January 1 2 3 4 5 6 7 8 9 10 11 12 13 14 15 16 17 18 19 20 21 22 23 24 25 26 27 28 29 30 31
Vayyiggash · Vayyechi · Shemot · Va-ayra · Bo
SHEVAT
Tevet 6 7 8 9 10 11 12 13 14 15 16 17 18 19 20 21 22 23 24 25 26 27 28 29 1 2 3 4 5 6 7

February 1 2 3 4 5 6 7 8 9 10 11 12 13 14 15 16 17 18 19 20 21 22 23 24 25 26 27 28
Beshallach · Tu b'Shevat · Yithro · SHABBAT SHEKALIM Mishpatim · Terumah
ADAR
Shevat 8 9 10 11 12 13 14 15 16 17 18 19 20 21 22 23 24 25 26 27 28 29 30 1 2 3 4 5

March 1 2 3 4 5 6 7 8 9 10 11 12 13 14 15 16 17 18 19 20 21 22 23 24 25 26 27 28 29 30 31
SHABBAT ZAKHOR Tezaveh · Purim · SHABBAT PARAH Ki Thissa · SHABBAT HA-HODESH Vayyakhel Pekudey · Vayyikra
NISAN
Adar 6 7 8 9 10 11 12 13 14 15 16 17 18 19 20 21 22 23 24 25 26 27 28 29 1 2 3 4 5 6 7

April 1 2 3 4 5 6 7 8 9 10 11 12 13 14 15 16 17 18 19 20 21 22 23 24 25 26 27 28 29 30
SHABBAT HA-GADOL Tzav · Passover · Hol ha-Mo'ed · Passover · Shemini · Yom Ha-Shoah · Thazria Metzora · Yom Ha-Atzma'ut
IYAR
Nisan 8 9 10 11 12 13 14 15 16 17 18 19 20 21 22 23 24 25 26 27 28 29 30 1 2 3 4 5 6 7

May 1 2 3 4 5 6 7 8 9 10 11 12 13 14 15 16 17 18 19 20 21 22 23 24 25 26 27 28 29 30 31
Acharey Mot Kedoshim · Emor · Lag b'Omer · Behar Bechukotai · Bamidbar · Shavuot
SIVAN
Iyar 8 9 10 11 12 13 14 15 16 17 18 19 20 21 22 23 24 25 26 27 28 29 1 2 3 4 5 6 7 8 9

June 1 2 3 4 5 6 7 8 9 10 11 12 13 14 15 16 17 18 19 20 21 22 23 24 25 26 27 28 29 30
Naso · Behaalotecha · Shelach · Korach
TAMMUZ
Sivan 10 11 12 13 14 15 16 17 18 19 20 21 22 23 24 25 26 27 28 29 30 1 2 3 4 5 6 7 8 9

July 1 2 3 4 5 6 7 8 9 10 11 12 13 14 15 16 17 18 19 20 21 22 23 24 25 26 27 28 29 30 31
Chukkat Balak · Pinchas · Mattot Massey · Devarim · Tisha b'Av · Va-ethchanan
AV
Tammuz 10 11 12 13 14 15 16 17 18 19 20 21 22 23 24 25 26 27 28 29 1 2 3 4 5 6 7 8 9 10 11

August 1 2 3 4 5 6 7 8 9 10 11 12 13 14 15 16 17 18 19 20 21 22 23 24 25 26 27 28 29 30 31
Ekev · Re'eh · Shofetim · Ki Thetze
ELUL
Av 12 13 14 15 16 17 18 19 20 21 22 23 24 25 26 27 28 29 30 1 2 3 4 5 6 7 8 9 10 11 12

September 1 2 3 4 5 6 7 8 9 10 11 12 13 14 15 16 17 18 19 20 21 22 23 24 25 26 27 28 29 30
Ki Thavo · Nitzavim Vayyelech · Rosh Hashanah · SHABBAT SHUVAH Haazinu · Yom Kippur
TISHRI
Elul 13 14 15 16 17 18 19 20 21 22 23 24 25 26 27 28 29 1 2 3 4 5 6 7 8 9 10 11 12 13

October 1 2 3 4 5 6 7 8 9 10 11 12 13 14 15 16 17 18 19 20 21 22 23 24 25 26 27 28 29 30 31
Sukkot · Shemini Azeret · Simchat Torah · Bereshit · Noach · Lech Lecha
HESHVAN
Tishri 14 15 16 17 18 19 20 21 22 23 24 25 26 27 28 29 30 1 2 3 4 5 6 7 8 9 10 11 12 13 14

November 1 2 3 4 5 6 7 8 9 10 11 12 13 14 15 16 17 18 19 20 21 22 23 24 25 26 27 28 29 30
Vayyera · Chayye Sarah · Toledot · Vayyetze
KISLEV
Heshvan 15 16 17 18 19 20 21 22 23 24 25 26 27 28 29 30 1 2 3 4 5 6 7 8 9 10 11 12 13 14

December 1 2 3 4 5 6 7 8 9 10 11 12 13 14 15 16 17 18 19 20 21 22 23 24 25 26 27 28 29 30 31
Vayyishlach · Chanukah · Vayyeshev · Mikketz · Vayyiggash
TEVET
Kislev 15 16 17 18 19 20 21 22 23 24 25 26 27 28 29 30 1 2 3 4 5 6 7 8 9 10 11 12 13 14 15

1983

5743/44

January 1 2 3 4 5 6 7 8 9 10 11 12 13 14 15 16 17 18 19 20 21 22 23 24 25 26 27 28 29 30 31
Vayyechi · Shemot · Va-ayra · Bo · Tu b'Shevat · Beshallach
SHEVAT
Tevet 16 17 18 19 20 21 22 23 24 25 26 27 28 29 1 2 3 4 5 6 7 8 9 10 11 12 13 14 15 16 17

February 1 2 3 4 5 6 7 8 9 10 11 12 13 14 15 16 17 18 19 20 21 22 23 24 25 26 27 28
Yithro · SHABBAT SHEKALIM Mishpatim · Terumah · SHABBAT ZAKHOR Tezaveh · Purim
ADAR
Shevat 18 19 20 21 22 23 24 25 26 27 28 29 30 1 2 3 4 5 6 7 8 9 10 11 12 13 14 15

March 1 2 3 4 5 6 7 8 9 10 11 12 13 14 15 16 17 18 19 20 21 22 23 24 25 26 27 28 29 30 31
SHABBAT PARAH Ki Thissa · SHABBAT HA-HODESH Vayyakhel Pekudey · Vayyikra · SHABBAT HA-GADOL Tzav · Passover
NISAN
Adar 16 17 18 19 20 21 22 23 24 25 26 27 28 29 1 2 3 4 5 6 7 8 9 10 11 12 13 14 15 16 17

April 1 2 3 4 5 6 7 8 9 10 11 12 13 14 15 16 17 18 19 20 21 22 23 24 25 26 27 28 29 30
Hol ha-Mo'ed · Passover · Yom Ha-Shoah · Shemini · Thazria Metzora · Yom Ha-Atzma'ut · Acharey Mot Kedoshim · Emor
IYAR
Nisan 18 19 20 21 22 23 24 25 26 27 28 29 30 1 2 3 4 5 6 7 8 9 10 11 12 13 14 15 16 17

May 1 2 3 4 5 6 7 8 9 10 11 12 13 14 15 16 17 18 19 20 21 22 23 24 25 26 27 28 29 30 31
Lag b'Omer · Behar Bechukotai · Bamidbar · Shavuot · Naso · Behaalotecha
SIVAN
Iyar 18 19 20 21 22 23 24 25 26 27 28 29 1 2 3 4 5 6 7 8 9 10 11 12 13 14 15 16 17 18 19

June 1 2 3 4 5 6 7 8 9 10 11 12 13 14 15 16 17 18 19 20 21 22 23 24 25 26 27 28 29 30
Shelach · Korach · Chukkat · Balak
TAMMUZ
Sivan 20 21 22 23 24 25 26 27 28 29 30 1 2 3 4 5 6 7 8 9 10 11 12 13 14 15 16 17 18 19

July 1 2 3 4 5 6 7 8 9 10 11 12 13 14 15 16 17 18 19 20 21 22 23 24 25 26 27 28 29 30 31
Pinchas · Mattot Massey · Devarim · Tisha b'Av · Va-ethchanan · Ekev
AV
Tammuz 20 21 22 23 24 25 26 27 28 29 1 2 3 4 5 6 7 8 9 10 11 12 13 14 15 16 17 18 19 20 21

August 1 2 3 4 5 6 7 8 9 10 11 12 13 14 15 16 17 18 19 20 21 22 23 24 25 26 27 28 29 30 31
Re'eh · Shofetim · Ki Thetze · Ki Thavo
ELUL
Av 22 23 24 25 26 27 28 29 30 1 2 3 4 5 6 7 8 9 10 11 12 13 14 15 16 17 18 19 20 21 22

September 1 2 3 4 5 6 7 8 9 10 11 12 13 14 15 16 17 18 19 20 21 22 23 24 25 26 27 28 29 30
Nitzavim Vayyelech · Rosh Hashanah · SHABBAT SHUVAH Haazinu · Yom Kippur · Sukkot · Hol ha-Mo'ed · Shemini Azeret · Simchat Torah
TISHRI
Elul 23 24 25 26 27 28 29 1 2 3 4 5 6 7 8 9 10 11 12 13 14 15 16 17 18 19 20 21 22 23

October 1 2 3 4 5 6 7 8 9 10 11 12 13 14 15 16 17 18 19 20 21 22 23 24 25 26 27 28 29 30 31
Bereshit · Noach · Lech Lecha · Vayyera · Chayye Sarah
HESHVAN
Tishri 24 25 26 27 28 29 30 1 2 3 4 5 6 7 8 9 10 11 12 13 14 15 16 17 18 19 20 21 22 23 24

November 1 2 3 4 5 6 7 8 9 10 11 12 13 14 15 16 17 18 19 20 21 22 23 24 25 26 27 28 29 30
Toledot · Vayyetze · Vayyishlach · Vayyeshev
KISLEV
Heshvan 25 26 27 28 29 30 1 2 3 4 5 6 7 8 9 10 11 12 13 14 15 16 17 18 19 20 21 22 23 24

December 1 2 3 4 5 6 7 8 9 10 11 12 13 14 15 16 17 18 19 20 21 22 23 24 25 26 27 28 29 30 31
Chanukah · Mikketz · Vayyiggash · Vayyechi · Shemot · Va-ayra
TEVET
Kislev 25 26 27 28 29 30 1 2 3 4 5 6 7 8 9 10 11 12 13 14 15 16 17 18 19 20 21 22 23 24 25

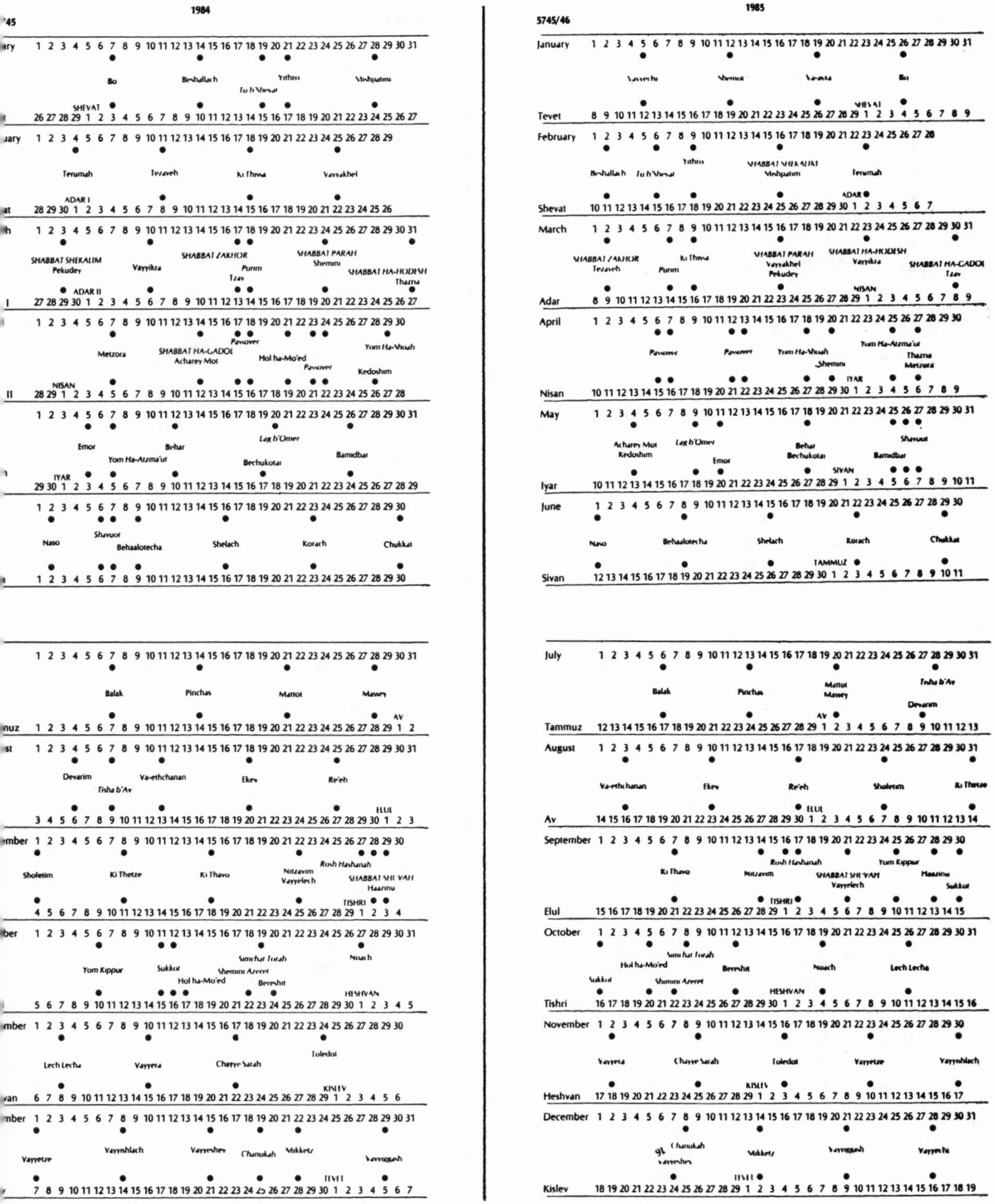

1984

'45

ary 1 2 3 4 5 6 7 8 9 10 11 12 13 14 15 16 17 18 19 20 21 22 23 24 25 26 27 28 29 30 31

Bo Beshallach Yithro Mishpatim
Tu b'Shevat

SHEVAT
26 27 28 29 1 2 3 4 5 6 7 8 9 10 11 12 13 14 15 16 17 18 19 20 21 22 23 24 25 26 27

ary 1 2 3 4 5 6 7 8 9 10 11 12 13 14 15 16 17 18 19 20 21 22 23 24 25 26 27 28 29

Terumah Tezaveh Ki Thissa Vayyakhel

ADAR I
at 28 29 30 1 2 3 4 5 6 7 8 9 10 11 12 13 14 15 16 17 18 19 20 21 22 23 24 25 26

h 1 2 3 4 5 6 7 8 9 10 11 12 13 14 15 16 17 18 19 20 21 22 23 24 25 26 27 28 29 30 31

SHABBAT SHEKALIM
Pekudey
Vayyikra
SHABBAT ZAKHOR
Purim
Tzav
SHABBAT PARAH
Shemini
SHABBAT HA-HODESH
Thazria

ADAR II
I 27 28 29 30 1 2 3 4 5 6 7 8 9 10 11 12 13 14 15 16 17 18 19 20 21 22 23 24 25 26 27

1 2 3 4 5 6 7 8 9 10 11 12 13 14 15 16 17 18 19 20 21 22 23 24 25 26 27 28 29 30

Metzora
SHABBAT HA-GADOL
Acharey Mot
Passover
Hol ha-Mo'ed
Passover
Yom Ha-Shoah
Kedoshim

NISAN
II 28 29 1 2 3 4 5 6 7 8 9 10 11 12 13 14 15 16 17 18 19 20 21 22 23 24 25 26 27 28

1 2 3 4 5 6 7 8 9 10 11 12 13 14 15 16 17 18 19 20 21 22 23 24 25 26 27 28 29 30 31

Emor
Yom Ha-Atzma'ut
Behar
Lag b'Omer
Bechukotai
Bamidbar

IYAR
29 30 1 2 3 4 5 6 7 8 9 10 11 12 13 14 15 16 17 18 19 20 21 22 23 24 25 26 27 28 29

1 2 3 4 5 6 7 8 9 10 11 12 13 14 15 16 17 18 19 20 21 22 23 24 25 26 27 28 29 30

Naso
Shavuot
Behaalotecha
Shelach
Korach
Chukkat

1 2 3 4 5 6 7 8 9 10 11 12 13 14 15 16 17 18 19 20 21 22 23 24 25 26 27 28 29 30

1 2 3 4 5 6 7 8 9 10 11 12 13 14 15 16 17 18 19 20 21 22 23 24 25 26 27 28 29 30 31

Balak Pinchas Mattot Masey

AV
nuz 1 2 3 4 5 6 7 8 9 10 11 12 13 14 15 16 17 18 19 20 21 22 23 24 25 26 27 28 29 1 2

st 1 2 3 4 5 6 7 8 9 10 11 12 13 14 15 16 17 18 19 20 21 22 23 24 25 26 27 28 29 30 31

Devarim
Tisha b'Av
Va-ethchanan
Ekev
Re'eh

ELUL
3 4 5 6 7 8 9 10 11 12 13 14 15 16 17 18 19 20 21 22 23 24 25 26 27 28 29 30 1 2 3

ember 1 2 3 4 5 6 7 8 9 10 11 12 13 14 15 16 17 18 19 20 21 22 23 24 25 26 27 28 29 30

Shofetim
Ki Thetze
Ki Thavo
Nitzavim
Vayyelech
Rosh Hashanah
SHABBAT SHUVAH
Haazinu

TISHRI
4 5 6 7 8 9 10 11 12 13 14 15 16 17 18 19 20 21 22 23 24 25 26 27 28 29 1 2 3 4

ber 1 2 3 4 5 6 7 8 9 10 11 12 13 14 15 16 17 18 19 20 21 22 23 24 25 26 27 28 29 30 31

Yom Kippur
Sukkot
Hol ha-Mo'ed
Shemini Azeret
Simchat Torah
Bereshit
Noach

HESHVAN
5 6 7 8 9 10 11 12 13 14 15 16 17 18 19 20 21 22 23 24 25 26 27 28 29 30 1 2 3 4 5

mber 1 2 3 4 5 6 7 8 9 10 11 12 13 14 15 16 17 18 19 20 21 22 23 24 25 26 27 28 29 30

Lech Lecha
Vayyera
Chayye Sarah
Toledot

KISLEV
van 6 7 8 9 10 11 12 13 14 15 16 17 18 19 20 21 22 23 24 25 26 27 28 29 1 2 3 4 5 6

mber 1 2 3 4 5 6 7 8 9 10 11 12 13 14 15 16 17 18 19 20 21 22 23 24 25 26 27 28 29 30 31

Vayyetze
Vayyishlach
Vayyeshev
Chanukah
Mikketz
Vayyiggash

TEVET
7 8 9 10 11 12 13 14 15 16 17 18 19 20 21 22 23 24 25 26 27 28 29 30 1 2 3 4 5 6 7

1985

5745/46

January 1 2 3 4 5 6 7 8 9 10 11 12 13 14 15 16 17 18 19 20 21 22 23 24 25 26 27 28 29 30 31

Vayyechi Shemot Va-era Bo

SHEVAT
Tevet 8 9 10 11 12 13 14 15 16 17 18 19 20 21 22 23 24 25 26 27 28 29 1 2 3 4 5 6 7 8 9

February 1 2 3 4 5 6 7 8 9 10 11 12 13 14 15 16 17 18 19 20 21 22 23 24 25 26 27 28

Beshallach
Tu b'Shevat
Yithro
SHABBAT SHEKALIM
Mishpatim
Terumah

ADAR
Shevat 10 11 12 13 14 15 16 17 18 19 20 21 22 23 24 25 26 27 28 29 30 1 2 3 4 5 6 7

March 1 2 3 4 5 6 7 8 9 10 11 12 13 14 15 16 17 18 19 20 21 22 23 24 25 26 27 28 29 30 31

SHABBAT ZAKHOR
Tezaveh
Purim
Ki Thissa
SHABBAT PARAH
Vayyakhel
Pekudey
SHABBAT HA-HODESH
Vayyikra
SHABBAT HA-GADOL
Tzav

NISAN
Adar 8 9 10 11 12 13 14 15 16 17 18 19 20 21 22 23 24 25 26 27 28 29 1 2 3 4 5 6 7 8 9

April 1 2 3 4 5 6 7 8 9 10 11 12 13 14 15 16 17 18 19 20 21 22 23 24 25 26 27 28 29 30

Passover
Passover
Yom Ha-Shoah
Shemini
Yom Ha-Atzma'ut
Thazria
Metzora

IYAR
Nisan 10 11 12 13 14 15 16 17 18 19 20 21 22 23 24 25 26 27 28 29 30 1 2 3 4 5 6 7 8 9

May 1 2 3 4 5 6 7 8 9 10 11 12 13 14 15 16 17 18 19 20 21 22 23 24 25 26 27 28 29 30 31

Acharey Mot
Kedoshim
Lag b'Omer
Emor
Behar
Bechukotai
Bamidbar
Shavuot

SIVAN
Iyar 10 11 12 13 14 15 16 17 18 19 20 21 22 23 24 25 26 27 28 29 1 2 3 4 5 6 7 8 9 10 11

June 1 2 3 4 5 6 7 8 9 10 11 12 13 14 15 16 17 18 19 20 21 22 23 24 25 26 27 28 29 30

Naso Behaalotecha Shelach Korach Chukkat

TAMMUZ
Sivan 12 13 14 15 16 17 18 19 20 21 22 23 24 25 26 27 28 29 30 1 2 3 4 5 6 7 8 9 10 11

July 1 2 3 4 5 6 7 8 9 10 11 12 13 14 15 16 17 18 19 20 21 22 23 24 25 26 27 28 29 30 31

Balak
Pinchas
Mattot
Masey
Tisha b'Av
Devarim

AV
Tammuz 12 13 14 15 16 17 18 19 20 21 22 23 24 25 26 27 28 29 1 2 3 4 5 6 7 8 9 10 11 12 13

August 1 2 3 4 5 6 7 8 9 10 11 12 13 14 15 16 17 18 19 20 21 22 23 24 25 26 27 28 29 30 31

Va-ethchanan Ekev Re'eh Shofetim Ki Thetze

ELUL
Av 14 15 16 17 18 19 20 21 22 23 24 25 26 27 28 29 30 1 2 3 4 5 6 7 8 9 10 11 12 13 14

September 1 2 3 4 5 6 7 8 9 10 11 12 13 14 15 16 17 18 19 20 21 22 23 24 25 26 27 28 29 30

Ki Thavo
Nitzavim
Rosh Hashanah
SHABBAT SHUVAH
Vayyelech
Yom Kippur
Haazinu
Sukkot

TISHRI
Elul 15 16 17 18 19 20 21 22 23 24 25 26 27 28 29 1 2 3 4 5 6 7 8 9 10 11 12 13 14 15

October 1 2 3 4 5 6 7 8 9 10 11 12 13 14 15 16 17 18 19 20 21 22 23 24 25 26 27 28 29 30 31

Sukkot
Hol ha-Mo'ed
Simchat Torah
Shemini Azeret
Bereshit
Noach
Lech Lecha

HESHVAN
Tishri 16 17 18 19 20 21 22 23 24 25 26 27 28 29 30 1 2 3 4 5 6 7 8 9 10 11 12 13 14 15 16

November 1 2 3 4 5 6 7 8 9 10 11 12 13 14 15 16 17 18 19 20 21 22 23 24 25 26 27 28 29 30

Vayyera Chayye Sarah Toledot Vayyetze Vayyishlach

KISLEV
Heshvan 17 18 19 20 21 22 23 24 25 26 27 28 29 1 2 3 4 5 6 7 8 9 10 11 12 13 14 15 16 17

December 1 2 3 4 5 6 7 8 9 10 11 12 13 14 15 16 17 18 19 20 21 22 23 24 25 26 27 28 29 30 31

Chanukah
Vayyeshev
Mikketz
Vayyiggash
Vayyechi

TEVET
Kislev 18 19 20 21 22 23 24 25 26 27 28 29 1 2 3 4 5 6 7 8 9 10 11 12 13 14 15 16 17 18 19

1986 — 5746/47

Month	Dates	Portions / Holidays	Hebrew month	Hebrew dates
January	1 2 3 4 5 6 7 8 9 10 11 12 13 14 15 16 17 18 19 20 21 22 23 24 25 26 27 28 29 30 31	Shemot; Va-era; Bo; Beshallach, Tu b'Shevat	Tevet (SHEVAT)	20 21 22 23 24 25 26 27 28 29 1 2 3 4 5 6 7 8 9 10 11 12 13 14 15 16 17 18 19 20 21
February	1 2 3 4 5 6 7 8 9 10 11 12 13 14 15 16 17 18 19 20 21 22 23 24 25 26 27 28	Yithro; Mishpatim; Terumah; Tezaveh	Shevat (ADAR I)	22 23 24 25 26 27 28 29 30 1 2 3 4 5 6 7 8 9 10 11 12 13 14 15 16 17 18 19
March	1 2 3 4 5 6 7 8 9 10 11 12 13 14 15 16 17 18 19 20 21 22 23 24 25 26 27 28 29 30 31	Ki Thissa; SHABBAT SHEKALIM Vayyakhel; Pekudey; SHABBAT ZAKHOR Vayyikra; Purim; SHABBAT PARAH Tzav	Adar I (ADAR II)	20 21 22 23 24 25 26 27 28 29 30 1 2 3 4 5 6 7 8 9 10 11 12 13 14 15 16 17 18 19 20
April	1 2 3 4 5 6 7 8 9 10 11 12 13 14 15 16 17 18 19 20 21 22 23 24 25 26 27 28 29 30	SHABBAT HA-HODESH Shemini; Thazria; SHABBAT HA-GADOL Metzora; Passover; Hol ha-Mo'ed; Passover	Adar II (NISAN)	21 22 23 24 25 26 27 28 29 1 2 3 4 5 6 7 8 9 10 11 12 13 14 15 16 17 18 19 20 21
May	1 2 3 4 5 6 7 8 9 10 11 12 13 14 15 16 17 18 19 20 21 22 23 24 25 26 27 28 29 30 31	Passover; Acharey Mot; Yom Ha-Shoah; Kedoshim; Yom Ha-Atzma'ut; Emor; Behar; Lag b'Omer; Bechukotai	Nisan (IYAR)	22 23 24 25 26 27 28 29 30 1 2 3 4 5 6 7 8 9 10 11 12 13 14 15 16 17 18 19 20 21 22
June	1 2 3 4 5 6 7 8 9 10 11 12 13 14 15 16 17 18 19 20 21 22 23 24 25 26 27 28 29 30	Bamidbar; Shavuot; Naso; Behaalotecha	Iyar (SIVAN)	23 24 25 26 27 28 29 1 2 3 4 5 6 7 8 9 10 11 12 13 14 15 16 17 18 19 20 21 22 23
July	1 2 3 4 5 6 7 8 9 10 11 12 13 14 15 16 17 18 19 20 21 22 23 24 25 26 27 28 29 30 31	Shelach; Korach; Chukkat Balak; Pinchas	Sivan (TAMMUZ)	24 25 26 27 28 29 30 1 2 3 4 5 6 7 8 9 10 11 12 13 14 15 16 17 18 19 20 21 22 23 24
August	1 2 3 4 5 6 7 8 9 10 11 12 13 14 15 16 17 18 19 20 21 22 23 24 25 26 27 28 29 30 31	Mattot Massey; Devarim; Tisha b'Av; Va-ethchanan; Ekev; Re'eh	Tammuz (AV)	25 26 27 28 29 1 2 3 4 5 6 7 8 9 10 11 12 13 14 15 16 17 18 19 20 21 21 21 24 25 26
September	1 2 3 4 5 6 7 8 9 10 11 12 13 14 15 16 17 18 19 20 21 22 23 24 25 26 27 28 29 30	Shofetim; Ki Thetze; Ki Thavo; Nitzavim Vayyelech	Av (ELUL)	27 28 29 30 1 2 3 4 5 6 7 8 9 10 11 12 13 14 15 16 17 18 19 20 21 22 23 24 25 26
October	1 2 3 4 5 6 7 8 9 10 11 12 13 14 15 16 17 18 19 20 21 22 23 24 25 26 27 28 29 30 31	Rosh Hashanah; SHABBAT SHUVAH Haazinu; Yom Kippur; Sukkot; Shemini Azeret; Simchat Torah	Elul (TISHRI)	27 28 29 1 2 3 4 5 6 7 8 9 10 11 12 13 14 15 16 17 18 19 20 21 22 23 24 25 26 27 28
November	1 2 3 4 5 6 7 8 9 10 11 12 13 14 15 16 17 18 19 20 21 22 23 24 25 26 27 28 29 30	Bereshit; Noach; Lech Lecha; Vayyera; Chayye Sarah	Tishri/Heshvan (HESHVAN)	29 30 1 2 3 4 5 6 7 8 9 10 11 12 13 14 15 16 17 18 19 20 21 22 23 24 25 26 27 28
December	1 2 3 4 5 6 7 8 9 10 11 12 13 14 15 16 17 18 19 20 21 22 23 24 25 26 27 28 29 30 31	Toledot; Vayyetze; Vayyishlach; Chanukah Vayyeshev	Heshvan/Kislev (KISLEV)	29 30 1 2 3 4 5 6 7 8 9 10 11 12 13 14 15 16 17 18 19 20 21 22 23 24 25 26 27 28 29

1987 — 5747/48

Month	Dates	Portions / Holidays	Hebrew month	Hebrew dates
January	1 2 3 4 5 6 7 8 9 10 11 12 13 14 15 16 17 18 19 20 21 22 23 24 25 26 27 28 29 3	Mikketz; Vayyiggash; Vayyechi; Shemot	Kislev/Tevet (TEVET)	30 1 2 3 4 5 6 7 8 9 10 11 12 13 14 15 16 17 18 19 20 21 22 23 24 25 26 27 28 2
February	1 2 3 4 5 6 7 8 9 10 11 12 13 14 15 16 17 18 19 20 21 22 23 24 25 26 27 28	Bo; Tu b'Shevat; Beshallach; Yithro; SHABBAT SHEKA Mishpatim	Shevat	2 3 4 5 6 7 8 9 10 11 12 13 14 15 16 17 18 29 20 21 22 23 24 25 26 27 28 29
March	1 2 3 4 5 6 7 8 9 10 11 12 13 14 15 16 17 18 19 20 21 22 23 24 25 26 27 28 29 3	Terumah; SHABBAT ZAKHOR Tezaveh; Purim; SHABBAT PARAH Ki Thissa; SHABBAT HA-HO Vayyakhel Pekudey	Shevat/Adar (ADAR)	30 1 2 3 4 5 6 7 8 9 10 11 12 13 14 15 16 17 18 19 20 21 22 23 24 25 26 27 28 2
April	1 2 3 4 5 6 7 8 9 10 11 12 13 14 15 16 17 18 19 20 21 22 23 24 25 26 27 28 29 3	Vayyikra; SHABBAT HA-GADOL Tzav; Passover; Hol ha-Mo'ed; Passover; Yom Ha-Shoah; Shemini	Nisan (IY)	2 3 4 5 6 7 8 9 10 11 12 13 14 15 16 17 18 19 20 21 22 23 24 25 26 27 28 29 30
May	1 2 3 4 5 6 7 8 9 10 11 12 13 14 15 16 17 18 19 20 21 22 23 24 25 26 27 28 29 3	Thazria Metzora; Yom Ha-Atzma'ut; Acharey Mot Kedoshim; Emor; Lag b'Omer; Behar Bechukotai; Bam	Iyar (SIVAN)	2 3 4 5 6 7 8 9 10 11 12 13 14 15 16 17 18 19 20 21 22 23 24 25 26 27 28 29 1
June	1 2 3 4 5 6 7 8 9 10 11 12 13 14 15 16 17 18 19 20 21 22 23 24 25 26 27 28 29 3	Shavuot; Naso; Behaalotecha; Shelach; Korach	Sivan (TAMMU)	4 5 6 7 8 9 10 11 12 13 14 15 16 17 18 19 20 21 22 23 24 25 26 27 28 29 30 1 2
July	1 2 3 4 5 6 7 8 9 10 11 12 13 14 15 16 17 18 19 20 21 22 23 24 25 26 27 28 29	Chukkat; Balak; Pinchas; Mattot Massey	Tammuz (AV)	4 5 6 7 8 9 10 11 12 13 14 15 16 17 18 19 20 21 22 23 24 25 26 27 28 29 1 2 3
August	1 2 3 4 5 6 7 8 9 10 11 12 13 14 15 16 17 18 19 20 21 22 23 24 25 26 27 28 29	Devarim; Tisha b'Av; Va-ethchanan; Ekev; Re'eh; Shofeti	Av (ELUL)	6 7 8 9 10 11 12 13 14 15 16 17 18 19 20 21 22 23 24 25 26 27 28 29 30 1 2 3 4
September	1 2 3 4 5 6 7 8 9 10 11 12 13 14 15 16 17 18 19 20 21 22 23 24 25 26 27 28 29	Ki Thetze; Ki Thavo; Nitzavim Vayyelech; Rosh Hashanah; SHABBAT SHUVA Haazinu	Elul (TISHRI)	7 8 9 10 11 12 13 14 15 16 17 18 19 20 21 22 23 24 25 26 27 28 29 1 2 3 4 5 6
October	1 2 3 4 5 6 7 8 9 10 11 12 13 14 15 16 17 18 19 20 21 22 23 24 25 26 27 28 29	Yom Kippur; Sukkot; Hol ha-Mo'ed; Shemini Azeret; Simchat Torah; Bereshit; Noach; Le	Tishri (HESHVAN)	8 9 10 11 12 13 14 15 16 17 18 19 20 21 22 23 24 25 26 27 28 29 30 1 2 3 4 5 6
November	1 2 3 4 5 6 7 8 9 10 11 12 13 14 15 16 17 18 19 20 21 22 23 24 25 26 27 28 29	Vayyera; Chayye Sarah; Toledot; Vayyetze	Heshvan (KISLEV)	9 10 11 12 13 14 15 16 17 18 19 20 21 22 23 24 25 26 27 28 29 1 2 3 4 5 6 7 8
December	1 2 3 4 5 6 7 8 9 10 11 12 13 14 15 16 17 18 19 20 21 22 23 24 25 26 27 28 29	Vayyishlach; Vayyeshev; Chanukah; Mikketz; Vayyiggash	Kislev (TEVET)	10 11 12 13 14 15 16 17 18 19 20 21 22 23 24 25 26 27 28 29 30 1 2 3 4 5 6 7 8

1988

3/49

uary 1 2 3 4 5 6 7 8 9 10 11 12 13 14 15 16 17 18 19 20 21 22 23 24 25 26 27 28 29 30 31
Vayyechi · Shemot · Va-era · Bo · Beshallach
et 11 12 13 14 15 16 17 18 19 20 21 22 23 24 25 26 27 28 29 SHEVAT 1 2 3 4 5 6 7 8 9 10 11 12

ruary 1 2 3 4 5 6 7 8 9 10 11 12 13 14 15 16 17 18 19 20 21 22 23 24 25 26 27 28 29
Tu b'Shevat · Yithro · SHABBAT SHEKALIM Mishpatim · Terumah · SHABBAT ZAKHOR Tetzaveh
vat 13 14 15 16 17 18 19 20 21 22 23 24 25 26 27 28 29 30 ADAR 1 2 3 4 5 6 7 8 9 10 11

rch 1 2 3 4 5 6 7 8 9 10 11 12 13 14 15 16 17 18 19 20 21 22 23 24 25 26 27 28 29 30 31
Purim · Ki Thissa · SHABBAT PARAH Vayyakhel Pekudey · SHABBAT HA-HODESH Vayyikra · SHABBAT HA-GADOL Tzav
r 12 13 14 15 16 17 18 19 20 21 22 23 24 25 26 27 28 29 NISAN 1 2 3 4 5 6 7 8 9 10 11 12 13

il 1 2 3 4 5 6 7 8 9 10 11 12 13 14 15 16 17 18 19 20 21 22 23 24 25 26 27 28 29 30
Passover · Passover · Yom Ha-Shoah · Shemini · Yom Ha-Atzma'ut · Thazria Metzora · Acharey Mot Kedoshim
an 14 15 16 17 18 19 20 21 22 23 24 25 26 27 28 29 30 IYAR 1 2 3 4 5 6 7 8 9 10 11 12 13

y 1 2 3 4 5 6 7 8 9 10 11 12 13 14 15 16 17 18 19 20 21 22 23 24 25 26 27 28 29 30 31
Lag b'Omer · Emor · Behar Bechukotai · Bamidbar · Shavuot · Naso
14 15 16 17 18 19 20 21 22 23 24 25 26 27 28 29 SIVAN 1 2 3 4 5 6 7 8 9 10 11 12 13 14 15

e 1 2 3 4 5 6 7 8 9 10 11 12 13 14 15 16 17 18 19 20 21 22 23 24 25 26 27 28 29 30
Behaalotecha · Shelach · Korach · Chukkat
n 16 17 18 19 20 21 22 23 24 25 26 27 28 29 30 TAMMUZ 1 2 3 4 5 6 7 8 9 10 11 12 13 14 15

y 1 2 3 4 5 6 7 8 9 10 11 12 13 14 15 16 17 18 19 20 21 22 23 24 25 26 27 28 29 30 31
Balak · Pinchas · Mattot Massey · Devarim · Tisha b'Av · Va-ethchanan
mmuz 16 17 18 19 20 21 22 23 24 25 26 27 28 29 AV 1 2 3 4 5 6 7 8 9 10 11 12 13 14 15 16 17

gust 1 2 3 4 5 6 7 8 9 10 11 12 13 14 15 16 17 18 19 20 21 22 23 24 25 26 27 28 29 30 31
Ekev · Re'eh · Shofetim · Ki Thetze
18 19 20 21 22 23 24 25 26 27 28 29 30 ELUL 1 2 3 4 5 6 7 8 9 10 11 12 13 14 15 16 17 18

ptember 1 2 3 4 5 6 7 8 9 10 11 12 13 14 15 16 17 18 19 20 21 22 23 24 25 26 27 28 29 30
Ki Thavo · Nitzavim · Rosh Hashnah · SHABBAT SHUVAH Vayyelech · Yom Kippur · Haazinu · Sukkot
l 19 20 21 22 23 24 25 26 27 28 29 TISHRI 1 2 3 4 5 6 7 8 9 10 11 12 13 14 15 16 17 18 19

tober 1 2 3 4 5 6 7 8 9 10 11 12 13 14 15 16 17 18 19 20 21 22 23 24 25 26 27 28 29 30 31
Hol ha-Mo'ed · Shemini Azeret · Simchat Torah · Bereshit · Noach · Lech Lecha · Vayyera
hri 20 21 22 23 24 25 26 27 28 29 30 HESHVAN 1 2 3 4 5 6 7 8 9 10 11 12 13 14 15 16 17 18 19 20

vember 1 2 3 4 5 6 7 8 9 10 11 12 13 14 15 16 17 18 19 20 21 22 23 24 25 26 27 28 29 30
Chayye Sarah · Toledot · Vayyetze · Vayyishlach
shvan 21 22 23 24 25 26 27 28 29 KISLEV 1 2 3 4 5 6 7 8 9 10 11 12 13 14 15 16 17 18 19 20 21

cember 1 2 3 4 5 6 7 8 9 10 11 12 13 14 15 16 17 18 19 20 21 22 23 24 25 26 27 28 29 30 31
Vayyeshev · Chanukah · Mikketz · Vayyiggash · Vayyechi · Shemot
lev 22 23 24 25 26 27 28 29 TEVET 1 2 3 4 5 6 7 8 9 10 11 12 13 14 15 16 17 18 19 20 21 22 23

1989

5749/50

January 1 2 3 4 5 6 7 8 9 10 11 12 13 14 15 16 17 18 19 20 21 22 23 24 25 26 27 28 29 30 31
Va-era · Bo · Tu b'Shevat Beshallach · Yithro
Tevet 24 25 26 27 28 29 SHEVAT 1 2 3 4 5 6 7 8 9 10 11 12 13 14 15 16 17 18 19 20 21 22 23 24 25

February 1 2 3 4 5 6 7 8 9 10 11 12 13 14 15 16 17 18 19 20 21 22 23 24 25 26 27 28
Mishpatim · Terumah · Tetzaveh · Ki Thissa
Shevat 26 27 28 29 30 ADAR I 1 2 3 4 5 6 7 8 9 10 11 12 13 14 15 16 17 18 19 20 21 22 23

March 1 2 3 4 5 6 7 8 9 10 11 12 13 14 15 16 17 18 19 20 21 22 23 24 25 26 27 28 29 30 31
SHABBAT SHEKALIM Vayyakhel · Pekudey · SHABBAT ZAKHOR Vayyikra · Purim · SHABBAT PARAH Tzav
Adar I 24 25 26 27 28 29 30 ADAR II 1 2 3 4 5 6 7 8 9 10 11 12 13 14 15 16 17 18 19 20 21 22 23 24

April 1 2 3 4 5 6 7 8 9 10 11 12 13 14 15 16 17 18 19 20 21 22 23 24 25 26 27 28 29 30
SHABBAT HA-HODESH Shemini · Thazria · SHABBAT HA-GADOL Metzora · Passover · Hol ha-Mo'ed · Passover · Acharey Mot
Adar II 25 26 27 28 29 NISAN 1 2 3 4 5 6 7 8 9 10 11 12 13 14 15 16 17 18 19 20 21 22 23 24 25

May 1 2 3 4 5 6 7 8 9 10 11 12 13 14 15 16 17 18 19 20 21 22 23 24 25 26 27 28 29 30 31
Yom Ha-Shoah · Kedoshim · Yom Ha-Atzma'ut · Emor · Behar · Lag b'Omer · Bechukotai
Nisan 26 27 28 29 30 IYAR 1 2 3 4 5 6 7 8 9 10 11 12 13 14 15 16 17 18 19 20 21 22 23 24 25 26

June 1 2 3 4 5 6 7 8 9 10 11 12 13 14 15 16 17 18 19 20 21 22 23 24 25 26 27 28 29 30
Bamidbar · Shavuot · Naso · Behaalotecha
Iyar 27 28 29 SIVAN 1 2 3 4 5 6 7 8 9 10 11 12 13 14 15 16 17 18 19 20 21 21 23 24 25 26 27

July 1 2 3 4 5 6 7 8 9 10 11 12 13 14 15 16 17 18 19 20 21 22 23 24 25 26 27 28 29 30 31
Shelach · Korach · Chukkat Balak · Pinchas · Mattot Massey
Sivan 28 29 30 TAMMUZ 1 2 3 4 5 6 7 8 9 10 11 12 13 14 15 16 17 18 19 20 21 22 23 24 25 26 27 28

August 1 2 3 4 5 6 7 8 9 10 11 12 13 14 15 16 17 18 19 20 21 22 23 24 25 26 27 28 29 30 31
Devarim · Tisha b'Av · Va-ethchanan · Ekev · Re'eh
Tammuz/Av 29 AV 1 2 3 4 5 6 7 8 9 10 11 12 13 14 15 16 17 18 19 20 21 22 23 24 25 26 27 28 29 30

September 1 2 3 4 5 6 7 8 9 10 11 12 13 14 15 16 17 18 19 20 21 22 23 24 25 26 27 28 29 30
Shofetim · Ki Thetze · Ki Thavo · Nitzavim Vayyelech · Rosh Hashanah
Elul 1 2 3 4 5 6 7 8 9 10 11 12 13 14 15 16 17 18 19 20 21 22 23 24 25 26 27 28 29 TISHRI 1

October 1 2 3 4 5 6 7 8 9 10 11 12 13 14 15 16 17 18 19 20 21 22 23 24 25 26 27 28 29 30 31
Rosh Hashanah · SHABBAT SHUVAH Haazinu · Yom Kippur · Sukkot · Shemini Azeret · Simchat Torah · Bereshit
Tishri 2 3 4 5 6 7 8 9 10 11 12 13 14 15 16 17 18 19 20 21 22 23 24 25 26 27 28 29 30 HESHVAN 1 2

November 1 2 3 4 5 6 7 8 9 10 11 12 13 14 15 16 17 18 19 20 21 22 23 24 25 26 27 28 29 30
Noach · Lech Lecha · Vayyera · Chayye Sarah
Heshvan 3 4 5 6 7 8 9 10 11 12 13 14 15 16 17 18 19 20 21 22 23 24 25 26 27 28 29 30 KISLEV 1 2

December 1 2 3 4 5 6 7 8 9 10 11 12 13 14 15 16 17 18 19 20 21 22 23 24 25 26 27 28 29 30 31
Toledot · Vayyetze · Vayyishlach · Chanukah Vayyeshev · Mikketz
Kislev 3 4 5 6 7 8 9 10 11 12 13 14 15 16 17 18 19 20 21 22 23 24 25 26 27 28 29 30 TEVET 1 2 3

1990

5750/51

January 1 2 3 4 5 6 7 8 9 10 11 12 13 14 15 16 17 18 19 20 21 22 23 24 25 26 27 28 29 30 31

Vayyiggash · Vayyechi · Shemot · Va-ayra

SHEVAT

Tevet 4 5 6 7 8 9 10 11 12 13 14 15 16 17 18 19 20 21 22 23 24 25 26 27 28 29 1 2 3 4 5

February 1 2 3 4 5 6 7 8 9 10 11 12 13 14 15 16 17 18 19 20 21 22 23 24 25 26 27 28

Bo · Tu b'Shevat Beshallach · Yithro · SHABBAT SHEKALIM Mishpatim

ADAR

Shevat 6 7 8 9 10 11 12 13 14 15 16 17 18 19 20 21 22 23 24 25 26 27 28 29 30 1 2 3

March 1 2 3 4 5 6 7 8 9 10 11 12 13 14 15 16 17 18 19 20 21 22 23 24 25 26 27 28 29 30 31

Terumah · Purim · SHABBAT ZAKHOR Tezaveh · SHABBAT PARAH Ki Thissa · SHABBAT HA-HODESH Vayyakhel Pekudey · Vayyikra

NISAN

Adar 4 5 6 7 8 9 10 11 12 13 14 15 16 17 18 19 20 21 22 23 24 25 26 27 28 29 1 2 3 4 5

April 1 2 3 4 5 6 7 8 9 10 11 12 13 14 15 16 17 18 19 20 21 22 23 24 25 26 27 28 29 30

Passover · Passover · Yom Ha-Shoah · Yom Ha-Atzma'ut · SHABBAT HA-GADOL Tzav · Hol ha-Mo'ed · Shemini · Thazria Metzora

IYAR

Nisan 6 7 8 9 10 11 12 13 14 15 16 17 18 19 20 21 22 23 24 25 26 27 28 29 30 1 2 3 4 5

May 1 2 3 4 5 6 7 8 9 10 11 12 13 14 15 16 17 18 19 20 21 22 23 24 25 26 27 28 29 30 31

Acharey Mot Kedoshim · Lag b'Omer · Emor · Behar Bechukotai · Bamidbar · Shavuot

SIVAN

Iyar 6 7 8 9 10 11 12 13 14 15 16 17 18 19 20 21 22 23 24 25 26 27 28 29 1 2 3 4 5 6 7

June 1 2 3 4 5 6 7 8 9 10 11 12 13 14 15 16 17 18 19 20 21 22 23 24 25 26 27 28 29 30

Naso · Behaalotecha · Shelach · Korach · Chukkat

TAMMUZ

Sivan 8 9 10 11 12 13 14 15 16 17 18 19 20 21 22 23 24 25 26 27 28 29 30 1 2 3 4 5 6 7

July 1 2 3 4 5 6 7 8 9 10 11 12 13 14 15 16 17 18 19 20 21 22 23 24 25 26 27 28 29 30 31

Balak · Pinchas · Mattot Massey · Devarim · Tisha b'Av

AV

Tammuz 8 9 10 11 12 13 14 15 16 17 18 19 20 21 22 23 24 25 26 27 28 29 1 2 3 4 5 6 7 8 9

August 1 2 3 4 5 6 7 8 9 10 11 12 13 14 15 16 17 18 19 20 21 22 23 24 25 26 27 28 29 30 31

Va-ethchanan · Ekev · Re'eh · Shofetim

ELUL

Av 10 11 12 13 14 15 16 17 18 19 20 21 22 23 24 25 26 27 28 29 30 1 2 3 4 5 6 7 8 9 10

September 1 2 3 4 5 6 7 8 9 10 11 12 13 14 15 16 17 18 19 20 21 22 23 24 25 26 27 28 29 30

Ki Thetze · Ki Thavo · Nitzavim Vayyelech · Rosh Hashanah · SHABBAT SHUVAH Haazinu · Yom Kippur

TISHRI

Elul 11 12 13 14 15 16 17 18 19 20 21 22 23 24 25 26 27 28 29 1 2 3 4 5 6 7 8 9 10 11

October 1 2 3 4 5 6 7 8 9 10 11 12 13 14 15 16 17 18 19 20 21 22 23 24 25 26 27 28 29 30 31

Sukkot · Hol ha-Mo'ed · Simchat Torah · Shemini Azeret · Bereshit · Noach · Lech Lecha

HESHVAN

Tishri 12 13 14 15 16 17 18 19 20 21 22 23 24 25 26 27 28 29 30 1 2 3 4 5 6 7 8 9 10 11 12

November 1 2 3 4 5 6 7 8 9 10 11 12 13 14 15 16 17 18 19 20 21 22 23 24 25 26 27 28 29 30

Vayyera · Chayye Sarah · Toledot · Vayyetze

KISLEV

Heshvan 13 14 15 16 17 18 19 20 21 22 23 24 25 26 27 28 29 1 2 3 4 5 6 7 8 9 10 11 12 13

December 1 2 3 4 5 6 7 8 9 10 11 12 13 14 15 16 17 18 19 20 21 22 23 24 25 26 27 28 29 30 31

Vayyishlach · Vayyeshev · Chanukah · Mikketz · Vayyiggash · Vayyechi

TEVET

Kislev 14 15 16 17 18 19 20 21 22 23 24 25 26 27 28 29 30 1 2 3 4 5 6 7 8 9 10 11 12 13 14

1991

5751/52

January 1 2 3 4 5 6 7 8 9 10 11 12 13 14 15 16 17 18 19 20 21 22 23 24 25 26 27 28 29 30 31

Shemot · Va-ayra · Bo · Beshallach · Tu b'Shevat

SHEVAT

Tevet 15 16 17 18 19 20 21 22 23 24 25 26 27 28 29 1 2 3 4 5 6 7 8 9 10 11 12 13 14 15 16

February 1 2 3 4 5 6 7 8 9 10 11 12 13 14 15 16 17 18 19 20 21 22 23 24 25 26 27 28

Yithro · SHABBAT SHEKALIM Mishpatim · Terumah · SHABBAT ZAKHOR Tezaveh · Purim

ADAR

Shevat 17 18 19 20 21 22 23 24 25 26 27 28 29 30 1 2 3 4 5 6 7 8 9 10 11 12 13 14

March 1 2 3 4 5 6 7 8 9 10 11 12 13 14 15 16 17 18 19 20 21 22 23 24 25 26 27 28 29 30 31

Ki Thissa · SHABBAT PARAH Vayyakhel Pekudey · SHABBAT HA-HODESH Vayyikra · SHABBAT HA-GADOL Tzav · Passover

NISAN

Adar 15 16 17 18 19 20 21 22 23 24 25 26 27 28 29 1 2 3 4 5 6 7 8 9 10 11 12 13 14 15 16

April 1 2 3 4 5 6 7 8 9 10 11 12 13 14 15 16 17 18 19 20 21 22 23 24 25 26 27 28 29 30

Passover · Yom Ha-Shoah · Shemini · Yom Ha-Atzma'ut · Thazria Metzora · Acharey Mot Kedoshim

IYAR

Nisan 17 18 19 20 21 22 23 24 25 26 27 28 29 30 1 2 3 4 5 6 7 8 9 10 11 12 13 14 15 16

May 1 2 3 4 5 6 7 8 9 10 11 12 13 14 15 16 17 18 19 20 21 22 23 24 25 26 27 28 29 30 31

Lag b'Omer · Emor · Behar Bechukotai · Bamidbar · Shavuot · Naso

SIVAN

Iyar 17 18 19 20 21 22 23 24 25 26 27 28 29 1 2 3 4 5 6 7 8 9 10 11 12 13 14 15 16 17 18

June 1 2 3 4 5 6 7 8 9 10 11 12 13 14 15 16 17 18 19 20 21 22 23 24 25 26 27 28 29 30

Behaalotecha · Shelach · Korach · Chukkat · Balak

TAMMUZ

Sivan 19 20 21 22 23 24 25 26 27 28 29 30 1 2 3 4 5 6 7 8 9 10 11 12 13 14 15 16 17 18

July 1 2 3 4 5 6 7 8 9 10 11 12 13 14 15 16 17 18 19 20 21 22 23 24 25 26 27 28 29 30 31

Pinchas · Mattot Massey · Devarim · Tisha b'Av · Va-ethchanan

AV

Tammuz 19 20 21 22 23 24 25 26 27 28 29 1 2 3 4 5 6 7 8 9 10 11 12 13 14 15 16 17 18 19 20

August 1 2 3 4 5 6 7 8 9 10 11 12 13 14 15 16 17 18 19 20 21 22 23 24 25 26 27 28 29 30 31

Ekev · Re'eh · Shofetim · Ki Thetze · Ki Th

ELUL

Av 21 22 23 24 25 26 27 28 29 30 1 2 3 4 5 6 7 8 9 10 11 12 13 14 15 16 17 18 19 20 21

September 1 2 3 4 5 6 7 8 9 10 11 12 13 14 15 16 17 18 19 20 21 22 23 24 25 26 27 28 29 30

Rosh Hashanah · Nitzavim · SHABBAT SHUVAH Vayyelech · Yom Kippur · Haazinu · Sukkot · Hol ha-Mo'ed · Shemini Aze

TISHRI

Elul 22 23 24 25 26 27 28 29 1 2 3 4 5 6 7 8 9 10 11 12 13 14 15 16 17 18 19 20 21 22

October 1 2 3 4 5 6 7 8 9 10 11 12 13 14 15 16 17 18 19 20 21 22 23 24 25 26 27 28 29 30 31

Simchat Torah · Bereshit · Noach · Lech Lecha · Vayyera

HESHVAN

Tishri 23 24 25 26 27 28 29 30 1 2 3 4 5 6 7 8 9 10 11 12 13 14 15 16 17 18 19 20 21 22 23

November 1 2 3 4 5 6 7 8 9 10 11 12 13 14 15 16 17 18 19 20 21 22 23 24 25 26 27 28 29 30

Chayye Sarah · Toledot · Vayyetze · Vayyishlach · Vayyeshev

KISLEV

Heshvan 24 25 26 27 28 29 30 1 2 3 4 5 6 7 8 9 10 11 12 13 14 15 16 17 18 19 20 21 22 23

December 1 2 3 4 5 6 7 8 9 10 11 12 13 14 15 16 17 18 19 20 21 22 23 24 25 26 27 28 29 30 31

Chanukah · Mikketz · Vayyiggash · Vayyechi · Shemot

TEVET

Kislev 24 25 26 27 28 29 30 1 2 3 4 5 6 7 8 9 10 11 12 13 14 15 16 17 18 19 20 21 22 23 24

1992

2/53

uary 1 2 3 4 5 6 7 8 9 10 11 12 13 14 15 16 17 18 19 20 21 22 23 24 25 26 27 28 29 30 31

Va-ayra Bo Beshallach Tu b'Shevat Yithro

SHEVAT

et 25 26 27 28 29 1 2 3 4 5 6 7 8 9 10 11 12 13 14 15 16 17 18 19 20 21 22 23 24 25 26

ruary 1 2 3 4 5 6 7 8 9 10 11 12 13 14 15 16 17 18 19 20 21 22 23 24 25 26 27 28 29

Mishpatim Terumah Tezaveh Ki Thissa SHABBAT SHEKALIM Vayyakhel

ADAR I

vat 27 28 29 30 1 2 3 4 5 6 7 8 9 10 11 12 13 14 15 16 17 18 19 20 21 22 23 24 25

rch 1 2 3 4 5 6 7 8 9 10 11 12 13 14 15 16 17 18 19 20 21 22 23 24 25 26 27 28 29 30 31

Pekudey SHABBAT ZAKHOR Vayyikra Purim Tzav SHABBAT PARAH Shemini

ADAR II

ar I 26 27 28 29 30 1 2 3 4 5 6 7 8 9 10 11 12 13 14 15 16 17 18 19 20 21 22 23 24 25 26

il 1 2 3 4 5 6 7 8 9 10 11 12 13 14 15 16 17 18 19 20 21 22 23 24 25 26 27 28 29 30

SHABBAT HA-HODESH Thazria SHABBAT HA-GADOL Metzora Passover Passover Yom Ha-Shoah

NISAN

ar II 27 28 29 1 2 3 4 5 6 7 8 9 10 11 12 13 14 15 16 17 18 19 20 21 22 23 24 25 26 27

y 1 2 3 4 5 6 7 8 9 10 11 12 13 14 15 16 17 18 19 20 21 22 23 24 25 26 27 28 29 30 31

Acharey Mot Yom Ha-Atzma'ut Kedoshim Emor Lag b'Omer Behar Bechukotai

IYAR

an 28 29 30 1 2 3 4 5 6 7 8 9 10 11 12 13 14 15 16 17 18 19 20 21 22 23 24 25 26 27 28

e 1 2 3 4 5 6 7 8 9 10 11 12 13 14 15 16 17 18 19 20 21 22 23 24 25 26 27 28 29 30

Bamidbar Shavuot Naso Behaalotecha Shelach

SIVAN

/Sivan 29 1 2 3 4 5 6 7 8 9 10 11 12 13 14 15 16 17 18 19 20 21 22 23 24 25 26 27 28 29

y 1 2 3 4 5 6 7 8 9 10 11 12 13 14 15 16 17 18 19 20 21 22 23 24 25 26 27 28 29 30 31

Korach Chukkat Balak Pinchas

TAMMUZ AV

ammuz 30 1 2 3 4 5 6 7 8 9 10 11 12 13 14 15 16 17 18 19 20 21 22 23 24 25 26 27 28 29 1

gust 1 2 3 4 5 6 7 8 9 10 11 12 13 14 15 16 17 18 19 20 21 22 23 24 25 26 27 28 29 30 31

Mattot Massey Tisha b'Av Devarim Va-ethchanan Ekev Re'eh

ELUL

2 3 4 5 6 7 8 9 10 11 12 13 14 15 16 17 18 19 20 21 22 23 24 25 26 27 28 29 30 1 2

tember 1 2 3 4 5 6 7 8 9 10 11 12 13 14 15 16 17 18 19 20 21 22 23 24 25 26 27 28 29 30

Shofetim Ki Thetze Ki Thavo Nitzavim Rosh Hashanah

TISHRI

3 4 5 6 7 8 9 10 11 12 13 14 15 16 17 18 19 20 21 22 23 24 25 26 27 28 29 1 2 3

tober 1 2 3 4 5 6 7 8 9 10 11 12 13 14 15 16 17 18 19 20 21 22 23 24 25 26 27 28 29 30 31

SHABBAT SHUVAH Vayyelech Yom Kippur Haazinu Sukkot Hol ha-Mo'ed Shemini Azeret Simchat Torah Bereshit Noach

HESHVAN

ri 4 5 6 7 8 9 10 11 12 13 14 15 16 17 18 19 20 21 22 23 24 25 26 27 28 29 30 1 2 3 4

vember 1 2 3 4 5 6 7 8 9 10 11 12 13 14 15 16 17 18 19 20 21 22 23 24 25 26 27 28 29 30

Lech Lecha Vayyera Chayye Sarah Toledot

KISLEV

hvan 5 6 7 8 9 10 11 12 13 14 15 16 17 18 19 20 21 22 23 24 25 26 27 28 29 1 2 3 4 5

ember 1 2 3 4 5 6 7 8 9 10 11 12 13 14 15 16 17 18 19 20 21 22 23 24 25 26 27 28 29 30 31

Vayyetze Vayyishlach Vayyeshev Chanukah Mikketz

TEVET

ev 6 7 8 9 10 11 12 13 14 15 16 17 18 19 20 21 22 23 24 25 26 27 28 29 1 2 3 4 5 6 7

1993

5753/54

January 1 2 3 4 5 6 7 8 9 10 11 12 13 14 15 16 17 18 19 20 21 22 23 24 25 26 27 28 29 30 31

Vayyiggash Vayyechi Shemot Va-ayra Bo

SHEVAT

Tevet 8 9 10 11 12 13 14 15 16 17 18 19 20 21 22 23 24 25 26 27 28 29 1 2 3 4 5 6 7 8 9

February 1 2 3 4 5 6 7 8 9 10 11 12 13 14 15 16 17 18 19 20 21 22 23 24 25 26 27 28

Tu b'Shevat Beshallach Yithro SHABBAT SHEKALIM Mishpatim Terumah

ADAR

Shevat 10 11 12 13 14 15 16 17 18 19 20 21 22 23 24 25 26 27 28 29 30 1 2 3 4 5 6 7

March 1 2 3 4 5 6 7 8 9 10 11 12 13 14 15 16 17 18 19 20 21 22 23 24 25 26 27 28 29 30 31

Purim SHABBAT ZAKHOR Tezaveh SHABBAT PARAH Ki Thissa SHABBAT HA-HODESH Vayyakhel Pekudey Vayyikra

NISAN

Adar 8 9 10 11 12 13 14 15 16 17 18 19 20 21 22 23 24 25 26 27 28 29 1 2 3 4 5 6 7 8 9

April 1 2 3 4 5 6 7 8 9 10 11 12 13 14 15 16 17 18 19 20 21 22 23 24 25 26 27 28 29 30

SHABBAT HA-GADOL Tzav Passover Hol ha-Mo'ed Passover Yom Ha-Shoah Shemini Thazria Metzora Yom Ha-Atzma'ut

IYAR

Nisan 10 11 12 13 14 15 16 17 18 19 20 21 22 23 24 25 26 27 28 29 30 1 2 3 4 5 6 7 8 9

May 1 2 3 4 5 6 7 8 9 10 11 12 13 14 15 16 17 18 19 20 21 22 23 24 25 26 27 28 29 30 31

Acharey Mot Kedoshim Emor Lag b'Omer Behar Bechukotai Bamidbar Shavuot Naso

SIVAN

Iyar 10 11 12 13 14 15 16 17 18 19 20 21 22 23 24 25 26 27 28 29 1 2 3 4 5 6 7 8 9 10 11

June 1 2 3 4 5 6 7 8 9 10 11 12 13 14 15 16 17 18 19 20 21 22 23 24 25 26 27 28 29 30

Behaalotecha Shelach Korach Chukkat

TAMMUZ

Sivan 12 13 14 15 16 17 18 19 20 21 22 23 24 25 26 27 28 29 30 1 2 3 4 5 6 7 8 9 10 11

July 1 2 3 4 5 6 7 8 9 10 11 12 13 14 15 16 17 18 19 20 21 22 23 24 25 26 27 28 29 30 31

Balak Pinchas Mattot Massey Devarim Tisha b'Av Va-ethchanan

AV

Tammuz 12 13 14 15 16 17 18 19 20 21 22 23 24 25 26 27 28 29 1 2 3 4 5 6 7 8 9 10 11 12 13

August 1 2 3 4 5 6 7 8 9 10 11 12 13 14 15 16 17 18 19 20 21 22 23 24 25 26 27 28 29 30 31

Ekev Re'eh Shofetim Ki Thetze

ELUL

Av 14 15 16 17 18 19 20 21 22 23 24 25 26 27 28 29 30 1 2 3 4 5 6 7 8 9 10 11 12 13 14

September 1 2 3 4 5 6 7 8 9 10 11 12 13 14 15 16 17 18 19 20 21 22 23 24 25 26 27 28 29 30

Ki Thavo Nitzavim Vayyelech Rosh Hashanah SHABBAT SHUVAH Haazinu Yom Kippur Sukkot

TISHRI

Elul 15 16 17 18 19 20 21 22 23 24 25 26 27 28 29 1 2 3 4 5 6 7 8 9 10 11 12 13 14 15

October 1 2 3 4 5 6 7 8 9 10 11 12 13 14 15 16 17 18 19 20 21 22 23 24 25 26 27 28 29 30 31

Sukkot Hol ha-Mo'ed Shemini Azeret Simchat Torah Bereshit Noach Lech Lecha Vayyera

HESHVAN

Tishri 16 17 18 19 20 21 22 23 24 25 26 27 28 29 30 1 2 3 4 5 6 7 8 9 10 11 12 13 14 15 16

November 1 2 3 4 5 6 7 8 9 10 11 12 13 14 15 16 17 18 19 20 21 22 23 24 25 26 27 28 29 30

Chayye Sarah Toledot Vayyetze Vayyishlach

KISLEV

Heshvan 17 18 19 20 21 22 23 24 25 26 27 28 29 30 1 2 3 4 5 6 7 8 9 10 11 12 13 14 15 16

December 1 2 3 4 5 6 7 8 9 10 11 12 13 14 15 16 17 18 19 20 21 22 23 24 25 26 27 28 29 30 31

Vayyeshev Chanukah Mikketz Vayyiggash Vayyechi

TEVET

Kislev 17 18 19 20 21 22 23 24 25 26 27 28 29 30 1 2 3 4 5 6 7 8 9 10 11 12 13 14 15 16 17

1994

5754/55

January 1 2 3 4 5 6 7 8 9 10 11 12 13 14 15 16 17 18 19 20 21 22 23 24 25 26 27 28 29 30 31
Tu b'Shevat
Shemot Va-era Bo Beshallach Yithro
SHEVAT
Tevet 18 19 20 21 22 23 24 25 26 27 28 29 1 2 3 4 5 6 7 8 9 10 11 12 13 14 15 16 17 18 19

February 1 2 3 4 5 6 7 8 9 10 11 12 13 14 15 16 17 18 19 20 21 22 23 24 25 26 27 28
Purim
Mishpatim SHABBAT SHEKALIM Terumah SHABBAT ZAKHOR Tetzaveh Ki Thissa
ADAR
Shevat 20 21 22 23 24 25 26 27 28 29 30 1 2 3 4 5 6 7 8 9 10 11 12 13 14 15 16 17

March 1 2 3 4 5 6 7 8 9 10 11 12 13 14 15 16 17 18 19 20 21 22 23 24 25 26 27 28 29 30 31
Passover
SHABBAT PARAH Vayyakhel SHABBAT HA-HODESH Pekudey Vayyikra SHABBAT HA-GADOL Tzav
NISAN
Adar 18 19 20 21 22 23 24 25 26 27 28 29 1 2 3 4 5 6 7 8 9 10 11 12 13 14 15 16 17 18 19

April 1 2 3 4 5 6 7 8 9 10 11 12 13 14 15 16 17 18 19 20 21 22 23 24 25 26 27 28 29 30
Yom Ha-Shoah Yom Ha-Atzma'ut Lag b'Omer
Passover Thazria Metzora Acharey Mot Kedoshim
Shemini Emor
IYAR
Nisan 20 21 22 23 24 25 26 27 28 29 30 1 2 3 4 5 6 7 8 9 10 11 12 13 14 15 16 17 18 19

May 1 2 3 4 5 6 7 8 9 10 11 12 13 14 15 16 17 18 19 20 21 22 23 24 25 26 27 28 29 30 31
Shavuot
Behar Bechukotai, Bamidbar Naso Behaalotecha
SIVAN
Iyar 20 21 22 23 24 25 26 27 28 29 1 2 3 4 5 6 7 8 9 10 11 12 13 14 15 16 17 18 19 20 21

June 1 2 3 4 5 6 7 8 9 10 11 12 13 14 15 16 17 18 19 20 21 22 23 24 25 26 27 28 29 30
Shelach Korach Chukkat Balak
TAMMUZ
Sivan 22 23 24 25 26 27 28 29 30 1 2 3 4 5 6 7 8 9 10 11 12 13 14 15 16 17 18 19 20 21

July 1 2 3 4 5 6 7 8 9 10 11 12 13 14 15 16 17 18 19 20 21 22 23 24 25 26 27 28 29 30 31
Devarim
Pinchas Mattot Massey Va-ethchanan Ekev
AV Tisha b'Av
Tammuz 22 23 24 25 26 27 28 29 1 2 3 4 5 6 7 8 9 10 11 12 13 14 15 16 17 18 19 20 21 22 23

August 1 2 3 4 5 6 7 8 9 10 11 12 13 14 15 16 17 18 19 20 21 22 23 24 25 26 27 28 29 30 31
Re'eh Shofetim Ki Thetze Ki Thavo
ELUL
Av 24 25 26 27 28 29 30 1 2 3 4 5 6 7 8 9 10 11 12 13 14 15 16 17 18 19 20 21 22 23 24

September 1 2 3 4 5 6 7 8 9 10 11 12 13 14 15 16 17 18 19 20 21 22 23 24 25 26 27 28 29 30
Rosh Hashanah Yom Kippur Shemini Atzeret
Nitzavim SHABBAT SHUVAH Vayyelech Sukkot Haazinu Hol ha-Mo'ed Simchat Torah
TISHRI
Elul 25 26 27 28 29 1 2 3 4 5 6 7 8 9 10 11 12 13 14 15 16 17 18 19 20 21 22 23 24 25

October 1 2 3 4 5 6 7 8 9 10 11 12 13 14 15 16 17 18 19 20 21 22 23 24 25 26 27 28 29 30 31
Bereshit Noach Lech Lecha Vayyera Chayye Sarah
HESHVAN
Tishri 26 27 28 29 30 1 2 3 4 5 6 7 8 9 10 11 12 13 14 15 16 17 18 19 20 21 22 23 24 25 26

November 1 2 3 4 5 6 7 8 9 10 11 12 13 14 15 16 17 18 19 20 21 22 23 24 25 26 27 28 29 30
Vayyeshev
Toledot Vayyetze Vayyishlach
Chanukah
KISLEV
Heshvan 27 28 29 1 2 3 4 5 6 7 8 9 10 11 12 13 14 15 16 17 18 19 20 21 22 23 24 25 26 27

December 1 2 3 4 5 6 7 8 9 10 11 12 13 14 15 16 17 18 19 20 21 22 23 24 25 26 27 28 29 30 31
Mikketz Vayyiggash Vayyechi Shemot Va-era
TEVET
Kislev 28 29 30 1 2 3 4 5 6 7 8 9 10 11 12 13 14 15 16 17 18 19 20 21 22 23 24 25 26 27 28

1995

5755/56

January 1 2 3 4 5 6 7 8 9 10 11 12 13 14 15 16 17 18 19 20 21 22 23 24 25 26 27 28 29 30
Bo Beshallach Yithro Mishpatim
Tu b'Shevat
SHEVAT
Tevet/Shevat 29 1 2 3 4 5 6 7 8 9 10 11 12 13 14 15 16 17 18 19 20 21 22 23 24 25 26 27 28 29

February 1 2 3 4 5 6 7 8 9 10 11 12 13 14 15 16 17 18 19 20 21 22 23 24 25 26 27 28
Terumah Tetzaveh Ki Thissa SHABBAT SHEKALIM Vayyakhel
Adar I 1 2 3 4 5 6 7 8 9 10 11 12 13 14 15 16 17 18 19 20 21 22 23 24 25 26 27 28

March 1 2 3 4 5 6 7 8 9 10 11 12 13 14 15 16 17 18 19 20 21 22 23 24 25 26 27 28 29 30
Pekudey Purim
SHABBAT ZAKHOR Vayyikra Tzav SHABBAT PARAH Shemini
ADAR II
Adar I/Adar II 29 30 1 2 3 4 5 6 7 8 9 10 11 12 13 14 15 16 17 18 19 20 21 22 23 24 25 26 27 28

April 1 2 3 4 5 6 7 8 9 10 11 12 13 14 15 16 17 18 19 20 21 22 23 24 25 26 27 28 29 30
Passover Passover
SHABBAT HA-HODESH Thazria SHABBAT HA-GADOL Metzora Yom Ha-Shoah
Acharey Mo
Nisan 1 2 3 4 5 6 7 8 9 10 11 12 13 14 15 16 17 18 19 20 21 22 23 24 25 26 27 28 29 30

May 1 2 3 4 5 6 7 8 9 10 11 12 13 14 15 16 17 18 19 20 21 22 23 24 25 26 27 28 29 30
Yom Ha-Atzma'ut
Emor Lag b'Omer Behar Bechukotai
Kedoshim
SIV
Iyar 1 2 3 4 5 6 7 8 9 10 11 12 13 14 15 16 17 18 19 20 21 22 23 24 25 26 27 28 29 1

June 1 2 3 4 5 6 7 8 9 10 11 12 13 14 15 16 17 18 19 20 21 22 23 24 25 26 27 28 29 30
Bamidbar Shavuot
Naso Behaalotecha Shelach
TAMMUZ
Sivan 3 4 5 6 7 8 9 10 11 12 13 14 15 16 17 18 19 20 21 22 23 24 25 26 27 28 29 30 1 2

July 1 2 3 4 5 6 7 8 9 10 11 12 13 14 15 16 17 18 19 20 21 22 23 24 25 26 27 28 29 30
Korach Chukkat Balak Pinchas Mattot Massey
AV
Tammuz 3 4 5 6 7 8 9 10 11 12 13 14 15 16 17 18 19 20 21 22 23 24 25 26 27 28 29 1 2 3

August 1 2 3 4 5 6 7 8 9 10 11 12 13 14 15 16 17 18 19 20 21 22 23 24 25 26 27 28 29 30
Tisha b'Av
Va-ethchanan Ekev Re'eh
Devarim
ELUL
Av 5 6 7 8 9 10 11 12 13 14 15 16 17 18 19 20 21 22 23 24 25 26 27 28 29 30 1 2 3 4

September 1 2 3 4 5 6 7 8 9 10 11 12 13 14 15 16 17 18 19 20 21 22 23 24 25 26 27 28 29 30
Rosh Hashanah
Shofetim Ki Thetze Ki Thavo Nitzavim SHABBAT SH
Vayyele
TISHRI
Elul 6 7 8 9 10 11 12 13 14 15 16 17 18 19 20 21 22 23 24 25 26 27 28 29 1 2 3 4 5 6

October 1 2 3 4 5 6 7 8 9 10 11 12 13 14 15 16 17 18 19 20 21 22 23 24 25 26 27 28 29 30
Yom Kippur Sukkot Shemini Azeret
Hol ha-Mo'ed Bereshit Noach
Haazinu Simchat Torah
HESHVAN
Tishri 7 8 9 10 11 12 13 14 15 16 17 18 19 20 21 22 23 24 25 26 27 28 29 30 1 2 3 4 5 6

November 1 2 3 4 5 6 7 8 9 10 11 12 13 14 15 16 17 18 19 20 21 22 23 24 25 26 27 28 29 30
Lech Lecha Vayyera Chayye Sarah Toledot
KISLEV
Heshvan 8 9 10 11 12 13 14 15 16 17 18 19 20 21 22 23 24 25 26 27 28 29 30 1 2 3 4 5 6 7

December 1 2 3 4 5 6 7 8 9 10 11 12 13 14 15 16 17 18 19 20 21 22 23 24 25 26 27 28 29 30
Vayyetze Vayyishlach Vayyeshev Mikketz Vayyig
Chanukah
TEVET
Kislev 8 9 10 11 12 13 14 15 16 17 18 19 20 21 22 23 24 25 26 27 28 29 30 1 2 3 4 5 6 7

1996

'56/57

nuary 1 2 3 4 5 6 7 8 9 10 11 12 13 14 15 16 17 18 19 20 21 22 23 24 25 26 27 28 29 30 31

Vayyechi · Shemot · Va-era · Bo

SHEVAT

evet 9 10 11 12 13 14 15 16 17 18 19 20 21 22 23 24 25 26 27 28 29 1 2 3 4 5 6 7 8 9 10

ebruary 1 2 3 4 5 6 7 8 9 10 11 12 13 14 15 16 17 18 19 20 21 22 23 24 25 26 27 28 29

Beshallach · *Tu b'Shevat* · Yithro · *SHABBAT SHEKALIM* Mishpatim · Terumah

ADAR

hevat 11 12 13 14 15 16 17 18 19 20 21 22 23 24 25 26 27 28 29 30 1 2 3 4 5 6 7 8 9

arch 1 2 3 4 5 6 7 8 9 10 11 12 13 14 15 16 17 18 19 20 21 22 23 24 25 26 27 28 29 30 31

SHABBAT ZAKHOR Tezaveh · *Purim* · *SHABBAT PARAH* Ki Thissa · *SHABBAT HA-HODESH* Vayyakhel Pekudey · Vayyikra · *SHABBAT HA-GADOL* Tzav

NISAN

dar 10 11 12 13 14 15 16 17 18 19 20 21 22 23 24 25 26 27 28 29 1 2 3 4 5 6 7 8 9 10 11

pril 1 2 3 4 5 6 7 8 9 10 11 12 13 14 15 16 17 18 19 20 21 22 23 24 25 26 27 28 29 30

Passover · Hol ha-Mo'ed · Passover · Shemini · *Yom Ha-Shoah* · Thazria Metzora · IYAR · *Yom Ha-Atzma'ut* · Acharey Mot Kedoshim

isan 12 13 14 15 16 17 18 19 20 21 22 23 24 25 26 27 28 29 30 1 2 3 4 5 6 7 8 9 10 11

ay 1 2 3 4 5 6 7 8 9 10 11 12 13 14 15 16 17 18 19 20 21 22 23 24 25 26 27 28 29 30 31

Emor · *Lag b'Omer* · Behar Bechukotai · Bamidbar · Shavuot

SIVAN

ar 12 13 14 15 16 17 18 19 20 21 22 23 24 25 26 27 28 29 1 2 3 4 5 6 7 8 9 10 11 12 13

ne 1 2 3 4 5 6 7 8 9 10 11 12 13 14 15 16 17 18 19 20 21 22 23 24 25 26 27 28 29 30

Naso · Behaalotecha · Shelach · Korach · Chukkat Balak

TAMMUZ

van 14 15 16 17 18 19 20 21 22 23 24 25 26 27 28 29 30 1 2 3 4 5 6 7 8 9 10 11 12 13

ly 1 2 3 4 5 6 7 8 9 10 11 12 13 14 15 16 17 18 19 20 21 22 23 24 25 26 27 28 29 30 31

Pinchas · Mattot Massey · Devarim · *Tisha b'Av* · Va-ethchanan

AV

ammuz 14 15 16 17 18 19 20 21 22 23 24 25 26 27 28 29 1 2 3 4 5 6 7 8 9 10 11 12 13 14 15

ugust 1 2 3 4 5 6 7 8 9 10 11 12 13 14 15 16 17 18 19 20 21 22 23 24 25 26 27 28 29 30 31

Ekev · Re'eh · Shofetim · Ki Thetze · Ki Thavo

ELUL

v 16 17 18 19 20 21 22 23 24 25 26 27 28 29 30 1 2 3 4 5 6 7 8 9 10 11 12 13 14 15 16

eptember 1 2 3 4 5 6 7 8 9 10 11 12 13 14 15 16 17 18 19 20 21 22 23 24 25 26 27 28 29 30

Nitzavim Vayyelech · *Rosh Hashanah* · *SHABBAT SHUVAH* Haazinu · *Yom Kippur* · Sukkot

TISHRI

ul 17 18 19 20 21 22 23 24 25 26 27 28 29 1 2 3 4 5 6 7 8 9 10 11 12 13 14 15 16 17

ctober 1 2 3 4 5 6 7 8 9 10 11 12 13 14 15 16 17 18 19 20 21 22 23 24 25 26 27 28 29 30 31

Shemini Azeret · *Simchat Torah* · Bereshit · Noach · Lech Lecha

HESHVAN

ishri 18 19 20 21 22 23 24 25 26 27 28 29 30 1 2 3 4 5 6 7 8 9 10 11 12 13 14 15 16 17 18

ovember 1 2 3 4 5 6 7 8 9 10 11 12 13 14 15 16 17 18 19 20 21 22 23 24 25 26 27 28 29 30

Vayyera · Chayye Sarah · Toledot · Vayyetze · Vayyishlach

KISLEV

eshvan 19 20 21 22 23 24 25 26 27 28 29 1 2 3 4 5 6 7 8 9 10 11 12 13 14 15 16 17 18 19

ecember 1 2 3 4 5 6 7 8 9 10 11 12 13 14 15 16 17 18 19 20 21 22 23 24 25 26 27 28 29 30 31

Chanukah · Vayyeshev · Mikketz · Vayyiggash · Vayyechi

TEVET

islev 20 21 22 23 24 25 26 27 28 29 1 2 3 4 5 6 7 8 9 10 11 12 13 14 15 16 17 18 19 20 21

1997

5757/58

January 1 2 3 4 5 6 7 8 9 10 11 12 13 14 15 16 17 18 19 20 21 22 23 24 25 26 27 28 29 30 31

Shemot · Va-era · Bo · *Tu b'Shevat* · Beshallach

SHEVAT

Tevet 22 23 24 25 26 27 28 29 1 2 3 4 5 6 7 8 9 10 11 12 13 14 15 16 17 18 19 20 21 22 23

February 1 2 3 4 5 6 7 8 9 10 11 12 13 14 15 16 17 18 19 20 21 22 23 24 25 26 27 28

Yithro · Mishpatim · Terumah · Tezaveh

ADAR I

Shevat 24 25 26 27 28 29 30 1 2 3 4 5 6 7 8 9 10 11 12 13 14 15 16 17 18 19 20 21

March 1 2 3 4 5 6 7 8 9 10 11 12 13 14 15 16 17 18 19 20 21 22 23 24 25 26 27 28 29 30 31

Ki Thissa · *SHABBAT SHEKALIM* Vayyakhel · Pekudey · *SHABBAT ZAKHOR* Vayyikra · *Purim* · *SHABBAT PARAH* Tzav

ADAR II

Adar I 22 23 24 25 26 27 28 29 30 1 2 3 4 5 6 7 8 9 10 11 12 13 14 15 16 17 18 19 20 21 22

April 1 2 3 4 5 6 7 8 9 10 11 12 13 14 15 16 17 18 19 20 21 22 23 24 25 26 27 28 29 30

SHABBAT HA-HODESH Shemini · Thazria · *SHABBAT HA-GADOL* Metzora · Passover · Hol ha-Mo'ed · Passover

NISAN

Adar II 23 24 25 26 27 28 29 1 2 3 4 5 6 7 8 9 10 11 12 13 14 15 16 17 18 19 20 21 22 23

May 1 2 3 4 5 6 7 8 9 10 11 12 13 14 15 16 17 18 19 20 21 22 23 24 25 26 27 28 29 30 31

Acharey Mot · *Yom Ha-Shoah* · Kedoshim · *Yom Ha-Atzma'ut* · Emor · Behar · *Lag b'Omer* · Bechukotai

IYAR

Nisan 24 25 26 27 28 29 30 1 2 3 4 5 6 7 8 9 10 11 12 13 14 15 16 17 18 19 20 21 22 23 24

June 1 2 3 4 5 6 7 8 9 10 11 12 13 14 15 16 17 18 19 20 21 22 23 24 25 26 27 28 29 30

Bamidbar · Shavuot · Naso · Behaalotecha · Shelach

SIVAN

Iyar 25 26 27 28 29 1 2 3 4 5 6 7 8 9 10 11 12 13 14 15 16 17 18 19 20 21 22 23 24 25

July 1 2 3 4 5 6 7 8 9 10 11 12 13 14 15 16 17 18 19 20 21 22 23 24 25 26 27 28 29 30 31

Korach · Chukkat · Balak · Pinchas

TAMMUZ

Sivan 26 27 28 29 30 1 2 3 4 5 6 7 8 9 10 11 12 13 14 15 16 17 18 19 20 21 22 23 24 25 26

August 1 2 3 4 5 6 7 8 9 10 11 12 13 14 15 16 17 18 19 20 21 22 23 24 25 26 27 28 29 30 31

Mattot Massey · Devarim · *Tisha b'Av* · Va-ethchanan · Ekev · Re'eh

AV

Tammuz 27 28 29 1 2 3 4 5 6 7 8 9 10 11 12 13 14 15 16 17 18 19 20 21 22 23 24 25 26 27 28

September 1 2 3 4 5 6 7 8 9 10 11 12 13 14 15 16 17 18 19 20 21 22 23 24 25 26 27 28 29 30

Shofetim · Ki Thetze · Ki Thavo · Nitzavim Vayyelech

ELUL

Av/Elul 29 30 1 2 3 4 5 6 7 8 9 10 11 12 13 14 15 16 17 18 19 20 21 22 23 24 25 26 27 28

October 1 2 3 4 5 6 7 8 9 10 11 12 13 14 15 16 17 18 19 20 21 22 23 24 25 26 27 28 29 30 31

Rosh Hashanah · *SHABBAT SHUVAH* Haazinu · *Yom Kippur* · Sukkot · Hol ha-Mo'ed · *Shemini Azeret* · *Simchat Torah* · Bereshit

TISHRI

Elul/Tishri 29 1 2 3 4 5 6 7 7 9 10 11 12 13 14 15 16 17 18 19 20 21 22 23 24 25 26 27 28 29 30

November 1 2 3 4 5 6 7 8 9 10 11 12 13 14 15 16 17 18 19 20 21 22 23 24 25 26 27 28 29 30

Noach · Lech Lecha · Vayyera · Chayye Sarah · Toledot

KISLEV

Heshvan 1 2 3 4 5 6 7 8 9 10 11 12 13 14 15 16 17 18 19 20 21 22 23 24 25 26 27 28 29 1

December 1 2 3 4 5 6 7 8 9 10 11 12 13 14 15 16 17 18 19 20 21 22 23 24 25 26 27 28 29 30 31

Vayyetze · Vayyishlach · Vayyeshev · *Chanukah* · Mikketz

TEVET

Kislev 2 3 4 5 6 7 8 9 10 11 12 13 14 15 16 17 18 19 20 21 22 23 24 25 26 27 28 29 30 1 2

5758/59 — 1998

January 1 2 3 4 5 6 7 8 9 10 11 12 13 14 15 16 17 18 19 20 21 22 23 24 25 26 27 28 29 30 31
Vayyiggash · Vayyechi · Shemot · Va-era · Bo
Tevet 3 4 5 6 7 8 9 10 11 12 13 14 15 16 17 18 19 20 21 22 23 24 25 26 27 28 29 SHEVAT 1 2 3 4

February 1 2 3 4 5 6 7 8 9 10 11 12 13 14 15 16 17 18 19 20 21 22 23 24 25 26 27 28
Beshallach · Tu b'Shevat · Yithro · SHABBAT SHEKALIM Mishpatim · Terumah
Shevat 5 6 7 8 9 10 11 12 13 14 15 16 17 18 19 20 21 22 23 24 25 26 27 28 29 30 ADAR 1 2

March 1 2 3 4 5 6 7 8 9 10 11 12 13 14 15 16 17 18 19 20 21 22 23 24 25 26 27 28 29 30 31
SHABBAT ZAKHOR Tezaveh · Purim · Ki Thissa · SHABBAT PARAH Vayyakhel Pekudey · SHABBAT HA-HODESH Vayyikra
Adar 3 4 5 6 7 8 9 10 11 12 13 14 15 16 17 18 19 20 21 22 23 24 25 26 27 28 29 NISAN 1 2 3 4

April 1 2 3 4 5 6 7 8 9 10 11 12 13 14 15 16 17 18 19 20 21 22 23 24 25 26 27 28 29 30
SHABBAT HA-GADOL Tzav · Passover · Passover · Yom Ha-Shoah · Shemini · Yom Ha-Atzma'ut
Nisan 5 6 7 8 9 10 11 12 13 14 15 16 17 18 19 20 21 22 23 24 25 26 27 28 29 30 IYAR 1 2 3 4

May 1 2 3 4 5 6 7 8 9 10 11 12 13 14 15 16 17 18 19 20 21 22 23 24 25 26 27 28 29 30 31
Thazria Metzora · Acharey Mot Kedoshim · Lag b'Omer · Emor · Behar Bechukotai · Bamidbar · Shavuot
Iyar 5 6 7 8 9 10 11 12 13 14 15 16 17 18 19 20 21 22 23 24 25 26 27 28 29 SIVAN 1 2 3 4 5 6

June 1 2 3 4 5 6 7 8 9 10 11 12 13 14 15 16 17 18 19 20 21 22 23 24 25 26 27 28 29 30
Shavuot · Naso · Behaalotecha · Shelach · Korach
Sivan 7 8 9 10 11 12 13 14 15 16 17 18 19 20 21 22 23 24 25 26 27 28 29 30 TAMMUZ 1 2 3 4 5 6

July 1 2 3 4 5 6 7 8 9 10 11 12 13 14 15 16 17 18 19 20 21 22 23 24 25 26 27 28 29 30 31
Chukkat · Balak · Pinchas · Mattot Massey
Tammuz 7 8 9 10 11 12 13 14 15 16 17 18 19 20 21 22 23 24 25 26 27 28 29 AV 1 2 3 4 5 6 7 8

August 1 2 3 4 5 6 7 8 9 10 11 12 13 14 15 16 17 18 19 20 21 22 23 24 25 26 27 28 29 30 31
Tisha b'Av · Devarim · Va-ethchanan · Ekev · Re'eh · Shofetim
Av 9 10 11 12 13 14 15 16 17 18 19 20 21 22 23 24 25 26 27 28 29 30 ELUL 1 2 3 4 5 6 7 8 9

September 1 2 3 4 5 6 7 8 9 10 11 12 13 14 15 16 17 18 19 20 21 22 23 24 25 26 27 28 29 30
Ki Thetze · Ki Thavo · Nitzavim · Rosh Hashanah · SHABBAT SHUVAH Vayyelech · Yom Kippur
Elul 10 11 12 13 14 15 16 17 18 19 20 21 22 23 24 25 26 27 28 29 TISHRI 1 2 3 4 5 6 7 8 9 10

October 1 2 3 4 5 6 7 8 9 10 11 12 13 14 15 16 17 18 19 20 21 22 23 24 25 26 27 28 29 30 31
Sukkot · Haazinu · Hol ha-Mo'ed · Shemini Azeret · Simchat Torah · Bereshit · Noach · Lech Lecha
Tishri 11 12 13 14 15 16 17 18 19 20 21 22 23 24 25 26 27 28 29 30 HESHVAN 1 2 3 4 5 6 7 8 9 10 11

November 1 2 3 4 5 6 7 8 9 10 11 12 13 14 15 16 17 18 19 20 21 22 23 24 25 26 27 28 29 30
Vayyera · Chayye Sarah · Toledot · Vayyetze
Heshvan 12 13 14 15 16 17 18 19 20 21 22 23 24 25 26 27 28 29 30 KISLEV 1 2 3 4 5 6 7 8 9 10 11

December 1 2 3 4 5 6 7 8 9 10 11 12 13 14 15 16 17 18 19 20 21 22 23 24 25 26 27 28 29 30 31
Vayyishlach · Vayyeshev · Chanukah · Mikketz · Vayyiggash
Kislev 12 13 14 15 16 17 18 19 20 21 22 23 24 25 26 27 28 29 30 TEVET 1 2 3 4 5 6 7 8 9 10 11 12

5759/60 — 1999

January 1 2 3 4 5 6 7 8 9 10 11 12 13 14 15 16 17 18 19 20 21 22 23 24 25 26 27 28 29 30 3
Vayyechi · Shemot · Va-era · Bo · Beshallac
Tevet 13 14 15 16 17 18 19 20 21 22 23 24 25 26 27 28 29 SHEVAT 1 2 3 4 5 6 7 8 9 10 11 12 13

February 1 2 3 4 5 6 7 8 9 10 11 12 13 14 15 16 17 18 19 20 21 22 23 24 25 26 27 28
Tu b'Shevat · Yithro · SHABBAT SHEKALIM Mishpatim · Terumah · SHABBAT ZAKHOR Tezaveh
Shevat 15 16 17 18 19 20 21 22 23 24 25 26 27 28 29 30 ADAR 1 2 3 4 5 6 7 8 9 10 11 12

March 1 2 3 4 5 6 7 8 9 10 11 12 13 14 15 16 17 18 19 20 21 22 23 24 25 26 27 28 29 30 3
Purim · SHABBAT PARAH Ki Thissa · SHABBAT HA-HODESH Vayyakhel Pekudey · Vayyikra · SHABBAT HA-GADOL Tzav
Adar 13 14 15 16 17 18 19 20 21 22 23 24 25 26 27 28 29 NISAN 1 2 3 4 5 6 7 8 9 10 11 12 13

April 1 2 3 4 5 6 7 8 9 10 11 12 13 14 15 16 17 18 19 20 21 22 23 24 25 26 27 28 29 30
Passover · Passover · Hol ha-Mo'ed · Yom Ha-Shoah · Shemini · Yom Ha-Atzma'ut · Thazria Metzora · Acharey Mot Kedoshim
Nisan 15 16 17 18 19 20 21 22 23 24 25 26 27 28 29 30 IYAR 1 2 3 4 5 6 7 8 9 10 11 12 13 14

May 1 2 3 4 5 6 7 8 9 10 11 12 13 14 15 16 17 18 19 20 21 22 23 24 25 26 27 28 29 30 3
Emor · Lag b'Omer · Behar Bechukotai · Bamidbar · Shavuot · Naso
Iyar 15 16 17 18 19 20 21 22 23 24 25 26 27 28 29 SIVAN 1 2 3 4 5 6 7 8 9 10 11 12 13 14 15 1

June 1 2 3 4 5 6 7 8 9 10 11 12 13 14 15 16 17 18 19 20 21 22 23 24 25 26 27 28 29 30
Behaalotecha · Shelach · Korach · Chukkat Balak
Sivan 17 18 19 20 21 22 23 24 25 26 27 28 29 30 TAMMUZ 1 2 3 4 5 6 7 8 9 10 11 12 13 14 15 16

July 1 2 3 4 5 6 7 8 9 10 11 12 13 14 15 16 17 18 19 20 21 22 23 24 25 26 27 28 29 30
Pinchas · Mattot Massey · Devarim · Tisha b'Av · Va-ethchanan · E
Tammuz 17 18 19 20 21 22 23 24 25 26 27 28 29 AV 1 2 3 4 5 6 7 8 9 10 11 12 13 14 15 16 17 1

August 1 2 3 4 5 6 7 8 9 10 11 12 13 14 15 16 17 18 19 20 21 22 23 24 25 26 27 28 29 30 3
Re'eh · Shofetim · Ki Thetze · Ki Thavo
Av 19 20 21 22 23 24 25 26 27 28 29 30 ELUL 1 2 3 4 5 6 7 8 9 10 11 12 13 14 15 16 17 18

September 1 2 3 4 5 6 7 8 9 10 11 12 13 14 15 16 17 18 19 20 21 22 23 24 25 26 27 28 29 30
Nitzavim Vayyelech · Rosh Hashanah · SHABBAT SHUVAH Haazinu · Yom Kippur · Sukkot
Elul 20 21 22 23 24 25 26 27 28 29 TISHRI 1 2 3 4 5 6 7 8 9 10 11 12 13 14 15 16 17 18 19 20

October 1 2 3 4 5 6 7 8 9 10 11 12 13 14 15 16 17 18 19 20 21 22 23 24 25 26 27 28 29 30 3
Shemini Azeret · Simchat Torah · Bereshit · Noach · Lech Lecha · Vayyera
Tishri 21 22 23 24 25 26 27 28 29 30 HESHVAN 1 2 3 4 5 6 7 8 9 10 11 12 13 14 15 16 17 18 19 20 2

November 1 2 3 4 5 6 7 8 9 10 11 12 13 14 15 16 17 18 19 20 21 22 23 24 25 26 27 28 29 30
Chayye Sarah · Toledot · Vayyetze · Vayyishlach
Heshvan 22 23 24 25 26 27 28 29 30 KISLEV 1 2 3 4 5 6 7 8 9 10 11 12 13 14 15 16 17 18 19 20 21

December 1 2 3 4 5 6 7 8 9 10 11 12 13 14 15 16 17 18 19 20 21 22 23 24 25 26 27 28 29 30 3
Chanukah Vayyeshev · Mikketz · Vayyiggash · Vayyechi
Kislev 22 23 24 25 26 27 28 29 30 TEVET 1 2 3 4 5 6 7 8 9 10 11 12 13 14 15 16 17 18 19 20 21 2

2000

/61

ary 1 2 3 4 5 6 7 8 9 10 11 12 13 14 15 16 17 18 19 20 21 22 23 24 25 26 27 28 29 30 31

Shemot Va-ayra Bo *Tu b'Shevat* Beshallach Yithro

SHEVAT

et 23 24 25 26 27 28 29 1 2 3 4 5 6 7 8 9 10 11 12 13 14 15 16 17 18 19 20 21 22 23 24

ruary 1 2 3 4 5 6 7 8 9 10 11 12 13 14 15 16 17 18 19 20 21 22 23 24 25 26 27 28 29

Mishpatim Terumah Tezaveh Ki Thissa

ADAR I

vat 25 26 27 28 29 30 1 2 3 4 5 6 7 8 9 10 11 12 13 14 15 16 17 18 19 20 21 22 23

ch 1 2 3 4 5 6 7 8 9 10 11 12 13 14 15 16 17 18 19 20 21 22 23 24 25 26 27 28 29 30 31

SHABBAT SHEKALIM Vayyakhel Pekudey SHABBAT ZAKHOR Vayyikra *Purim* SHABBAT PARAH Tzav

ADAR II

r I 24 25 26 27 28 29 30 1 2 3 4 5 6 7 8 9 10 11 12 13 14 15 16 17 18 19 20 21 22 23 24

l 1 2 3 4 5 6 7 8 9 10 11 12 13 14 15 16 17 18 19 20 21 22 23 24 25 26 27 28 29 30

Passover *Passover*

SHABBAT HA-HODESH Shemini Thazria SHABBAT HA-GADOL Metzora Hol ha-Mo'ed Acharey Mot

NISAN

r II 25 26 27 28 29 1 2 3 4 5 6 7 8 9 10 11 12 13 14 15 16 17 18 19 20 21 22 23 24 25

y 1 2 3 4 5 6 7 8 9 10 11 12 13 14 15 16 17 18 19 20 21 22 23 24 25 26 27 28 29 30 31

Yom Ha-Shoah Kedoshim *Yom Ha-Atzma'ut* Emor Behar *Lag b'Omer* Bechukotai

IYAR

an 26 27 28 29 30 1 2 3 4 5 6 7 8 9 10 11 12 13 14 15 16 17 18 19 20 21 22 23 24 25 26

e 1 2 3 4 5 6 7 8 9 10 11 12 13 14 15 16 17 18 19 20 21 22 23 24 25 26 27 28 29 30

Bamidbar Shavuot Naso Behaalotecha

SIVAN

27 28 29 1 2 3 4 5 6 7 8 9 10 11 12 13 14 15 16 17 18 19 20 21 22 23 24 25 26 27

1 2 3 4 5 6 7 8 9 10 11 12 13 14 15 16 17 18 19 20 21 22 23 24 25 26 27 28 29 30 31

Shelach Korach Chukkat Balak Pinchas Mattot Massey

TAMMUZ

an 28 29 30 1 2 3 4 5 6 7 8 9 10 11 12 13 14 15 16 17 18 19 20 21 22 23 24 25 26 27 28

gust 1 2 3 4 5 6 7 8 9 10 11 12 13 14 15 16 17 18 19 20 21 22 23 24 25 26 27 28 29 30 31

Devarim *Tisha b'Av* Va-ethchanan Ekev Re'eh

AV

muz/Av 29 1 2 3 4 5 6 7 8 9 10 11 12 13 14 15 16 17 18 19 20 21 22 23 24 25 26 27 28 29 30

tember 1 2 3 4 5 6 7 8 9 10 11 12 13 14 15 16 17 18 19 20 21 22 23 24 25 26 27 28 29 30

Shofetim Ki Thetze Ki Thavo Nitzavim Vayyelech *Rosh Hashanah*

TISHRI

l 1 2 3 4 5 6 7 8 9 10 11 12 13 14 15 16 17 18 19 20 21 22 23 24 25 26 27 28 29 1

tober 1 2 3 4 5 6 7 8 9 10 11 12 13 14 15 16 17 18 19 20 21 22 23 24 25 26 27 28 29 30 31

Rosh Hashanah SHABBAT SHUVAH Haazinu *Yom Kippur* *Sukkot* *Shemini Azeret* *Simchat Torah* Bereshit

HESHVAN

hri 2 3 4 5 6 7 8 9 10 11 12 13 14 15 16 17 18 19 20 21 22 23 24 25 26 27 28 29 30 1 2

vember 1 2 3 4 5 6 7 8 9 10 11 12 13 14 15 16 17 18 19 20 21 22 23 24 25 26 27 28 29 30

Noach Lech Lecha Vayyera Chayye Sarah

KISLEV

shvan 3 4 5 6 7 8 9 10 11 12 13 14 15 16 17 18 19 20 21 22 23 24 25 26 27 28 29 1 2 3

cember 1 2 3 4 5 6 7 8 9 10 11 12 13 14 15 16 17 18 19 20 21 22 23 24 25 26 27 28 29 30 31

Toledot Vayyetze Vayyishlach *Chanukah* Vayyeshev Mikketz

TEVET

slev 4 5 6 7 8 9 10 11 12 13 14 15 16 17 18 19 20 21 22 23 24 25 26 27 28 29 1 2 3 4 5

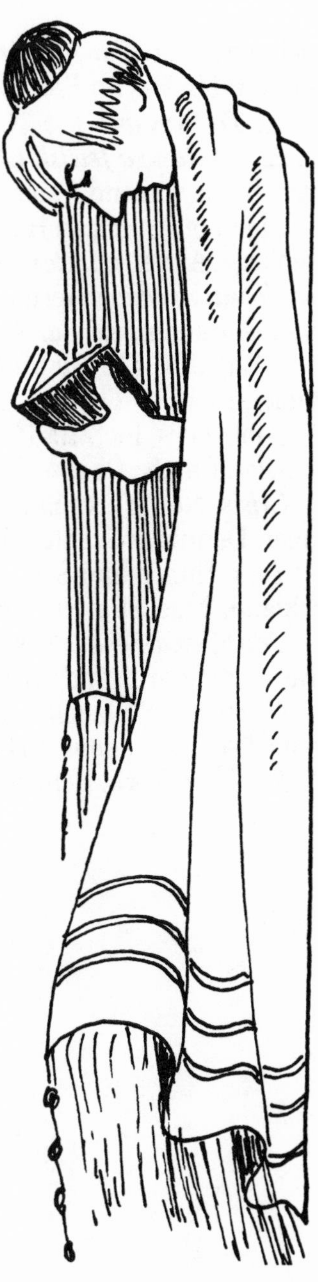

Bibliography

Chiel, Arthur. *Guide to Sidrot and Haftarot.* New York: K'tav, 1971.

Donin, Rabbi Hayim Halevy. *To Be a Jew.* New York: Basic Books, Inc., 1972.

______. *To Pray as a Jew.* New York: Basic Books, Inc., 1980.

______. *To Raise a Jewish Child.* New York: Basic Books, Inc., 1977.

Efron, Benjamin and Rubin, Alvan. *Coming of Age: Your Bar or Bat Mitzvah.* New York: Union of American Hebrew Congregations, 1977.

Eisenberg, Azriel, ed. *Bar Mitzvah Treasury.* New York: Behrman House, 1962.

Encyclopedia Judaica. Jerusalem: Keter Publishing, 1972.

Katsh, Abraham, ed. *Bar Mitzvah Illustrated.* New York: Shengold Publishers, 1955.

Kitov, Eliyahu. *The Jew and His Home.* New York: Shengold Publishers, 1963.

Mandel, Morris. *Thirteen: A Teenage Guide to Judaism.* New York: Jonathan David Publishers, Inc., 1961.

Pelcovitz, Ralph. *Danger and Opportunity: Essays on Traditional Judaism in a Time of Crisis.* New York: Shengold Publishers, 1976.

Prager, Dennis and Telushkin, Joseph. *Nine Questions People Ask about Judaism.* New York: Simon and Schuster, 1981.

Rockland, Mae Shafter. *The Jewish Party Book: A Contemporary Guide to Customs, Crafts, and Foods.* New York: Schocken Books, 1978.

Strassfeld, Sharon and Strassfeld, Michael, eds. *The Second Jewish Catalog: Sources and Resources.* Philadelphia: The Jewish Publication Society, 1976.

Trepp, Leo. *The Complete Book of Jewish Observance: A Practical Manual for the Modern Jew.* New York: Behrman House, 1980.

Index

IN APPRECIATION OF
THE LOVE, KINDNESS AND CARING OF
MRS. ADOLPH FINE
FROM
LIZ FREIDMAN DOUGLIS &
CINDY FREIDMAN SUTTON